DEVELOPMENTS IN SOIL MECHANICS AND FOUNDATION ENGINEERING—2

Stress–Strain Modelling of Soils

CONTENTS OF VOLUME 1

Volume 1: Model Studies

DEVELOPMENTS IN SOIL MECHANICS AND FOUNDATION ENGINEERING—2

Stress–Strain Modelling of Soils

Edited by

P. K. BANERJEE

*Department of Civil Engineering,
State University of New York at Buffalo,
New York, USA*

and

R. BUTTERFIELD

*Department of Civil Engineering,
University of Southampton, UK*

ELSEVIER APPLIED SCIENCE PUBLISHERS
LONDON and NEW YORK

ELSEVIER APPLIED SCIENCE PUBLISHERS LTD
Crown House, Linton Road, Barking, Essex IG11 8JU, England

Sole Distributor in the USA and Canada
ELSEVIER SCIENCE PUBLISHING CO., INC.
52 Vanderbilt Avenue, New York, NY 10017, USA

British Library Cataloguing in Publication Data

Developments in soil mechanics and foundation
engineering.—2
1. Soil mechanics
624.1′5136′05   TA710

ISBN 0-85334-345-4
ISSN 0266-2507

WITH 15 TABLES AND 158 ILLUSTRATIONS

© ELSEVIER APPLIED SCIENCE PUBLISHERS LTD 1985

Printed in Great Britain by Galliard (Printers) Ltd, Great Yarmouth

PREFACE

Whereas Volume 1 in this series was principally concerned with the use of physical models of soils and soil systems to elucidate the behaviour of a variety of foundation structures, the present volume focuses on advances in the numerical modelling of soil response to changes in applied stress. This is a field which has progressed rapidly in the past few years as constitutive equations, and the computer algorithms interpreting them, have become more and more sophisticated in attempts to reproduce adequately the complexities of real soil behaviour. The book presents some of the more powerful numerical soil-modelling techniques in a sufficiently rigorous mechanics framework whilst, at the same time, providing the reader with critical analyses, in two chapters, of the ever-present problems of soil parameter determination. The final chapter is a comprehensive review of the development, performance and measurements obtained from *in situ* pressure-meter tests which serves to keep in perspective the inevitable gap between the reality of the soil profile on a construction site and the world of the numerical modeller—a gap which, we hope, this book will, in a small way, help to bridge.

The chapters themselves fall into three groups. Chapters 1, 2 and 3 are all concerned with improved numerical modelling of the static stress–strain behaviour of soils. In Chapter 1 an incremental plasticity model is introduced for anisotropically consolidated clays, and their subsequent stress dependent alteration. Comparisons with laboratory data show that it predicts satisfactorily various aspects of both the drained and undrained response of K_0-consolidated clays. Chapter 2 provides an overview of elasto-plastic models, with either isotropic or kinematic hardening, leading to a general anisotropic hardening model, predictions from which are compared with experimentally determined data. An alternative, visco-plastic, model is presented in Chapter 3. This leads to a 'multi-laminate' (i.e. one in which particular attention is paid to laws of sliding and closing or separation of intergranular boundaries within the soil skeleton) for-mulation of the well-known Critical State Model. Chapters 4 and 5 introduce cyclic load behaviour, the former concentrating on a Critical State Model (of clay) augmented by a single fatigue parameter related to the generation of pore-water pressures under cyclic loading. A novel feature of this work is the consideration of 'intermittent' loading in which batches of undrained loading cycles are separated by drainage periods. The results obtained are discussed in relation to laboratory test results and in relation to the behaviour of a hypothetical offshore gravity oil-platform. Chapter 5 presents a review of the cyclic-response numerical models available with particular emphasis on the realistic incorporation of hysteretic (inelastic) phenomena.

The remaining chapters deal with experimental measurement of some of the parameters required by the numerical models. Chapter 6 offers an exhaustive analysis of the strengths and shortcomings of the Cambridge simple-shear apparatus leading to a practically useful set of corrections, to improve the precision of the raw test-data, based on comprehensive measurements made on highly instrumented shear boxes. In rather the same spirit Chapter 7 considers drained triaxial compression tests on granular materials and, in particular, an analytical exploration of the effects of efficient end-platten lubrication and the resultant stress-induced non-uniformities. Bifurcation theory is introduced to explore and explain both the diffuse and the localised inhomogeneities observed experimentally in triaxial tests and their effects on the parameters measured. Chapter 8, as mentioned previously, brings us home to real *in situ* soil parameter determination with an authoritative overview of the development and application of the Self-Boring Pressuremeter.

We hope that, by ranging from esoteric mathematical modelling to a review of the, still severely limited, precision of a modern *in situ* soil testing device, the book will serve to encourage communication and understanding between workers in disciplines which are, all too often, considered in isolation.

P. K. BANERJEE
R. BUTTERFIELD

CONTENTS

LIST OF CONTRIBUTORS

D. W. AIREY
Research Assistant, Cambridge Soil Mechanics Group, University Engineering Department, Trumpington Street, Cambridge CB2 1PZ, UK.

P. K. BANERJEE
Professor, Department of Civil Engineering, State University of New York at Buffalo, Buffalo, NY 14260, USA.

J. BENOIT
Assistant Professor, Department of Civil Engineering, Kingsbury Hall, University of New Hampshire, Durham, NH 03824, USA.

M. BUDHU
Assistant Professor, Department of Civil Engineering, State University of New York at Buffalo, Buffalo, NY 14260, USA.

G. WAYNE CLOUGH
Professor and Head, Department of Civil Engineering, Virginia Polytechnic Institute and State University, Blacksburg, Virginia 24061, USA.

C. S. DESAI
Professor, Department of Civil Engineering and Engineering Mechanics, University of Arizona, Tucson, Arizona 85721, USA.

A. DRESCHER
Professor, Department of Civil and Mineral Engineering, University of Minnesota, Minneapolis, Minnesota 55455-0220, USA.

M. O. FARUQUE
Assistant Professor, Department of Civil Engineering, University of Rhode Island, Kingston, Rhode Island 02881, USA.

G. N. PANDE
Lecturer, Department of Civil Engineering, University College of Swansea, Swansea SA2 8PP, UK.

S. PIETRUSZCZAK
Assistant Professor, Department of Civil Engineering and Engineering Mechanics, McMaster University, Hamilton, Ontario L8S 4L7, Canada.

H. B. POOROOSHASB
Professor, Department of Civil Engineering, Concordia University, Montreal, Quebec H3G 1M8, Canada.

D. POTTS
Lecturer, Department of Civil Engineering, Imperial College of Science and Technology, Imperial College Road, London SW7 2BU, UK.

S. SOMASUNDARAM
Graduate Student, Department of Civil Engineering and Engineering Mechanics, University of Arizona, Tucson, Arizona 85721, USA.

A. S. STIPHO
Assistant Professor, Department of Civil Engineering, University of Riyadh, P.O. Box 2454, Riyadh, Saudi Arabia.

I. G. VARDOULAKIS
Associate Professor, Department of Civil and Mineral Engineering, University of Minnesota, Minneapolis, Minnesota 55455–0220, USA.

D. M. WOOD
Lecturer, Cambridge Soil Mechanics Group, University Engineering Department, Trumpington Street, Cambridge CB2 1PZ, UK.

N. B. YOUSIF
Graduate Student, Department of Civil Engineering, State University of New York at Buffalo, Buffalo, NY 14260, USA.

Chapter 1

A THEORETICAL AND EXPERIMENTAL INVESTIGATION OF THE BEHAVIOUR OF ANISOTROPICALLY CONSOLIDATED CLAY

P. K. Banerjee,* A. S. Stipho† and N. B. Yousif*

** Department of Civil Engineering,
State University of New York at Buffalo, USA*

*† Department of Civil Engineering,
University of Riyadh, Saudi Arabia*

1 INTRODUCTION

The mechanical behaviour of real soils is extremely complex. Even in a completely saturated soil system the behaviour is strongly affected by the pore water pressure, the effective stress state and the stress history of loading. In addition the effects of micro-structural fabric and rate dependence (creep effects) need to be accounted for in some problems. Therefore, one cannot hope to develop an understanding of real soil behaviour from laboratory studies alone without having a conceptual model of sufficient generality.

The need for such a generalised model has become even greater with the emergence of the Finite Element and the Boundary Element Methods where without a proper soil model the results of the analyses would be essentially meaningless.

It is not surprising, therefore, that during the last decade a significant part of the research effort has been directed towards developing the theories of nonlinear mechanics for providing the description of the mechanical behaviour of real soils. Of these, plasticity based concepts perhaps lead to the most general theory for the development of a proper model for the mechanical behaviour of real soils.

1

Drücker, Gibson and Henkel (1957) were the first to suggest that soil may be modelled as an elasto-plastic material with work hardening or work softening effects. Based on these ideas and the concept of critical void ratio (first proposed by Casagrande (1936) for sand), Roscoe, Schofield and Wroth (1958) developed an isotropic strain hardening model which was subsequently modified by Burland (1967) and Roscoe and Burland (1968).

Although these models provide a very good basis for understanding the stress path dependent behaviour of soils they are fundamentally applicable only to remoulded soils consolidated under an isotropic stress state. For most natural deposits (sedimented under K_0 conditions) these models do not predict correctly the differences in the stiffness and shear strengths under compression and extension tests. Although the use of a Mohr–Coulomb failure surface can partially correct some of these limitations (as was shown by Zienkiewicz et al. (1975)) these major differences can only be corrected by anisotropic models which can take account of the soil fabric developed during deposition and its alteration during the subsequent loading.

Geotechnical processes and the stresses relevant to the formation of naturally deposited soils are mainly responsible for the development of the 'inherent anisotropy'. Subsequent application of a given stress history introduces further anisotropy ('induced anisotropy') in the mechanical response of real soils. Some of the earliest discussions of such behaviour can be found in Casagrande and Carillo (1944). Inherent anisotropy is developed as a result of the applied stresses at the time of formation of the soil deposit. The relative magnitude and symmetry of these stresses determine the nature of the inherent fabric. It is conceivable that if the subsequent applied stress system is much lower than the formation stresses, the nature of the inherent fabric will dominate the observed behaviour. On the other hand, if the applied stresses during this subsequent loading are higher than the formation stresses the inherent fabric will gradually reorganize during the loading. The effective stress ratios of such loading relate the degree of this reorganization and the symmetry of the induced structure. This particular organization and alignment of soil fabric has been clearly observed during microscopic examination of the soil structure (Barden, 1972; Kirkpatrick and Rennie, 1972; Mitchell, 1966, 1970).

An extensive programme of experimental and theoretical research was undertaken by the authors during the mid-seventies to develop a consistent model which can explain the above mentioned features of a naturally deposited soil (Stipho, 1978; Banerjee and Stipho, 1978, 1979; Yousif, 1980 and Banerjee et al., 1981). This chapter essentially summarises these

developments and presents recent work relating to the generalisation of
the ideas developed in earlier works.

2 THE PROPOSED MODEL IN q–p'–e SPACE

The development of a general model for anisotropic elasto-plastic
behaviour of soils requires a treatment in six-dimensional stress space. In
this section, however, we shall restrict ourselves to a simplified treatment
for a bi-axial stress state such as that which occurs under 'triaxial' stress

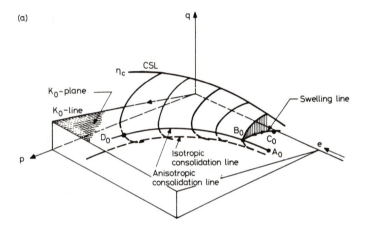

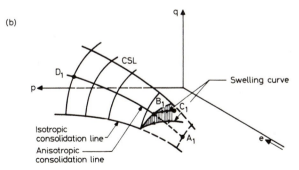

FIG. 1.   (a) Anisotropic state boundary surface; (b) state boundary surface after
Schofield and Wroth (1968).

conditions (i.e., $\sigma_1, \sigma_2 = \sigma_3$). Under such stress conditions the locus of the boundary between the elastic and elasto-plastic states of an anisotropically consolidated soil deposit may be described by a surface in a three-dimensional space, having water contents or void ratios as one axis and two effective stress components $(p = (\sigma_1 + \sigma_2 + \sigma_3)/3, \; q = \sigma_1 - \sigma_3)$ on the other two axes.

An anisotropic consolidation test, in which (q/p) is assumed constant, is represented by $A_0B_0C_0B_0D_0$ (Fig. 1(a)). This path lies in the $q_0/p_0 = $ constant, or the K_0-plane. An important feature of this new state boundary surface is that for each consolidation history ($q_0/p_0 = $ constant) a different state boundary surface is created.

Although the consolidation curves in e–$\log p$ space for samples consolidated under constant stress ratio are parallel and similar to each

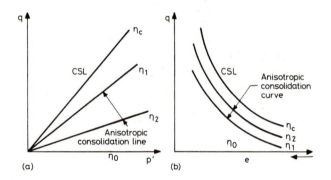

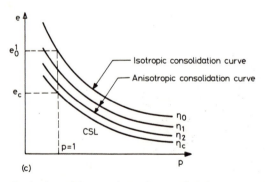

FIG. 2.   Projection of the state boundary surface for various degrees of anisotropy (η) on the (a) q–p plane; (b) q–e plane; (c) e–p plane.

other, they lie on different planes in $(e-p-q)$ space, as shown in Fig. 2. The inclination of each of these planes is dependent on the magnitude of shear (deviator stress) applied during the consolidation. Therefore, these anisotropic consolidation curves do not lie on the state boundary surface as represented by $A_1B_1C_1B_1D_1$ (Fig. 1(b)) for isotropic materials as suggested by Roscoe, Schofield and Wroth (1958). The state boundary surface for each degree of anisotropy will be different and these surfaces will no longer be symmetrical about the p-axis but would be oriented along the K_0 consolidation line in the $p-q$ space. These rotated yield surfaces are assumed to account for the initial anisotropy developed during the (q_0/p_0) consolidation. In the context of such an idealisation, an anisotropic hardening rule must be used to take account of the simultaneous expansions and rotations of the yield surface which result from further plastic deformation. For a general analysis it is no longer possible to represent the yield surface in the principal stress space; all aspects of the material behaviour must be represented in a six-dimensional stress space (see, for example, Baker and Desai (1984)).

3 GENERALISATION OF THE MODEL

3.1 Definitions
In that which follows all stresses are assumed to be effective stresses, unless otherwise stated.

Adopting the compressive stresses and strains as positive, the effective stress state in soil can be described in terms of three invariants:

$$J_1 = \tfrac{1}{3}\sigma_{ii} \qquad J_2 = (\tfrac{1}{2}s_{ij}s_{ij})^{1/2} \quad \text{and} \quad J_3 = \tfrac{1}{3}s_{ij}s_{jk}s_{ki} \qquad (1)$$

where $s_{ij} = \sigma_{ij} - \tfrac{1}{3}\delta_{ij}\sigma_{kk}$ denotes the stress deviator and δ_{ij} is the Kronecker delta.

Further, we introduce the angular measure of the third invariant J_3:

$$\theta = \tfrac{1}{3}\sin^{-1}\left(\frac{3\sqrt{3}}{2}\frac{J_3}{J_2^3}\right) \qquad \pi/6 \geq \theta \geq -\pi/6 \qquad (2)$$

The Lode angle θ can be identified in the octahedral π-plane ($J_1 = \text{constant}$). In this plane the magnitude of the vector represents the second stress invariant J_2.

For the triaxial state, $\sigma_2 = \sigma_3$, we have: $p = J_1$, $q = \sqrt{3}J_2$ and $\theta = \pi/6$.

3.2 The Yield Function

The proposed yield surface is assumed to be of approximately the same shape as that in the modified Cam-clay model and the hardening rule adopted here is a combination of isotropic and kinematic hardening rules. Due to the kinematic hardening the material develops a new state of anisotropy at every stage of the loading process. In order to characterise this anisotropy a new tensor q_{ij} defined with respect to the apex of the yield surface (σ_{ij}^0) is introduced (Fig. 3):

$$q_{ij} = \sigma_{ij}^0 - \tfrac{1}{3}\delta_{ij}\sigma_{kk}^0 \tag{3}$$

With the above definitions the yield function defining the family of evolving yield surfaces can take the form:

$$f(\sigma_{ij}, q_{ij}, p_0) = \frac{3}{2g^2(\bar{\theta})}\left[\bar{s}_{ij}\bar{s}_{ij} - \frac{1}{9}\frac{p}{p_0}q_{ij}q_{ij}\right] - pp_0 + p^2 = 0 \tag{4}$$

where

$$g(\bar{\theta}) = \frac{2kg(\pi/6)}{(1+k) - (1-k)\sin 3\bar{\theta}}$$

$$k = \frac{3 - \sin\phi}{3 + \sin\phi}$$

$$g(\pi/6) = \frac{6\sin\phi}{3 - \sin\phi}$$

$$\bar{\theta} = \tfrac{1}{3}\sin^{-1}\left(\frac{3\sqrt{3}}{2}\frac{\bar{J}_3}{\bar{J}_2^3}\right)$$

$$\bar{J}_2 = [\tfrac{1}{2}\bar{s}_{ij}\bar{s}_{ij}]^{1/2}$$

$$\bar{J}_3 = \tfrac{1}{3}\bar{s}_{ij}\bar{s}_{jk}\bar{s}_{ki}$$

$$\bar{s}_{ij} = s_{ij} - \tfrac{2}{3}(p/p_0)q_{ij}$$

$$p = \tfrac{1}{3}\sigma_{ii}$$

$$p_0 = \tfrac{1}{3}\sigma_{ii}^0$$

and

$$\phi = \text{the Coulomb friction angle.}$$

Equation (4) represents a family of asymmetric distorted ellipsoids oriented in the direction of the K_0 consolidation line in an axisymmetric stress plane $(\sigma_2 = \sigma_3)$ as shown in Fig. 3(b).

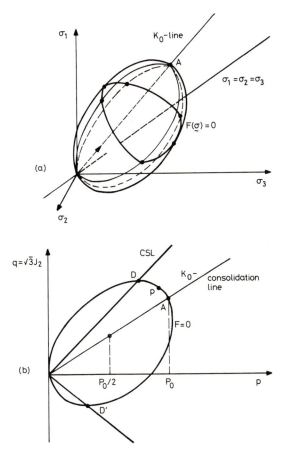

FIG. 3. Anisotropic model: (a) yield surface in general stress space; (b) yield surface in $(p-q)$ space.

It is evident that the tensor $\bar{s}_{ij}$ is a reduced state of the deviatoric stress tensor s_{ij} and the translational tensor q_{ij} specifies the instantaneous orientation of the yield surface with respect to the space diagonal. For the isotropic model (isotropically consolidated soil) the tensor q_{ij} vanishes and the well known form of the evolution equation for the modified Cam-clay model is recovered:

$$f(\sigma_{ij}, p_0) = \frac{3}{2g(\theta)^2} s_{ij}s_{ij} - pp_0 + p^2 \qquad (5)$$

which for a triaxial state takes the form:

$$f(p, q, p_0) = \frac{q^2}{M^2} - pp_0 + p^2 \tag{6}$$

where

$$M = g(\theta) = \frac{6 \sin \phi}{3 \mp \sin \phi}$$

3.3 Anisotropic Hardening Rule

The simultaneous expansion and translation built into eqn (4) simulate the changes in the void ratio as well as the development of the fabric structure during consolidation.

Extensive experimental studies (Namy, 1970; Parry and Nadarajah, 1974 and Stipho, 1978) indicate that the void ratio during anisotropic consolidation is not only a function of the mean effective pressure p but also of the stress ratio (q/p). Accordingly a general expression for the void ratio changes may be written as

$$e = e_0^1 - \lambda \ln p + \alpha q/p \tag{7}$$

where e_0^1 is a reference void ratio, α is a coefficient and $q = [\frac{3}{2} q_{ij} q_{ij}]^{1/2}$.

Similarly experimental studies by Stipho (1978) show that the equation for the swelling line can be expressed as:

$$e = e_0^2 - \kappa \ln p \tag{8}$$

where e_0^2 is a reference void ratio.

These equations governing the change of void ratio during anisotropic consolidation suggest that the change of hardening parameters p_0 and q_{ij} can be expressed by

$$dp_0 = \frac{1 + e_0}{\lambda - \kappa} p_0 \, d\varepsilon_{ii}^p \tag{9}$$

$$dq_{ij} = \frac{1 + e_0}{\lambda - \kappa} s_{ij} \, d\varepsilon_{kk}^p \tag{10}$$

where e_0 is the initial void ratio.

The resulting incremental stress strain relations when applied to the case of anisotropic consolidation predict the change of void ratio in accord with eqn (7), where α becomes a state dependent parameter and not an independent soil parameter (such as λ and κ) as implied there. The current stress state as well as the characteristic soil parameters λ and κ uniquely determine the response during an anisotropic consolidation.

3.4 Incremental Stress–Strain Relations for Monotonic Loading

By decomposing the elastic and plastic strains in the usual manner the correct stresses $d\boldsymbol{\sigma}$ can be obtained from Hooke's law as

$$d\boldsymbol{\sigma} = \mathbf{D}^e \, d\boldsymbol{\varepsilon}^e \qquad \text{or} \qquad d\boldsymbol{\sigma} = \mathbf{D}^e(d\boldsymbol{\varepsilon} - d\boldsymbol{\varepsilon}^p) \tag{11}$$

where $\mathbf{D}^e$ is the elastic constitutive matrix and $d\boldsymbol{\varepsilon}$ is the total strain rate.

The consistency relation requiring the stress state to remain on the yield surface is

$$df = \left(\frac{\partial f}{\partial \boldsymbol{\sigma}}\right)^{\mathrm{T}} d\boldsymbol{\sigma} + \left(\frac{\partial f}{\partial \mathbf{q}}\right)^{\mathrm{T}} d\mathbf{q} + \left(\frac{\partial f}{\partial p_0}\right) dp_0 = 0 \tag{12}$$

Assuming the associated plastic flow we have

$$d\boldsymbol{\varepsilon}^p = d\lambda \frac{\partial f}{\partial \boldsymbol{\sigma}} \tag{13}$$

where $d\lambda$ is a flow factor.

From eqns (9) to (13) the state dependent flow factor $d\lambda$ can be determined and the plastic strain $d\boldsymbol{\varepsilon}^p$ can be then expressed as:

$$d\boldsymbol{\varepsilon}^p = \frac{\left(\dfrac{\partial f}{\partial \boldsymbol{\sigma}}\right)^{\mathrm{T}} \mathbf{D}^e(d\boldsymbol{\varepsilon})}{H_p + H_e} \left(\frac{\partial f}{\partial \boldsymbol{\sigma}}\right) \tag{14}$$

where

$$H_e = \left(\frac{\partial f}{\partial \boldsymbol{\sigma}}\right)^{\mathrm{T}} \mathbf{D}^e \left(\frac{\partial f}{\partial \boldsymbol{\sigma}}\right) \quad \text{and} \quad H_p = -\left(\frac{1+e_0}{\lambda - \kappa}\right) \mathrm{tr} \left(\frac{\partial f}{\partial \boldsymbol{\sigma}}\right) \left[p_0 \frac{\partial f}{\partial p_0} + \mathbf{s}^{\mathrm{T}} \frac{\partial f}{\partial \mathbf{q}}\right]$$

Accordingly the constitutive equation for a general stress state is given by

$$d\boldsymbol{\sigma} = \left[\mathbf{D}^e - \frac{\mathbf{D}^e \left(\dfrac{\partial F}{\partial \boldsymbol{\sigma}}\right)\left(\dfrac{\partial F}{\partial \boldsymbol{\sigma}}\right)^{\mathrm{T}} \mathbf{D}^e}{H_p + H_e} \right] d\boldsymbol{\varepsilon} \tag{15}$$

Explicit expressions for the gradient vector $\partial f/\partial \boldsymbol{\sigma}$ to the surface $f = 0$ and the hardening moduli H_p and H_e are derived in the Appendix.

Once again the isotropic response can be easily recovered from eqn (15) by setting $\mathbf{q} = 0$. Equation (15) together with eqns (9) and (10) allow us to predict the material response at any stage of a loading process providing the initial status of the state variables q_{ij}, σ_{ij} and p_0 are defined and the characteristic material parameters λ, κ, e_0, ϕ and v are specified. Equation (15) can be then integrated along a specified loading path to obtain the stress–strain response at every stage of the loading.

It should be noted that in the above derivation no restriction was placed on the elastic behaviour which can either be anisotropic or isotropic; although for the purposes of defining the behaviour with a minimum number of soil parameters we have assumed isotropic elasticity. The value of Young's modulus can be then easily shown to be

$$E = \frac{3p(1 + e_0)(1 - 2v)}{\kappa} \qquad (16)$$

where v is the Poisson's ratio of the soil skeleton.

It is interesting to recall that by comparing the swelling behaviour of anisotropically consolidated clays and those of an ideal cross-anisotropic elastic skeleton, Stipho (1978) obtained an expression for Young's modulus in the vertical direction as

$$E_1 = p(1 + e_0)\left[1 - 4v_{12} + \frac{2}{N}(1 - v_{22})\right]\Big/ \kappa \qquad (17)$$

where v_{12} and v_{22} are Poisson's ratios (where 1 and 2 refer to the vertical and horizontal axes, respectively). $N = E_2/E_1 = \sigma_1^0/\sigma_2^0$, the degree of anisotropy, which is assumed to be identical to the stress ratio during the formation.

For the isotropic state, $v_{12} = v_{22} = v$ and $N = 1$, eqn (17) becomes identical to eqn (16).

3.5 Extension of the Model to Cyclic Loading

One of the major problems in soil mechanics is the description of the response of soils under cyclic loading. Soils in general undergo both elastic and plastic deformation simultaneously at every stage of the loading process. The constitutive model based on clearly defined elastic and elasto-plastic behaviour outlined above is inadequate for cyclic loading since experimental results show very clearly that within the elastic domain bounded by the state boundary surface small plastic deformation occurs. The cumulative effects of these residual inelastic strains which often exist at the micro-structural level may lead to the total collapse of the soil structure.

Recently a number of researchers have developed and proposed various material models for elucidating the cyclic behaviour of soils (Pande and Zienkiewicz, 1982; Mroz et al., 1979, 1981; Pietruszczak and Mroz, 1981, 1983 and Prevost, 1977, 1978). Most of these models involve the use of the 'nested yield surface' concept of Mroz (1967). The major problem with these models is, of course, the identification of the soil parameters from conventional soil tests and accordingly they are rather difficult to use for practical problems.

A less complex and potentially practical model for cyclic loading based on the basic ideas expressed by Mroz (1967) was introduced by Dafalias and Popov (1974, 1975) and Krieg (1975) where an enclosed yield surface within the bounding surface (which characterises gross yielding) was used for cyclic deformation of metals. This yield surface was later abandoned in order to model materials with no defined ideal elastic behaviour (Dafalias and Popov, 1975, 1977).

A form of bounding surface/yield surface plasticity formulation for soils was discussed by Mroz et al. (1978) which was subsequently developed further by Mroz et al. (1979) within the framework of the modified Cam-clay model. The case of a vanishing elastic region was also discussed. More recently, Dafalias and Herrmann (1980) developed a simpler bounding surface plasticity model with a vanishing elastic region.

In the present work we shall make use of the basic concepts developed by Dafalias and Herrmann to extend the anisotropic soil plasticity model developed earlier to deal with cyclic loading.

It is assumed that initial consolidation process defines the bounding surface which is identical to the yield surface defined in the monotonic loading case discussed in the previous section. This surface preserves the memory of the previous formation stress history. A stress state σ_{ij}^* is assumed to lie always on the bounding surface defined by

$$F(\sigma_{ij}^*, q_{ij}, p_0) = 0 \tag{18}$$

Equation (18) is essentially identical to eqn (4) with σ_{ij} replaced by σ_{ij}^*.

To each current stress point σ_{ij} within the bounding surface, a unique σ_{ij}^* on $F = 0$ is defined according to a specific rule. Here σ_{ij}^* is the intersection of the line joining the origin 0 and the stress point σ_{ij} extended to the bounding surface (see Fig. 4) such that

$$\sigma_{ij}^* = \beta \sigma_{ij} \tag{19}$$

where β is a scale factor obtained from the condition $F(\beta\sigma_{ij}, q_{ij}, p_0) = 0$.

The gradient tensor $\partial F/\partial \sigma_{ij}^*$ defined at σ_{ij}^* determines the direction of the

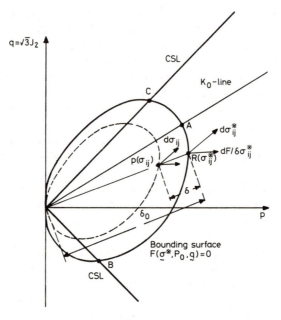

FIG. 4.   Bounding surface in p–q space.

plastic strain rate $d\varepsilon_{ij}^{p}$ at the stress point σ_{ij}; whence eqn (14) can be rewritten for determining the irrecoverable strain components as:

$$d\varepsilon^{p} = \frac{\left(\dfrac{\partial F}{\partial \sigma^{*}}\right)^{\mathrm{T}} \mathbf{D}^{e}(d\varepsilon)}{H_{p} + H_{e}} \left(\frac{\partial F}{\partial \sigma^{*}}\right) \tag{20}$$

where H_{p} is the actual plastic hardening modulus associated with the stress point σ_{ij} and

$$H_{e} = \left(\frac{\partial F}{\partial \sigma^{*}}\right)^{\mathrm{T}} \mathbf{D}^{e} \left(\frac{\partial F}{\partial \sigma^{*}}\right)$$

From the definition of the gradient tensor it follows that at each point σ_{ij}, an imaginary surface identical to the bounding surface is indirectly defined. This surface defines a quasi-elastic domain but is not a yield surface, since the stress point may move first elastically upon unloading, i.e.:

$$dL = \frac{\partial f}{\partial \sigma} d\sigma < 0 \tag{21}$$

and then reloading ($dL > 0$) causes plastic strains to develop even before the original surface is reached. This is obviously quite contrary to the original plasticity theory proposed by Drücker (1951). The continually changing distance δ in the stress space between the stress state σ_{ij} and the corresponding point σ_{ij}^* on the bounding surface, as well as the initial value $\delta_0 = (\sigma_{ij}^* \sigma_{ij}^*)^{1/2}$, determines the value of the actual plastic modulus H_p as:

$$H_p = H_p(\delta, \delta_0)$$

$$= H_r + H_0 \left(\frac{\delta}{\delta_0 - \delta} \right)^\mu \tag{22}$$

where $\delta = [\mathrm{tr}\,(\sigma_{ij}^* - \sigma_{ij})^2]^{1/2}$, the scaled distance between P and R

μ = a material parameter

H_r = the plastic modulus at R on the bounding surface

H_0 = a reference modulus which we have taken as the maximum value of H_r (at the point A).

The value of plastic modulus H_r is given by the equation:

$$H_r = -\left(\frac{1 + e_0}{\lambda - \kappa} \right) \mathrm{tr} \left(\frac{\partial F}{\partial \boldsymbol{\sigma}^*} \right) \left(p_0 \frac{\partial F}{\partial p_0} + \mathbf{s}^{*\mathrm{T}} \frac{\partial F}{\partial \mathbf{q}} \right) \tag{23}$$

where $\mathbf{s}^* = \boldsymbol{\sigma}^* - \frac{1}{3} \mathrm{tr}\, \boldsymbol{\sigma}^*$.

The resulting incremental stress–strain relations for a general stress state σ_{ij} is then given by

$$d\boldsymbol{\sigma} = \left[\mathbf{D}^e - \frac{\mathbf{D}^e \left(\dfrac{\partial F}{\partial \boldsymbol{\sigma}^*} \right) \left(\dfrac{\partial F}{\partial \boldsymbol{\sigma}^*} \right)^{\mathrm{T}} \mathbf{D}^e}{H_p + H_e} \right] d\varepsilon \tag{24}$$

Equation (24) differs from eqn (15) only when the stress state σ_{ij} is inside the bounding surface. As the stress state reaches the bounding surface σ_{ij} becomes identical to σ_{ij}^* and functions f and F also become identical. Since the distance δ vanishes on the bounding surface the hardening parameter H_p equals H_r. If the stress state σ_{ij} is inside the bounding surface, depending on the distance δ and the chosen material parameter for cyclic loading μ, the plastic modulus H_p can become considerably larger than that at a corresponding point on the bounding surface. The magnitude of the plastic strain predicted reduces accordingly.

It should be noted that by setting $q_{ij} = 0$ in eqn (24) we can recover the isotropic bounding surface model for the monotonic and cyclic loading, and by setting H_0 to a suitably large value we can recover the elasto-plastic model for monotonic loading discussed earlier (see eqn (15)). The bounding surface then behaves as an ordinary yield surface.

4 EXPERIMENTAL INVESTIGATION

The motivation for the development of the anisotropic plasticity model, described in the preceding section, was generated by an experimental research program on the stress–strain behaviour of saturated samples of Kaolin consolidated under isotropic and anisotropic stress systems. The complete details of this experimental work can be found in the PhD thesis of Stipho (1978). The results of the research on the isotropically consolidated series were reported by Banerjee and Stipho (1978, 1979), where they were compared with those obtained from the Cam-clay and modified Cam-clay models. The experimental program is briefly outlined below.

A quantity of oven-dried Kaolin (LL = 52, PL = 26) was mixed with distilled water in ratio of 1:1 by weight. The slurry sample was then transferred into a vacuum chamber where a suction of 13 psi was applied for about 2 h during which the chamber was shaken every 10 min to allow all entrapped air to migrate. The slurry was then spooned into a special consolidation cell designed for this investigation, details of which are given in Stipho (1978). The consolidation cell once filled with slurry was left on a vibrating plate for 1 h to remove all the entrapped air that was possible. The consolidation cell was then sealed and a hydraulic pressure system was applied to the top of a rigid diaphragm in increments of 2 psi. Each increment was left for 24 h to allow for the dissipation of the excess pore water pressure. The final consolidation pressure of 8 psi was kept on the sample for 4 days. The pressure was then released and the cell dismantled.

A specimen of 3 in diameter, 6 in long was trimmed from the sample and then mounted under water in a triaxial cell for further consolidation. During this mounting all the necessary precautions and care were taken to prevent the possibility of air being trapped between the rubber membrane and the sample. A special mounting frame was also designed to support this soft sample before the cell pressure and the deviatoric loading system could be applied. Indeed, inspite of these precautions a number of samples did collapse under the weight of the end plattens and had to be discarded. The lateral stress was applied through the surrounding chamber fluid by an automatic air pressure system controlled by manostats having a sensitivity of 0·1 psi. The deviatoric consolidation stress was applied through a plunger controlled through another air pressure system.

The volume change during this second stage of consolidation was measured and the radial deformation of the sample was calculated from the volume change and the compression of the sample, i.e. assuming, of course, an uniform radial deformation. The use of lubricated end plattens ensured the uniform radial deformation which was visible in all tests.

Depending on the applied stress system the entire test programme was classified into I, A and T series. In the I-series (isotropic) the samples were consolidated isotropically in pressure increments of 10 psi applied at 24 h intervals until the desired states were reached. In the A-series the principal stress ratios ($N = \sigma_1^0/\sigma_3^0$) of 1·25, 1·5 and 1·75 were applied in simultaneous increments of 3 psi and were allowed to consolidate fully before the next increments were applied. The swelling of the samples to the desired overconsolidation ratios (OCR) were also accomplished under the same stress ratio. In the T-series the samples were first consolidated isotropically in increments of 10 psi until the desired lateral stress is reached when it was consolidated further by an incremental axial loading of 3 psi to achieve the desired stress ratio N. This second stage consolidation for all three series was carried out under a back pressure of 20 psi to ensure maximum saturation during all stages of loading and unloading. Before the commencement of the undrained triaxial compression and extension tests (designated by the letters C and E, respectively in Tables 1 and 2) a small mean pressure was applied to the sample to investigate if their pore water pressure responses were satisfactory.

TABLE 1

TEST PROGRAM FOR ISOTROPIC SERIES

Test no.	p_0	p	OCR	Types of test	$w\%$
IC-1	60·0	60·0	1·0	Compression	35·2
IC-2	53·0	53·0	1·0	Compression	35·4
IC-3	30·0	30·0	1·0	Compression	38·4
IC-4	37·0	37·0	1·0	Compression	37·2
IC-5	35·0	35·0	1·0	Compression	37·9
IC-6	53·0	44·0	1·2	Compression	35·9
IC-7	56·0	28·0	2·0	Compression	36·8
IC-8	55·0	11·0	5·0	Compression	35·3
IC-9	56·0	7·0	8·0	Compression	38·5
IC-10	60·0	5·0	12·0	Compression	38·8
IE-1	56·0	56·0	1·0	Extension	35·3
IE-1R	56·0	56·0	1·0	Extension	35·5
IE-2	60·0	60·0	1·0	Extension	35·2
IE-3	60·0	30·0	2·0	Extension	36·3
IE-4	60·0	50·0	1·2	Extension	35·3
IE-5	80·0	13·3	6·0	Extension	38·0
IE-6	60·0	6·0	10·0	Extension	39·0

TABLE 2

TEST PROGRAM FOR THE ANISOTROPIC SERIES

Test no.	p_0	p	N	OCR	Type of test	$w\%$
AC-1	30·0	30·0	1·25	1	Compression	38·2
AC-2	30·0	15·0	1·25	2	Compression	38·8
AC-3	30·0	7·5	1·25	4	Compression	40·5
AC-4	50·0	12·5	1·25	4	Compression	40·0
AC-5	80·0	10·0	1·25	8	Compression	37·4
AC-6	30·0	30·0	1·50	1	Compression	37·9
AC-7	30·0	15·0	1·50	2	Compression	39·9
AC-8	30·0	7·5	1·50	4	Compression	40·3
AC-9	80·0	10·0	1·50	8	Compression	37·2
AC-10	30·0	30·0	1·75	1	Compression	37·6
AC-11	30·0	15·0	1·75	2	Compression	39·3
AC-12	30·0	7·5	1·75	4	Compression	40·1
AC-13	50·0	12·5	1·75	4	Compression	39·7
AC-14	80·0	10·0	1·75	8	Compression	37·2
AE-15	30·0	30·0	1·25	1	Extension	38·1
AE-16	30·0	15·0	1·25	2	Extension	39·5
AE-17	50·0	12·5	1·25	4	Extension	40·5
AE-18	80·0	10·0	1·25	8	Extension	38·2
AE-19	30·0	30·0	1·50	1	Extension	37·8
AE-19R	30·0	30·0	1·50	1	Extension	37·6
AE-20	30·0	15·0	1·50	2	Extension	39·5
AE-21	50·0	12·5	1·50	4	Extension	40·2
AE-22	80·0	10·0	1·50	8	Extension	38·0
AE-23	30·0	30·0	1·75	1	Extension	37·6
AE-24	30·0	15·0	1·75	2	Extension	39·4
AE-25	50·0	12·5	1·75	4	Extension	40·0
AE-25R	50·0	12·5	1·75	4	Extension	39·8
AE-26	80·0	10·0	1·75	8	Extension	38·1
TC-1	30·0	30·0	1·25	1	Compression	38·0
TC-2	30·0	30·0	1·50	1	Compression	37·8
TC-3	30·0	30·0	1·75	1	Compression	37·8

All tests were carried out under stress controlled conditions. In the case of compression tests an increment $\dot\sigma_1$ of 3 psi was applied at 1 h intervals to allow for complete equalisation of the pore water pressures. Extension tests were also carried out in a similar manner. There are some drawbacks in these stress controlled tests, as described by Parry and Nadarajah (1974), particularly in extension tests where the determined failure point cannot be precise. Indeed, in all extension tests of the A-series on overconsolidated clays the stress paths seem to continue beyond the failure envelope of the normally consolidated soil. Similar observations were also reported by Parry and Nadarajah (1974) as well as Ladd *et al.* (1971).

Tables 1 and 2 show the details of the samples that were tested under this program of experimental work. Samples IC-1 to IC-5 and IE-1 to IE-2 were used to investigate the repeatability and reproducibility of the test results. The normalised stress–strain plots (q/p_0 vs. ε_1) were within $\pm 2\%$ of the mean results indicating the general quality of the experimental data. It should be emphasised that in natural deposits the consolidation and swelling histories would be different from those used in this experimental program. The different stress ratios N used during the consolidation were designed to give the soil a variety of defined structures during the formation.

5   COMPARISON OF THE EXPERIMENTAL RESULTS AND MODEL PREDICTIONS

In order to evaluate the usefulness and the applicability of the model developed in Sections 2 and 3, the predicted results were compared with the data from the experimental investigation outlined in the preceding section.

The soil parameters needed for the model are λ, κ, ϕ, v, e_0 and μ. Of these only two (v and μ) were not determined from the laboratory tests. Accordingly for all the comparisons reported in this section these were assumed to be 0·3 and 5, respectively. The remaining parameters determined from tests were:

$$\lambda = 0\cdot14 \qquad \kappa = 0\cdot05 \qquad e_0 = wG_s \qquad G_s = 2\cdot65$$
$$\phi = 26\cdot5^\circ \text{ (for I-series)} \qquad \phi = 29\cdot5^\circ \text{ (for A-series)}$$

5.1 Comparisons with the I-series

The effective stress paths, stress–strain curves and pore water pressure responses are compared with the corresponding experimental results in Figs 5–9. It is evident that the model predictions are reasonably close to experimental data for OCR > 1·2. The predicted stress paths for OCR = 1 and 1·2, especially in compression tests, are stiffer than the experimental data because of the choice of an elliptical shape of the consolidation surface (bounding surface).

The form of the undrained stress paths (Fig. 5) deserves some attention since it depends strongly on the relative values of the hardening modulus H_p and the relative distance δ from the bounding surface. The smooth undrained stress paths for all OCR values (Fig. 5) indicate plastic

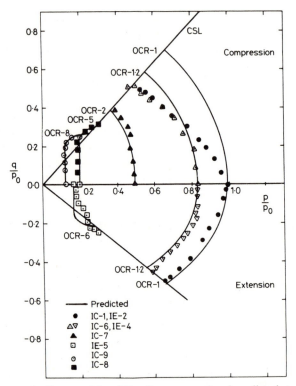

FIG. 5.   Isotropically consolidated Kaolin: measured and predicted stress paths in undrained triaxial compression and extension tests.

deformation within the bounding surface at the very early stage of loading. In a classical yield surface formulation (see Banerjee and Stipho, 1978, 1979) the stress paths would have been vertical within the bounding surface until they reach the surface when the plastic deformation occurs.

For OCR = 1 and 1·2, the stress state reaches the bounding surface and moves with it as a result of its subsequent expansion and rotation in the stress space, until it reaches the failure surface when unconstrained plastic flow occurs. For OCR > 2 the initial behaviour is dominantly elastic until the bounding surface is approached when the dilatant behaviour is observed.

5.2 Comparison with the A-series
Figures 10, 11 and 12 show the comparisons between the theoretical and experimental stress paths in compression and extension tests for

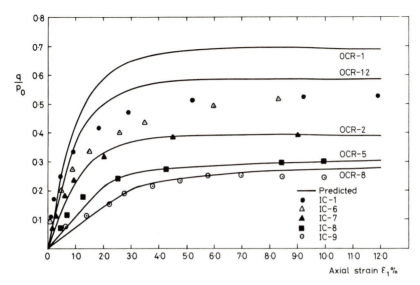

FIG. 6.   Isotropically consolidated Kaolin: measured and predicted stress–strain relations in undrained triaxial compression tests.

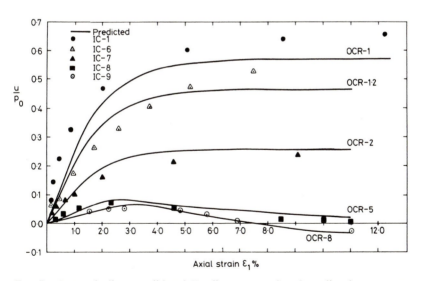

FIG. 7.   Isotropically consolidated Kaolin: measured and predicted pore water pressure responses in undrained triaxial compression tests.

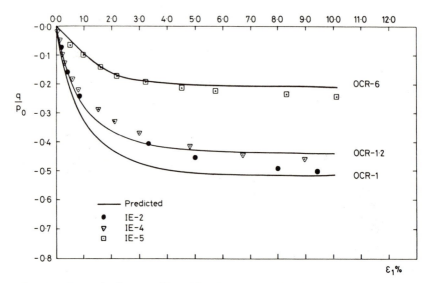

FIG. 8.   Isotropically consolidated Kaolin: measured and predicted stress–strain relations in undrained triaxial extension tests.

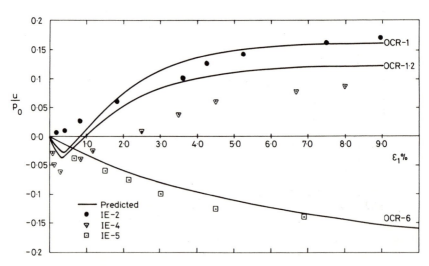

FIG. 9.   Isotropically consolidated Kaolin: measured and predicted pore water pressure responses in undrained triaxial extension tests.

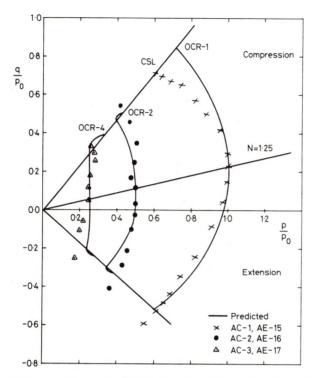

FIG. 10. Anisotropically consolidated Kaolin: measured and predicted undrained stress paths for $N = 1·25$ in compression and extension tests.

anisotropically consolidated samples (OCR = 1, 2 and 4) for different degrees of anisotropy $N = 1·25$, $1·5$ and $1·75$, respectively. The predicted paths are in good agreement with the experimental data except for extension tests where the experimental data appear to continue outside the extension failure envelope. Similar data have also been reported in the literature (e.g. Parry and Nadarajah, 1974; Ladd et al., 1971) and is widely believed to be of doubtful validity.

Figures 13 to 16 show the comparisons between the experimentally observed stress–strain and pore water pressure responses in compression tests and the corresponding theoretical predictions. Only two cases of anisotropy $N = 1·25$ and $1·75$ have been considered since the results for $1·5$ lie somewhat in between these two cases. For overconsolidated clays it is the early part of the stress–strain response which is dominated by the elastic stiffness and is not predicted very well by the theory. This is probably due to

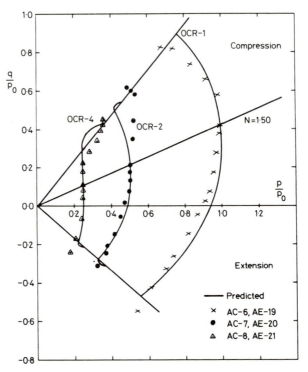

FIG. 11. Anisotropically consolidated Kaolin: measured and predicted undrained stress paths for $N = 1.50$ in compression and extension tests.

the anisotropic elastic behaviour which was not included in the present
calculations. Indeed, the results presented in Stipho (1978), which include
the effects of elastic anisotropy, are in better agreement with the
experimental data. Introduction of the elastic anisotropy will of course
require at least three additional elastic constants and therefore will reduce
the usefulness of the model in practice.

General trends of the stiffnesses and the pore water pressure responses
are quite well predicted by the model.

The experimental results for the T-series were also compared with the
present model but are not presented here. The stress–strain and pore water
pressure responses were predicted quite well. This is not surprising since
the initial isotropic consolidation quite possibly reduced the anisotropy in
the elastic stiffnesses, particularly for the $N = 1.25$ state. In general the
experimental stress–strain curves for the T-series were less stiff than those
of the A-series.

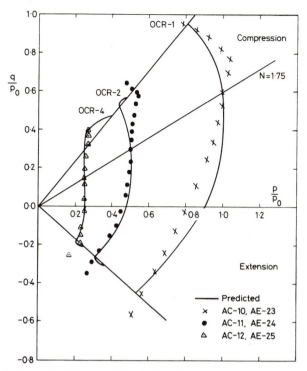

FIG. 12. Anisotropically consolidated Kaolin: measured and predicted undrained stress paths for $N = 1.75$ in compression and extension tests.

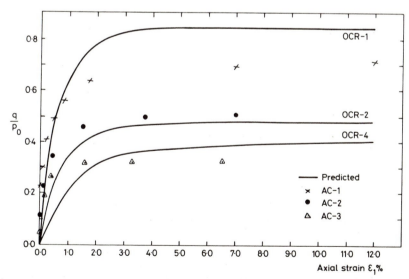

FIG. 13. Anisotropically consolidated Kaolin: $N = 1.25$, measured and predicted stress–strain relations in undrained triaxial compression tests.

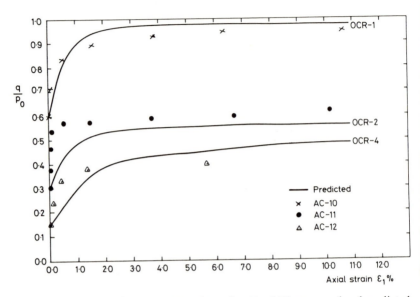

FIG. 14.   Anisotropically consolidated Kaolin: $N = 1.75$, measured and predicted stress–strain relations in undrained triaxial compression tests.

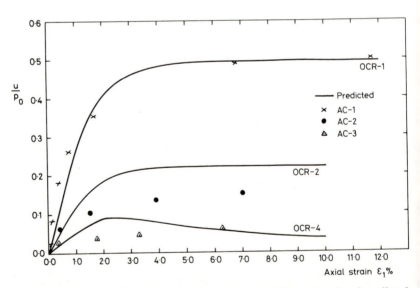

FIG. 15.   Anisotropically consolidated Kaolin: $N = 1.25$, measured and predicted pore water pressure responses in undrained triaxial compression tests.

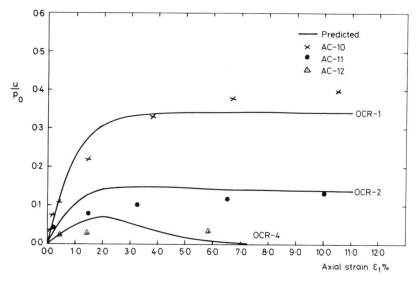

FIG. 16.   Anisotropically consolidated Kaolin: $N = 1.75$, measured and predicted
pore water pressure responses in undrained triaxial compression tests.

6   COMPARISON WITH OTHER EXPERIMENTAL DATA

6.1   Undrained Triaxial Tests after K_0 Consolidation

Nadarajah (1973) has provided a set of interesting test data from undrained
compression and extension tests on soils initially consolidated one-
dimensionally (K_0) in a triaxial cell to the stress state of $p = p_0 =
418\,\mathrm{k\,N\,m^{-2}}$, $q = q_0 = 198\,\mathrm{k\,N\,m^{-2}}$ with $K_0 = 0.64$.

The prediction of the theoretical results are based on the following soil
parameters (as reported by Nadarajah), the slope of the consolidation line
$\lambda = 0.27$, that of the swelling line $\kappa = 0.06$, the initial void ratio $e_0 = 0.95$
and the slope of the failure line $\phi = 20.8°$. The value of $\nu = 0.3$ was
assumed.

The predicted and the observed stress–strain relations for K_0-
consolidated samples sheared in compression and extension tests are
presented in Fig. 17. The general agreement is satisfactory.

During an undrained extension test the stress point moves elastically for
the first increment, due to unloading $(\mathrm{d}L < 0)$, and then causes plastic
deformation within the bounding surface. Upon reaching the surface the
stress point will move with it until the failure line is reached. Due to the

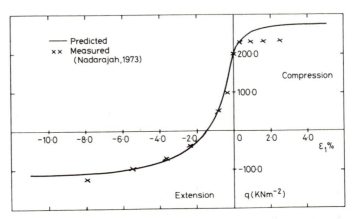

FIG. 17. K_0-normally consolidated Kaolin: predicted and measured stress–strain behaviour in undrained triaxial compression and extension tests.

kinematic hardening and the application of a stress path which is different from the previous consolidation history, the material develops a new state of anisotropy and this is reflected in the magnitude of the translational tensor q_{ij}. It is also of considerable interest to note that the stiffness and strength in extension test are considerably lower than those in compression.

6.2 K_0 Swelling Test

The stress history for unloading under K_0-conditions is very important in soil mechanics. In order to understand the *in situ* effective stress distribution within the soil and the change that occurs when natural deposits are unloaded during geological events, it is essential to determine the value of K_0 ($\sigma_h = \sigma_v K_0$). Several workers have attempted to determine the magnitude of K_0 from experimental studies (Skempton, 1961; Brooker and Ireland, 1965; Nadarajah, 1973; Singh *et al.*, 1973). They observed that during K_0-unloading the influence of stress history is best expressed in terms of the overconsolidation ratio (OCR). The value of K_0 is generally found to increase steadily with increasing OCR. Although many empirical expressions for evaluating K_0 are available (for instance, Jaky, 1944, 1948; Wroth, 1975; Alpan, 1967) for a wide range of OCR values, none of them is based on any sound theoretical foundation.

The effectiveness of the model in predicting the value of K_0 during one-dimensional swelling is evaluated by comparing it with observed results on samples which were first consolidated one-dimensionally and were then allowed to swell back, as reported by Nadarajah (1973). The theoretical

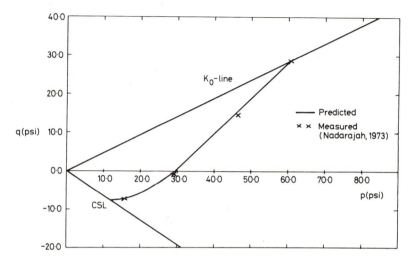

Fig. 18. K_0-normally consolidated Kaolin: measured and predicted stress path in K_0-unloading.

predictions depicted in Figs 18 and 19 were obtained using the same material parameters and loading history described earlier. Highly consistent agreement between the theoretical and the observed stress paths are shown in Fig. 18. The increase of the K_0 value during unloading with the increasing overconsolidation ratio has also been predicted satisfactorily, as shown in Fig. 19. The isotropic critical state model will not reproduce this behaviour.

It is interesting to observe that the predicted stress path shown in Fig. 18 lies totally within the bounding surface. The stress point moves first elastically due to unloading ($dL < 0$), and then loading ($dL > 0$) causes plastic deformation to develop until the stress point reaches the failure line. The initial anisotropy is fully preserved during the K_0 unloading.

6.3 Perfect Sampling and Testing

Skempton and Sowa (1963) reported the results of a laboratory investigation of the stresses and strains associated with the 'perfect' sampling of anisotropically (K_0) consolidated samples. They concluded that the undrained shear strengths for triaxial compression of 'perfect' samples are approximately equal to those of anisotropically consolidated in-ground samples, provided that the strains during sampling are not sufficiently large to cause significant micro-structural changes. Ladd and

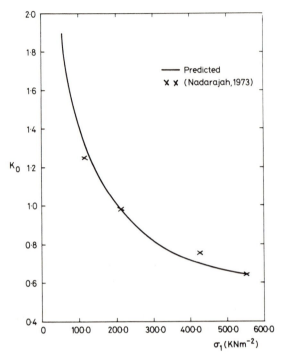

FIG. 19. K_0-normally consolidated Kaolin: measured and predicted K_0-values in K_0-unloading.

Bailey (1964) also examined the effects of sampling disturbance and the stress path to failure. They produced results to support those of Skempton and Sowa.

The model predictions shown here are based on the initial stress state of $\sigma_1 = 90 \cdot 1$ psi, and σ_3 being obtained with $K_0 = 0 \cdot 59$. The other soil parameters are: $\lambda = 0 \cdot 093$, $\kappa = 0 \cdot 035$, $\phi = 26°$, $e_0 = 0 \cdot 92$ (initial void ratio for the perfect sample, test 63), and $e_0 = 0 \cdot 91$ (initial void ratio for the undisturbed sample, test 64).

The observed and predicted stress paths, stress–strain and pore water pressure responses are shown in Figs 20 to 22. The stress path AB represents the effects of taking a naturally deposited (K_0 consolidated) sample out of ground by a 'perfect sampling' operation where the sample loses its deviator stress under completely undrained unloading. If an undrained compression test is now carried out on a sample from this state the stress path would rise initially vertically until it approaches the

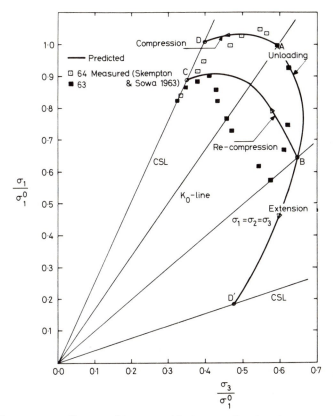

FIG. 20. K_0-normally consolidated weald clay: predicted and measured stress paths during sampling and testing.

bounding surface when it will bend due to plastic deformation and fail at the point C. If it were possible to carry out a compression test from the *in situ* state A, the stress path followed for an undrained compression test can be represented by AD (Fig. 20). Although the shear strengths of two samples are not dramatically different, there will be a major difference in the stiffnesses of the two samples.

The theoretical results show a general qualitative agreement with the experimental data. The differences stem mainly from the stress point B not moving far enough towards the origin of the p axis. This is a direct consequence of the elliptical shape of bounding surface.

As noted earlier, there would be major differences in the shear strength

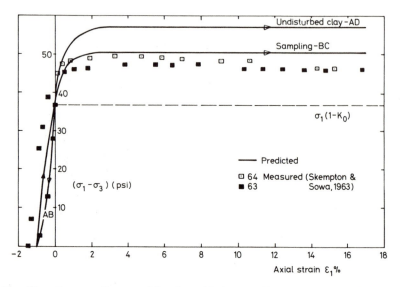

FIG. 21. K_0-normally consolidated weald clay: predicted and measured stress–strain relations during sampling and testing.

and the stiffness of the sample tested under triaxial compression and extension tests starting from the point B (the end of a perfect sampling operation). During a compression test, the path followed can be represented by BC as shown in Fig. 20. In an extension test, however, since the point B is on the bounding surface already, the stress path followed would be quite close to the shape of the lower part of the rotated bounding surface. The failure state would be close to a point such as D′ shown in Fig. 20. The resulting shear strength as well as the stiffness of the sample in an extension test would be considerably lower than those in a compression test (by as much as 100%). Cairncross and James (1977) observed similar differences in the behaviour of undisturbed samples in compression and extension tests. Such differences in the observed behaviour cannot be reproduced by the Cam-clay or the modified Cam-clay models, where the difference in strengths in compression and extension is only due to the values of the critical state parameter M.

6.4 Isotropic Consolidation of a K_0 Consolidation Sample
In this section, we shall examine, by using the present model, how an anisotropically consolidated clay can, under some subsequent loading

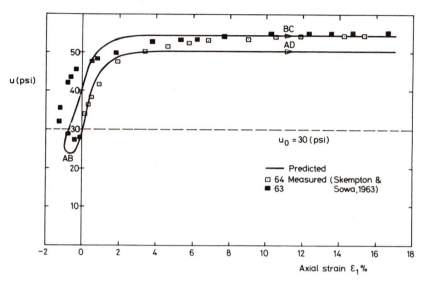

FIG. 22. K_0-normally consolidated weald clay: predicted and measured pore
water pressures during sampling and testing.

history, behave similarly to an isotropically consolidated clay, as was
observed by Balasubramaniam (1969).

Balasubramaniam prepared three specimens of Kaolin consolidated
from the slurry state, initially under K_0 condition with $\sigma_1 = 22$ psi. These
specimens were subsequently consolidated isotropically to $p = 30$, 60 and
90 psi and sheared under a constant p condition. The comparisons between
the theoretical results and those obtained by Balasubramaniam, were based
on the initial stress distribution at the end of the one-dimensional
consolidation ($\sigma_1 = 22$ psi) as an input data for the model; the
corresponding value of σ_3 was calculated using a K_0 value of 0·64 (as
measured by Balasubramaniam). The material constants required by the
present model were taken (as reported for the tested Kaolin) as: $\lambda = 0·24$,
$\kappa = 0·06$, $e_0 = 1·05$ (at the end of one-dimensional consolidation) and
$\phi = 23°$. These are the only parameters (together with $v = 0$) needed in the
present model.

The theoretical results were obtained by using the analysis in two stages.
During the first stage the data at the end of K_0 consolidation were input as
the initial condition for the isotropic drained loading. The stress states and
the positions of the yield surfaces for the three samples at the end of this

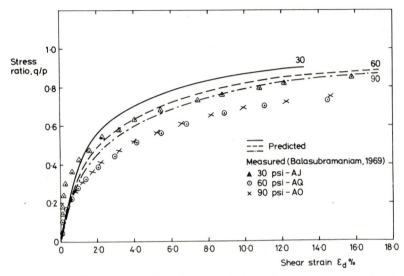

FIG. 23.   Predicted and measured $(q/p, \varepsilon_d)$ relations of specimens prepared under 1-D stress of 22 psi and sheared under constant p-drained test from isotropic stresses of 30, 60 and 90 psi.

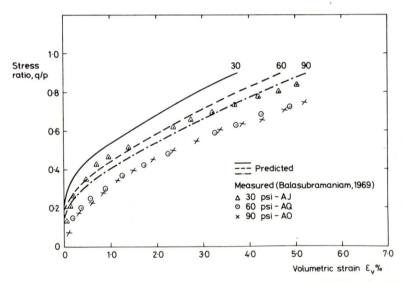

FIG. 24.   Predicted and measured $(q/p, \varepsilon_v)$ relations of specimens prepared under 1-D stress of 22 psi and sheared under constant p-drained test from isotropic stresses of 30, 60 and 90 psi.

loading were then input as the initial data for the $p = $ constant drained loading case.

Theoretically predicted stress–strain relations for the three samples sheared under constant p tests ($dp = 0$ and $dq > 0$) are compared with experimentally observed results as shown in Figs 23 and 24 in $(q/p, \varepsilon_d)$ and $(q/p, \varepsilon_v)$ plots, respectively. The model predictions are reasonably satisfactory for all three samples.

The initial K_0 consolidation results in a developed clay particle orientation characterised by the orientation tensor q_{ij}/p_0. During the subsequent isotropic consolidation the magnitude of this orientation tensor reduces and for the longer isotropic consolidation (60 psi and 90 psi) the initial memory of q_{ij}/p_0 is considerably reduced. Without this memory the normalised results of all three samples would have been identical.

7 APPLICATION OF THE MODEL TO CYCLIC LOADING

The effects of cyclic loading are most important when the soil is loaded and unloaded in an undrained condition. In this section, we shall briefly discuss some qualitative feature of the model prediction in the case of two-way strain controlled cyclic loading. Our major interest will be concentrated on (a) the variation of excess pore water pressure during the cyclic loading, (b) the variation of the stiffness after a prescribed number of cycles, and (c) the evolution of hysteresis loops with associated growth of accumulated irreversible deformation. Energy dissipation through hysteresis is probably the major portion of actual material damping in most dynamic problems. The accumulated irreversible strains lead to the increase of pore water pressure and the possible liquefaction.

Typical results of the model prediction for a two-way-cyclic triaxial test are summarised in Fig. 25, for which the axial strain was varied continuously in the range $-0.003 \leq \varepsilon_1 \leq 0.003$. The material parameters used for an isotropically consolidated ($\sigma_{ij} = 0$) sample are selected as: $\lambda = 0.24$, $\kappa = 0.045$, $\phi = 23°$, $e_0 = 1.27$, $p = p_0 = 60$ psi, $\nu = 0.3$ and $\mu = 5$. It is seen that, the stress path moves towards the origin and an almost steady state is reached after 25 cycles. In this test case the strain amplitude prescribed is not sufficient to cause failure. However, in a boundary value problem the material state reached at the end of this 25 cycles of loading may have reduced the safety factors considerably. A reduction in the mean effective stress and increase in the pore water pressures is clearly seen in Fig. 25.

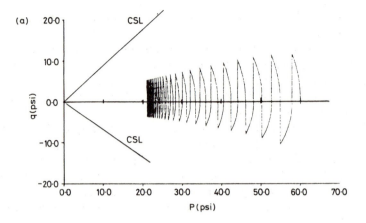

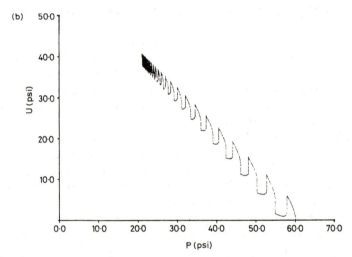

FIG. 25.   Prediction for a two-way strain controlled undrained triaxial test on normally consolidated soil.

The rate of increase in the excess pore water pressure and that of the decrease in the mean effective stress increase with higher amplitude of shear strain as was observed in experimental studies of Taylor and Bacchus (1969), Seed and Idriss (1970), Hardin and Drenvich (1972) and Andersen (1975).

Taylor and Bacchus (1969) conducted triaxial tests on artificially

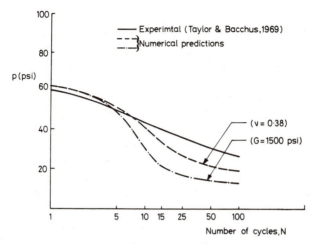

FIG. 26.   Comparison of model predictions with test results for a two-way, strain controlled undrained triaxial test.

prepared samples of clay. The model predictions for one of their results for which the material parameters (calculated from their reported results) were: $\lambda = 0 \cdot 132$, $\kappa = 0 \cdot 021$, $\phi = 36 \cdot 9$, $e_0 = 0 \cdot 963$ and $p_0 = 64$ psi, are compared with the experimental data in Fig. 26. The strain amplitude in the experiment was varied continuously in the range $-0 \cdot 003 \leq \varepsilon_1 \leq 0 \cdot 003$. The response of such strain controlled tests is likely to be very dependent on the adopted elastic parameters. The reduction of mean effective pressure, as the number of cycles N is increased, is compared with two sets of results: one in which the elastic modulus G was kept constant and the bulk modulus was calculated as $(K = (1 + e_0)p/\kappa)$ throughout and the other in which the Young's modulus was varied with the mean effective stress p according to eqn (16). The Poisson's ratio was calculated from $G = 1500$ psi and used in the second prediction. Both predictions overestimate the increase in pore water pressure but the overall quality of the predicted result, by adopting the variable modulus, is reasonably satisfactory.

8   DISCUSSION AND CONCLUSIONS

The model presented in this chapter combines properties of isotropic and kinematic hardening theories of plasticity. The yield (consolidation) surface is represented by a family of distorted and rotated ellipsoids in a general stress-space. For anisotropically consolidated clays, the yield surface is initially oriented along the K_0-consolidation axis representing the fabric anisotropy during the formation. The subsequent changes in the anisotropy are accounted for through translation and rotation of this surface in the stress-space.

In order to simulate the inelastic material behaviour at the microstructural level under monotonic and cyclic loading more realistically, the concept of a bounding surface is introduced. The basic feature of the bounding surface formulation is that the plastic deformation may occur for stress-state within the surface with the plastic modulus being a decreasing function of the distance of the stress-point from a corresponding point on the bounding surface. For any stress-point inside the surface a unique image point is defined on the surface by a specific rule.

The combined model is thus able to predict the behaviour of isotropically and anisotropically consolidated, normally consolidated and over-consolidated soils under monotonic and cyclic loading conditions. The predicted inelastic behaviour has been compared with the available experimental test results for a large number of triaxial compression and extension tests, K_0-swelling, K_0-consolidation, variation of K_0 values with OCR, pore water pressure build up in cyclic-undrained tests, etc., and generally the agreement was found to be satisfactory. Only six material parameters are needed to characterise a particular soil. Five of these parameters are identical to those required for the critical state model (that is, λ, κ, ϕ, e_0 and v). The most important limitation of this model is its inability to model properly the hysteretic loop in an isotropic cyclic consolidation test. From a practical standpoint it is not a serious limitation. Although some of the errors in predictions occur due to the choice of the distorted ellipsoid as the bounding surface it was thought to be a more convenient surface than other usable alternative forms.

It is also possible to improve the performance of the model by incorporating anisotropic elasticity, which of course requires at least three additional deformation parameters.

REFERENCES

ALPAN, I. (1967). The empirical evaluation of the coefficient K_0 and K_{or}, *Soils and Foundation*, 7(1), 31.

ANDERSEN, K. H. (1975). *Repeated loading on clay—summary and interpretation of test results*, Norwegian Geotechnical Inst., Report 74037-9, Oslo.

BAKER, R. and DESAI, C. S. (1984). Induced anisotropy during plastic straining, *Int. J. Num. Anal. Meth. in Geomech.*, **8**, 167.

BALASUBRAMANIAM, A. S. (1969). Some factors influencing the stress–strain behaviour of clays, Ph.D. Thesis, University of Cambridge, UK.

BANERJEE, P. K. and STIPHO, A. S. (1978). Associated and non-associated constitutive relations for undrained behaviour of isotropic soft clays, *Int. J. Num. Meth. in Geomech.*, **2**(1), 35–52.

BANERJEE, P. K. and STIPHO, A. S. (1979). An elasto-plastic model for undrained behaviour of heavily overconsolidated clays, *Int. J. Num. Meth. in Geomech.*, **3**(1), 97–103.

BANERJEE, P. K., STIPHO, A. A. and YOUSIF, N. B. (1981). A simple analytical model of the bi-axial stress–strain behaviour of anisotropically consolidated clays, *Implementation of computer procedure and stress–strain laws in geotechnical engineering*, Desai and Saxena, Eds, Acorn Press, North Carolina, 535–45.

BARDEN, L. (1972). Influence of structure on deformation and failure of clay soils, *Geotechnique*, **22**(1), 159–63.

BROOKER, E. W. and IRELAND, H. O. (1965). Earth pressure at rest related to stress history, *Can. Geotech. J.*, **2**, 1–15.

BURLAND, J. B. (1967). Deformation of soft clays, Ph.D. Thesis, University of Cambridge, UK.

CAIRNCROSS, A. M. and JAMES, R. G. (1977). Anisotropy in overconsolidated clays, *Geotechnique*, **27**(1), 31–6.

CASAGRANDE, A. (1936). Characteristics of cohesionless soils affecting the stability of slopes and earth fills, *J. Boston Soc. Civil Engrs.*, **23**(1), 13–32.

CASAGRANDE, A. and CARILLO, N. (1944). Shear failure of anisotropic material, *Contributions to Soil Mech.*, Boston Soc. Civil Engrs., 122–35.

DAFALIAS, Y. F. and HERRMANN, L. R. (1980). A bounding surface soil plasticity model, *Int. Symp. on Soils under Cyclic and Transient Loadings*, Swansea, pp. 335–45.

DAFALIAS, Y. F. and POPOV, E. P. (1974). A model of nonlinearly hardening materials for complex loadings, *Proc. 7th US National Congress of Appl. Mech.*, Boulder, 149 (Abstract), 1974 and *Acta Mech.*, **21**, 173–92.

DAFALIAS, Y. F. and POPOV, E. P. (1975). A simple constitutive law for artificial graphite-like materials, *Trans. 3rd SMIRT*, C 1/5, London.

DAFALIAS, Y. F. and POPOV, E. P. (1977). Cyclic loading for materials with vanishing elastic region, *Nucl. Engng. Design*, **41**(2), 293–302.

DRÜCKER, D. C. (1951). A more fundamental approach to plastic stress–strain relations, *Proc. 1st US Nat. Cong. Appl. Mech. ASME*, pp. 487–91.

DRÜCKER, D. C., GIBSON, R. E. and HENKEL, D. J. (1957). Soil mechanics and work-hardening theories of plasticity, *Trans. ASCE*, **122**, 338–46.

HARDIN, B. O. and DRENVICH, V. P. (1972). Shear modulus and damping in soils: Measurements and parameter effects, *J. S.MF.E., ASCE*, **98**(SM5), 603–24.

JAKY, J. (1944). The coefficients of earth pressure at rest, *J. Hung. Arch. Engrs. Soc.*, Budapest, pp. 355–8.

JAKY, J. (1948). Pressure in soil, *Proc. 2nd Int. Conf. Soil Mech. Found. Engng.*, Rotterdam, **1**, pp. 103–7.

KIRKPATRICK, W. M. and RENNIE, I. A. (1972). Directional properties of consolidated Kaolin, *Geotech.*, **22**(1), 166–9.

KRIEG, R. D. (1975). A practical two surface plasticity theory, *J. Appl. Mech. Trans. ASCE*, **E42**, 641–6.

LADD, C. C. and BAILEY, W. A. (1964). Correspondence on the behaviour of saturated clays during sampling and testing by Skempton and Sowa, *Geotech.*, **14**(4), 353–8.

LADD, C. C., BOVEE, R. B., EDGERS, L. and RIXNER, J. J. (1971). *Consolidated undrained plane strain shear tests on Boston Blue Clay*, Report No. 71-13, M.I.T., Cambridge, USA.

MITCHELL, J. K. (1966). The fabric of natural clays and its relation to engineering properties, *Proc. Highway Res. Bd.*, Washington, DC, **35**, pp. 693–713.

MITCHELL, R. J. (1970). On the yielding and mechanical strength of Leda clays, *Can. Geotech. J.*, **7**, 297–312.

MROZ, Z. (1967). On the description of anisotropic work hardening, *J. Mech. Phys. Solids*, **15**, 163–75.

MROZ, Z., NORRIS, V. A. and ZIENKIEWICZ, O. C. (1978). An anisotropic hardening model for soils and its application to cyclic loading, *Int. J. Num. Anal. Meth. in Geomech.*, **2**, 203–321.

MROZ, Z., NORRIS, V. A. and ZIENKIEWICZ, O. C. (1979). Application of an anisotropic hardening model in the analysis for the elastoplastic deformation of soils, *Geotech.*, **29**, 1–34.

MROZ, Z., NORRIS, V. A. and ZIENKIEWICZ, O. C. (1981). An anisotropic critical state model for soils subjected to cyclic loading, *Geotech.*, **31**, 451–69.

NAMY, D. (1970). An investigation of certain aspects of stress–strain relationships of clay soils, Ph.D. Thesis, Cornell University.

NADARAJAH, V. (1973). Stress–strain properties of lightly overconsolidated clays, Ph.D. Thesis, Cambridge University.

PANDE, G. N. and ZIENKIEWICZ, O. C. (1982) (eds). *Soil mechanics, transient and cyclic loads*. John Wiley and Sons, Ltd, London.

PARRY, R. H. and NADARAJAH, N. (1974). Observation on laboratory prepared lightly overconsolidated specimens of Kaolin, *Geotech.*, **24**(3), 345–58.

PIETRUSZCZAK, S. and MROZ, Z. (1981). Description of anisotropic consolidation of clays. In: *Mechanical behaviour of anisotropic soils*, Ed. Boehler, J. P., Int. Publ., Noordhoff.

PIETRUSZCZAK, S. and MROZ, Z. (1983). On hardening anisotropy of K_0-consolidated clays, *Int. J. Num. Anal. Meth. in Geomech.*, **7**(1), 19.

PREVOST, J. H. (1977). Mathematical modelling of monotonic and cyclic undrained clay behaviour, *Int. J. Num. Anal. Meth. in Geomech.*, **1**, 195–216.

PREVOST, J. H. (1978). Plasticity theory for soil stress–strain behaviour, *J. Eng. Mech. Div., ASCE*, **104**(EM5), 1177–94.

ROSCOE, K. H. and BURLAND, J. B. (1968). On the generalised stress–strain behaviour of wet clay, *Engineering plasticity*, Eds Hayman, J. V. and Leckie, F. A., Cambridge University Press, Cambridge, pp. 535–609.

ROSCOE, K. H., SCHOFIELD, A. N. and WROTH, C. P. (1958). On yielding of soils, *Geotech.*, **8**(1), 22–53.

SINGH, R., HENKEL, D. J. and SANGERY, D. A. (1973). Shear and K_0-swelling of overconsolidated clay, *Proc. 9th ICSMFE*, Moscow, **1**, pp. 367–76.

SKEMPTON, A. W. (1961). Horizontal stresses in an overconsolidated Eocene clay, *Proc. 5th ICSMFE, Paris*, pp. 351–7.

SKEMPTON, A. W. and SOWA, V. A. (1963). The behaviour of saturated clays during sampling and testing, *Geotech.*, **13**(4), 269–90.
STIPHO, A. S. (1978). Theoretical and experimental investigation of the anisotropically consolidated Kaolin, Ph.D. Thesis, University College, Cardiff.
SEED, H. B. and IDRISS, I. M. (1970). *Soil moduli and damping factors for dynamic response analysis*, Earthquake Engng. Research Centre EERC, Report No. EERC 70–10, University of California, Berkeley.
TAYLOR, P. W. and BACCHUS, D. R. (1969). Dynamic cyclic strain test on a clay, *Proc. 7th ICSMFE*, Mexico, **1**, pp. 40–9.
WROTH, C. P. (1975). *In situ* measurements of initial stress and deformation characteristics, State-of-the-Art paper, *Proc. ASCE Spec. Conf.* in situ *Measurements of Soil Properties*, Raleigh, Vol. II, pp. 181–230.
YOUSIF, N. B. (1980). Interpretation of soil behaviour in terms of isotropic and anisotropic hardening theories of plasticity, M.Sc. Thesis, University College, Cardiff.
ZIENKIEWICZ, O. C., HUMPHESON, C. and LEWIS, R. W. (1975). Associated and non-associated visco-plasticity and plasticity in soil mechanics, *Geotechnique*, **25**, 671–89.

APPENDIX A

For a general plane strain case the stresses and strains are defined as follows:

$$(\boldsymbol{\sigma})^T = (\sigma_y, \sigma_x, \sigma_z, \tau_{xy}) \qquad (\boldsymbol{\varepsilon})^T = (\varepsilon_y, \varepsilon_x, \varepsilon_z, \gamma_{xy}) \qquad \varepsilon_z = 0 \qquad \text{(A1)}$$

and for axisymmetric system they are defined as:

$$(\boldsymbol{\sigma})^T = (\sigma_z, \sigma_r, \sigma_\theta, \tau_{rz}) \qquad (\boldsymbol{\varepsilon})^T = (\varepsilon_z, \varepsilon_r, \varepsilon_\theta, \gamma_{rz}) \qquad \text{(A2)}$$

Other relevant quantities $(\mathbf{q})^T$ and $(\mathbf{s})^T$ are defined similarly.

Recalling the expressions for the invariants and yield surface

$$\bar{J}_2 = (\tfrac{1}{2}\bar{s}_{ij}\bar{s}_{ij})^{1/2} = \left[\frac{1}{2}\left(s_{ij} - \frac{2}{3}\frac{p}{p_0}q_{ij}\right)\left(s_{ij} - \frac{2}{3}\frac{p}{p_0}q_{ij}\right)\right]$$

$$\bar{J}_3 = \tfrac{1}{3}\bar{s}_{ij}\bar{s}_{jk}\bar{s}_{ki}$$

and

$$f(\sigma_{ij}, q_{ij}, p_0) = \frac{3}{2g^2(\bar{\theta})}\left(\bar{s}_{ij}\bar{s}_{ij} - \frac{1}{9}\frac{p}{p_0}q_{ij}q_{ij}\right) - pp_0 + p^2 = 0$$

the gradient vector $\partial f/\partial \boldsymbol{\sigma}$ can be obtained from

$$\frac{\partial f}{\partial \boldsymbol{\sigma}} = \frac{\partial f}{\partial p}\frac{\partial p}{\partial \boldsymbol{\sigma}} + \frac{\partial f}{\partial \bar{J}_2}\frac{\partial \bar{J}_2}{\partial \boldsymbol{\sigma}} + \frac{\partial f}{\partial \bar{\theta}}\frac{\partial \bar{\theta}}{\partial \boldsymbol{\sigma}} \qquad \text{(A3)}$$

where

$$\frac{\partial \bar{\theta}}{\partial \boldsymbol{\sigma}} = \left[-\frac{\tan 3\bar{\theta}}{\bar{J}_2} \frac{\partial \bar{J}_2}{\partial \boldsymbol{\sigma}} + \frac{\sqrt{3}}{2 \cos 3\bar{\theta}} \frac{1}{\bar{J}_2^3} \frac{\partial \bar{J}_3}{\partial \boldsymbol{\sigma}} \right] \tag{A4}$$

Substituting (A4) in (A3) gives

$$\frac{\partial f}{\partial \boldsymbol{\sigma}} = C_1 \frac{\partial p}{\partial \boldsymbol{\sigma}} + C_2 \frac{\partial \bar{J}_2}{\partial \boldsymbol{\sigma}} + C_3 \frac{\partial \bar{J}_3}{\partial \boldsymbol{\sigma}} \tag{A5}$$

where

$$C_1 = \frac{\partial f}{\partial p} = -\frac{1}{g^2(\bar{\theta})p_0} [2\mathbf{q}^{\mathrm{T}}\bar{\mathbf{s}} + \tfrac{1}{6}\mathbf{q}^{\mathrm{T}}\mathbf{q}] - p_0 + 2p$$

$$C_2 = \frac{\partial f}{\partial \bar{J}_2} - \frac{\tan 3\bar{\theta}}{\bar{J}_2} \frac{\partial f}{\partial \bar{\theta}} \qquad \bar{\theta} = \tfrac{1}{3}\sin^{-1}\left[\frac{3\sqrt{3}}{2} \frac{\bar{J}_3}{\bar{J}_2^3} \right]$$

$$C_3 = \frac{\sqrt{3}}{2\cos 3\bar{\theta}} \frac{1}{\bar{J}_2^3} \frac{\partial f}{\partial \bar{\theta}}$$

$$\frac{\partial f}{\partial \bar{J}_2} = \frac{6\bar{J}_2}{g^2(\bar{\theta})}$$

$$\frac{\partial f}{\partial \bar{\theta}} = -\frac{3\cos 3\bar{\theta}}{g(\bar{\theta})} \bar{J}_2^2$$

$$g(\bar{\theta}) = \frac{6\sin\phi}{3 - \sin\phi \sin 3\bar{\theta}}$$

The components of each of the vectors on the right hand side of eqn (A5) can be then recovered for a plane strain case as

$$\left(\frac{\partial p}{\partial \boldsymbol{\sigma}}\right)^{\mathrm{T}} = (1, 1, 1, 0) \tag{A6}$$

$$\left(\frac{\partial \bar{J}_2}{\partial \boldsymbol{\sigma}}\right)^{\mathrm{T}} = \frac{1}{2\bar{J}_2} (\bar{s}_y, \bar{s}_x, \bar{s}_z, 2\bar{\tau}_{xy})$$

$$\left(\frac{\partial \bar{J}_3}{\partial \boldsymbol{\sigma}}\right)^{\mathrm{T}} = \left[\left(\bar{s}_x\bar{s}_z + \frac{\bar{J}_2^2}{3}\right), \left(\bar{s}_y\bar{s}_z + \frac{\bar{J}_2^2}{3}\right), \left(\bar{s}_x\bar{s}_y - \bar{\tau}_{xy}^2 + \frac{\bar{J}_2^2}{3}\right), (-2\bar{s}_z\bar{\tau}_{xy}) \right]$$

Equations (A5) and (A6) provide the components of the gradient vector at a point σ_{ij} on the bounding surface.

The hardening modulus H_p is given by

$$H_p = -\left(\frac{1+e_0}{\lambda-\kappa}\right) \text{tr} \frac{\partial f}{\partial \boldsymbol{\sigma}} \left[p_0 \frac{\partial f}{\partial p_0} + \mathbf{s}^{\mathrm{T}} \frac{\partial f}{\partial \mathbf{q}} \right] \tag{A7}$$

where

$$\frac{\partial f}{\partial p_0} = \frac{1}{g^2(\theta)} \left[2\frac{p}{p_0^2} \mathbf{q}^{\mathrm{T}}\bar{\mathbf{s}} + \frac{1}{6}\frac{p}{p_0^2} \mathbf{q}^{\mathrm{T}}\mathbf{q} \right] - p$$

$$\frac{\partial f}{\partial \mathbf{q}} = -\frac{1}{g^2(\theta)} \left[2\frac{p}{p_0}\bar{\mathbf{s}} + \frac{1}{3}\frac{p}{p_0}\mathbf{q} \right]$$

The constitutive matrix relating an increment of stress $d\boldsymbol{\sigma}$ for a prescribed increment of strain $d\varepsilon$ from a stress point $\boldsymbol{\sigma}$ which lies on the yield surface $f = 0$ can be then obtained from

$$d\boldsymbol{\sigma} = \mathbf{D}^{ep}(\boldsymbol{\sigma}, \mathbf{q}, p_0) \, d\varepsilon \tag{A8}$$

where $\boldsymbol{\sigma}$ is the stress state, $\mathbf{q}$ is the current value of the orientation tensor and p_0 is the maximum mean consolidation pressure. If the stress state σ_{ij} is within the bounding surface and σ_{ij}^* is the corresponding reference point on that surface, eqn (A8) takes the form

$$d\boldsymbol{\sigma} = D^{ep}(\boldsymbol{\sigma}^*, \mathbf{q}, p_0) \, d\varepsilon \tag{A9}$$

where the left hand side of eqn (A7) becomes H_r and all the stress parameters $\mathbf{s}$, $\bar{\mathbf{s}}$ and p in eqns (A5), (A6) and (A7) are calculated by assuming $\boldsymbol{\sigma}$ in these equations are identical to $\boldsymbol{\sigma}^*$.

Chapter 2

CONSTITUTIVE MODELLING OF GEOLOGICAL MATERIALS: A GENERAL PROCEDURE

C. S. DESAI, S. SOMASUNDARAM

Department of Civil Engineering & Engineering Mechanics,
University of Arizona, Tucson, USA

and

M. O. FARUQUE

Department of Civil Engineering,
University of Rhode Island, Kingston, USA

1 INTRODUCTION

A variety of quasilinear or nonlinear elastic and elastic-plastic models have been proposed for characterising stress-deformation behaviour of geological materials. Since the behaviour is complex owing to effect of factors such as initial state of stress, stress path, change in physical state (volume) and the type of loading, it is necessary to modify or improve the models based on the conventional elasticity and plasticity theories. Reviews of available models for geological materials are available in a number of publications such as Desai and Siriwardane (1984); only a limited number of publications will be referenced herein.

Developments towards incorporation of continuously yielding (isotropic hardening) behaviour of geological materials include models classified as critical state (soil mechanics) (Schofield and Wroth, 1968) and Cap (DiMaggio and Sandler, 1971). Based on comprehensive series of laboratory tests on soils, Lade (1977), and Matsuoka and Nakai (1974) proposed models that allow for isotropic hardening and nonassociative behaviour. Most of these models can be referred to as two-surface models since they involve an (expanding) yield surface that merges with a failure or critical state surface.

Models to account for kinematic and isotropic hardening have been proposed and used by various investigators: Baltov and Sawczuk (1965); Dafalias and Popov (1977); Ishlinski (1954); Mroz (1967); Mroz et al. (1978); Prager (1956); Prevost (1977, 1978) and Ziegler (1919). One of the aspects of these models has been to devise a geometrical mechanism to permit movement (translation) of the yield surfaces together with change in their sizes (expansion), starting from an initial yield surface.

Most of the previous models, particularly in geotechnical engineering research, have been developed based on laboratory test results for given material(s). The procedure proposed herein involves postulation of a generalised concept, and development of appropriate specialised models on the basis of comprehensive laboratory tests for given classes of materials. The procedure proposed is considered to be capable of including isotropic hardening, softening and anisotropic hardening through use of internal physical variables.

2 PROPOSED MODEL

A general expression for a constitutive equation (for a yield function) can be written as

$$F = F(\sigma_{ij}, \varepsilon_{ij}^p, \alpha_n) = 0 \tag{1}$$

For an initially isotropic material, using the principle of material invariance leading to form invariance of the constitutive laws, this equation can be expressed in terms of invariants as (Baker and Desai, 1984; Desai, 1980; Desai and Faruque, 1983, 1984; Desai and Siriwardane, 1980; Faruque, 1983; Green and Naghdi, 1965; Rivlin and Ericksen, 1955 and Shrivastava et al., 1973)

$$F = F(J_i, I_i^p, K_j, \alpha_n) = 0 \tag{2}$$

where J_i $(i = 1, 2, 3)$ = invariants of the stress tensor, σ_{ij}, I_i^p $(i = 1, 2, 3)$ = invariants of the plastic strain tensor, ε_{ij}^p, K_j $(j = 1, 2, 3)$ = joint or mixed invariants of the stress and plastic strain tensor, $K_1 = \sigma_{ij}\varepsilon_{ij}^p, K_2 = \sigma_{ij}\varepsilon_{jk}^p\varepsilon_{ki}^p$ and $K_3 = \sigma_{ij}\sigma_{jk}\varepsilon_{ki}^p$, and α_n $(n = 1, 2, \ldots, m)$ are (scalar) valued internal variables such as plastic work. It is shown that in the context of the theory of plasticity, eqn (2) can provide and include representation of yield functions for a number of idealisations of the material behaviour as (Baker and Desai, 1984; Desai, 1980; Desai and Siriwardane, 1984)

Ideal plastic

$$F = F(J_i, k) = 0 \tag{3a}$$

where k = constant.

Plastic isotropic hardening

$$F = F[J_i, I_i^p, k(W^p, \xi)] \tag{3b}$$

where W^p = plastic work, ξ = trajectory of plastic strains = $\int (d\varepsilon_{ij}^p d\varepsilon_{ij}^p)^{1/2}$.

Plastic isotropic and kinematic hardening

$$F = F(J_i, I_i^p, K_j, k(W^p, \xi)) \tag{3c}$$

In this chapter, we consider some explicit forms of eqn (3c) and show the generality of the proposed concept. Typical examples of development and implementation of the models for some geological material are also included.

An expression for F as a (complete) polynomial of a given order, in terms J_i, I_i^p and K_j can be written as

$$F = \alpha_0 + \alpha_1 J_1 + \alpha_2 J_2^{1/2} + \alpha_3 J_3^{1/3} + \alpha_4 I_i^p + \alpha_5 I_2^p + \alpha_6 I_3^p$$
$$+ \alpha_7 K_1 + \alpha_8 K_2 + \alpha_9 K_3^{1/2} + \alpha_{10} J_1^2 + \alpha_{11} J_2 + \alpha_{12} J_3^{2/3} + \cdots \tag{4}$$

Here α_i's = $\alpha_i(W^p, \xi)$ = material parameters. It can be shown that only nine of the ten invariants (six direct invariants J_i and I_i^p and three mixed invariants K_j) are independent. Hence, only nine of the invariants are included in eqn (4). A special form of eqn (4) only in terms of J_1, $J_2^{1/2}$ and $J_3^{1/3}$ with α's expressed as functions of $\xi(W^p)$ has been used previously to develop isotropic hardening models (Desai, 1980; Desai and Faruque, 1983, 1984; Desai and Siriwardane, 1980; Faruque, 1983). The form in eqn (4) is capable of incorporating change in shape and orientation (rotation) and translation of the yield surface in addition to isotropic hardening.

The initial motivation for the development of the concept proposed herein is derived from the identification of a number of truncated forms of $F(J_1)$ by Desai (1980). Here it was shown that a number of the truncated forms assumed invariant values at ultimate state of stress, irrespective of the stress path followed. The ultimate stress or ultimate yield condition is defined as the states of stress corresponding to the asymptotes to observed

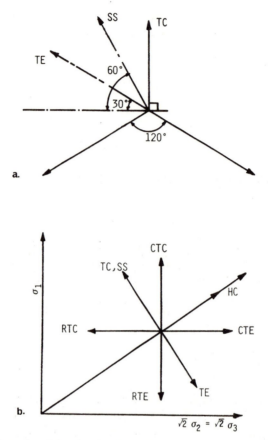

FIG. 1.   Schematic of the commonly used stress paths: (a) stress paths on the octahedral plane, (b) stress paths in triaxial plane.

stress–strain curves under different stress paths, Fig. 1. The conventionally used states such as failure and critical are usually lower than or coincide with the ultimate state.

3 ISOTROPIC HARDENING MODELS

A form of eqn (4) can be obtained by expressing F as a complete polynomial in terms of J_1, $J_2^{1/2}$, $J_3^{1/3}$ or J_1, $J_{2D}^{1/2}$, $J_{3D}^{1/3}$ which are invariants of the total and deviatoric stress tensors, respectively (Desai, 1980). Here the coefficients of the polynomial can represent the hardening behaviour. Details of this representation are given in various publications (Desai, 1980; Desai and Faruque, 1983, 1984; Desai and Siriwardane, 1980; Faruque, 1983); here we present only a brief description.

One of the functions that was studied in detail is given by (from the above references)

$$F = J_{2D} + \alpha J_1^2 - \beta J_1 J_3^{1/3} - \gamma J_1 - k^2 = 0 \tag{5}$$

where α, β, γ and k are response functions. For convenience, α, γ and k were related to the ultimate condition, whereas β was chosen as growth or hardening (softening) function. For isotropic hardening behaviour of initially isotropic materials, the function in eqn (5) plots as continuous and convex in stress space, Fig. 2; here $k = 0$ is assumed for convenience. Since it is continuous, it involves no discontinuity at the intersection of the progressive yield and ultimate yield surfaces. In the previous two surface models (Schofield and Wroth, 1968; DiMaggio and Sandler, 1971; Lade, 1977), the intersection involves a discontinuity. The function intersects the J_1-axis orthogonally; that is, behaviour of isotropic materials under hydrostatic loading is simulated. Alternatively, the function can be modified to yield nonorthogonal intersection with the J_1-axis.

4   GROWTH OR HARDENING (SOFTENING) FUNCTION

The growth function β is expressed as (Desai and Faruque, 1983, 1984; Desai and Siriwardane, 1980; Faruque, 1983)

$$\beta(\xi, r_D) = \beta_u \left[1 - \frac{\beta_a}{i + \xi^{\eta_1}\{1 - \beta_b(r_D)^{\eta_2}\}} \right] \tag{6a}$$

where β_u = value of β at the ultimate state ($= 3\alpha$), β_a, η_1, β_b and η_2 are material constants, i = limit of elastic behaviour, r_D is given by

$$r_D = \frac{\xi_D}{\xi} \tag{6b}$$

and ξ_D = trajectory of deviatoric plastic strains, E_{ij}^p:

$$\xi_D = \int (dE_{ij}^p dE_{ij}^p)^{1/2} \tag{6c}$$

The motivation for eqn (6a) was derived from the plots of r_v vs r_D for a number of geological materials: sand, clays and concrete (Baker and Desai, 1984; Desai and Faruque, 1983, 1984: Desai and Salami, in prep.; Desai

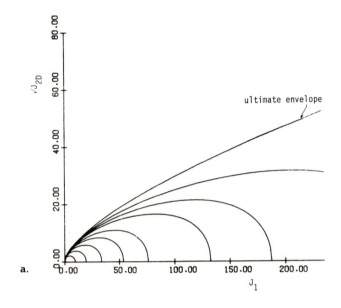

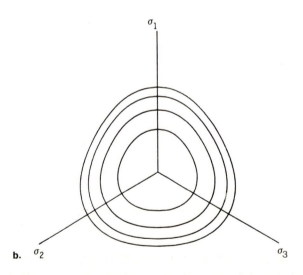

FIG. 2.   Plots of F, eqn (5): (a) in $J_1 - \sqrt{J_{2D}}$ space, (b) in principal stress space.

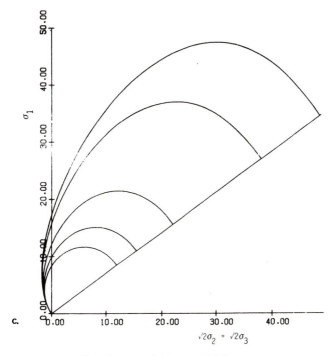

FIG. 2.—*contd.* (c) on triaxial space.

and Siriwardane, 1980; Faruque, 1983); here r_v = trajectory of volumetric plastic strains, ε_{kk}^p:

$$r_v = \frac{1}{\sqrt{3}} \int d\varepsilon_{kk}^p \qquad (6d)$$

Figure 3 shows that irrespective of the stress paths followed, the relation between r_v and r_D is essentially invariant for a given material with given initial density. The test data for the materials [silty sand (Desai *et al.*, 1982), artificial soil (Desai *et al.*, 1981), Ottawa sand (Mould, 1979), agricultural soil (Samford, 1981) and 'Munich' sand (Scheele and Desai, 1983)] were obtained from a series of laboratory tests under different stress paths by using the multiaxial testing device (Desai *et al.*, 1982; Sture and Desai, 1979). The use of ξ and r_D in eqn (6a) allows for the effect of coupling between volumetric and shear responses, and of stress paths.

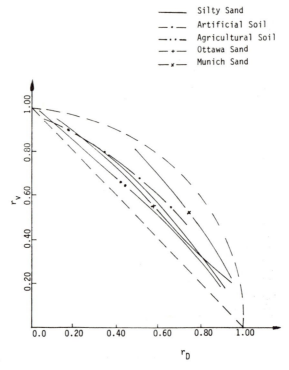

	Silty Sand
	Artificial Soil
	Agricultural Soil
	Ottawa Sand
	Munich Sand

FIG. 3.   Averages of $r_v - r_D$ plots from tests with different stress paths for five materials.

4.1 Parameters

The isotropic hardening model has been used for a wide range of materials such as clays, sands, and concrete. The material parameters required involve: (1) *For elastic behaviour:* elastic modulus, E and Poisson's ratio, ν, (2) *For plastic behaviour:* (a) for ultimate condition; α, γ, k, and (b) for hardening, $\beta_a, \eta_1, \beta_b, \eta_2$. Their determination from given laboratory tests is straightforward (Desai and Faruque, 1983, 1984; Faruque, 1983).

The elastic constants are found from unloading/reloading responses, often from results of conventional triaxial compression (CTC) tests. The constants α, γ and k are obtained by fitting the ultimate envelope through observed ultimate stress states, say in the $J_1 - \sqrt{J_{2D}}$ space (for given J_{3D}), Fig. 2.

The constants β_a and η_1 are obtained by plotting $\ln(\xi_v)$ vs $\ln(1 - \beta/\beta_u)$, Fig. 4(a), from hydrostatic compression (HC) tests. Plots of $\ln(r_D)$ vs

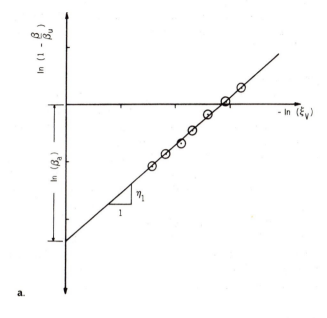

a.

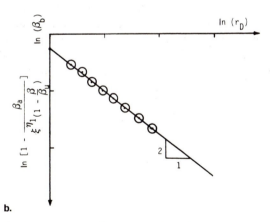

b.

FIG. 4. Plots for determination of hardening (growth) constants: (a) for β_a and η_1, (b) for β_b and η_2.

$\ln[1 - (\beta_a/\xi^{\eta_1}(1 - \beta/\beta_u))]$, Fig. 4(b), from shear tests under other stress paths, Fig. 1, provide values of β_b and η_2. It is found that approximate and satisfactory values of β_b and η_b can be found simply from (three) CTC tests Desai and Faruque, 1984).

4.2 Implementation

The above model is implemented (a) for prediction of observed stress–strain responses and (b) in two- and three-dimensional finite element procedures to predict the behaviour of boundary value problems (Desai and Faruque, 1984; Faruque, 1983; Faruque and Desai, in press).

The values of constants for a number of soils are given in Baker and Desai (1984), Desai and Faruque, (1983, 1984), Faruque (1983) and Faruque and Desai (in press). Typical comparisons between predictions of stress–strain and volumetric behaviour for different stress paths for different soils (artificial soil, agricultural soil, silty sand, Munich sand) are given in Figs 5 to 8 (Desai and Faruque, 1984; Faruque, 1983; Muqtadir, 1984). The correlation is found to be satisfactory. The deviations, particularly near ultimate conditions, can be due to factors such as (induced) anisotropy and nonassociative characteristics.

4.3 Softening

The growth function β can be used to define softening behaviour also. During hardening, the function reaches the ultimate state with an ultimate value of $\beta_u = 3\alpha$. Usually, somewhere before the ultimate state, the material reaches the peak state, Fig. 9(a). Hence at the peak, the growth function $\beta_p \leq \beta_u$. The subsequent softening behaviour can be simulated by referring to β_s as the softening function. Thus, the growth function is given by

Hardening: same as in eqn (6a):

$$\beta_b = \beta(\xi, r_D) \tag{7a}$$

At peak:

$$\beta_p \leq \beta_u \tag{7b}$$

During softening:

$$\beta_s = \beta(\beta_p, \xi, r_v, r_D) \tag{7c}$$

A schematic of growth functions, corresponding to the above states, is shown in Fig. 9(b). As a simplification, the term, γ, associated with J_1 in eqn (5) can be treated as a softening function. Both the above approaches are currently under investigation.

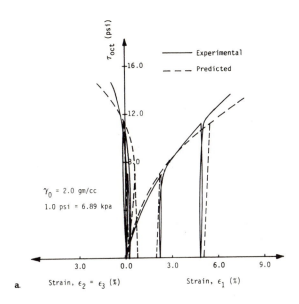

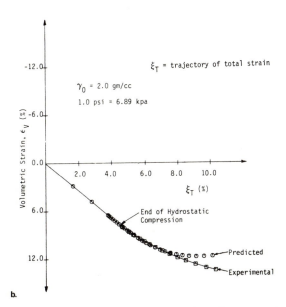

FIG. 5. Comparison of predictions and observations for conventional triaxial compression (CTC) test; artificial soil ($\sigma_0 = 20 \cdot 0$ psi): (a) stress–strain response, (b) volumetric response.

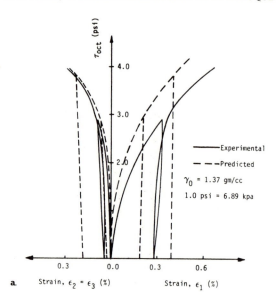

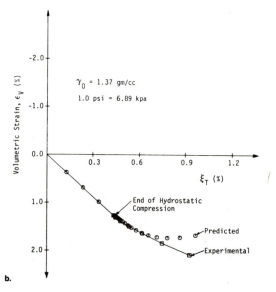

FIG. 6.   Comparison of predictions and observations for responses of triaxial compression (TC) test; agricultural soil ($\sigma_0 = 5 \cdot 0$ psi): (a) stress–strain response, (b) volumetric response.

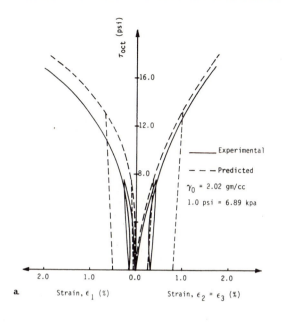

a.

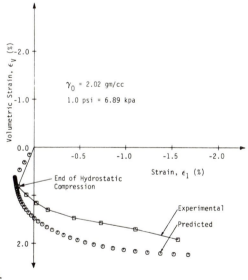

b.

FIG. 7. Comparison of predictions and observations for conventional triaxial extension (CTE) test; silty sand ($\sigma_0 = 20 \cdot 0$ psi): (a) stress–strain response, (b) volumetric response.

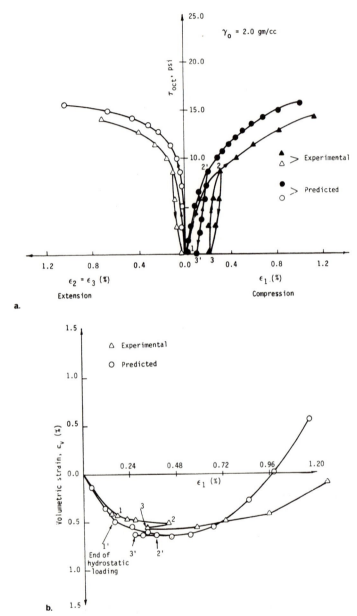

FIG. 8.   Comparisons of predictions and observations for triaxial compression test; Munich sand ($\sigma_0 = 13$ psi): (a) stress–strain response, (b) volumetric response.

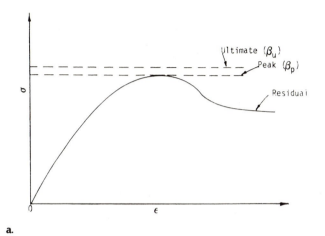

a.

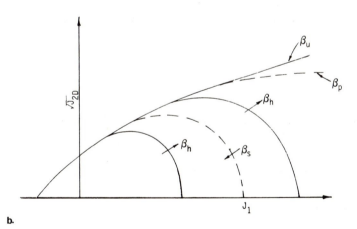

b.

FIG. 9.   Softening behaviour: (a) symbolic stress–strain curve, (b) growth functions in $J_1 - \sqrt{J_{2D}}$ space at constant J_{3D}.

4.4 Nonassociative Behaviour

The above concept can be used to consider nonassociative behaviour by using the idea of a correction function, $h_n(J_i, \xi)$ as (Baker & Desai, 1982; Desai and Faruque, 1983; Desai and Siriwardane, 1980)

$$Q = F + h_n(J_i, \xi) \tag{8}$$

5 PORE WATER PRESSURE

Here the effective stress tensor, σ'_{ij}, is written as

$$\sigma'_{ij} = \sigma_{ij} - p\delta_{ij} \tag{9a}$$

The invariants of which may be written as

$$J'_1 = \sigma'_{11} + \sigma'_{22} + \sigma'_{33} \tag{9b}$$

$$J'_2 = \tfrac{1}{2}\sigma'_{ij}\sigma'_{ij} \tag{9c}$$

$$J'_3 = \tfrac{1}{3}\sigma'_{im}\sigma'_{mj}\sigma'_{ji} \tag{9d}$$

where p = pore water pressure. Substitution of the modified quantities in eqn (5) will lead to the yield function including pore water pressures.

6 ANISOTROPIC HARDENING

In general, (an initially isotropic) material may experience anisotropic (hardening) behaviour during (plastic) straining. This may be represented by translation, change in orientation (rotation) and/or change in shape of the (initial) yield surface together with change in its size. It is possible to evolve representations for these modes on the basis of eqn (4).

6.1 Translation

Models that allow for the first mode, translation, are usually called kinematic (hardening) models (Ishlinski, 1954; Prager, 1956; Ziegler, 1919). When combined with isotropic hardening, they are referred to as isotropic and kinematic hardening models (Mroz, 1967; Mroz et al., 1978; Prevost, 1977, 1978; Dafalias and Popov, 1977). Here the yield surface expands and translates without change in shape and orientation. In the following, we describe briefly how these models can be derived from eqn (4).

A yield surface that translates in the stress space may be expressed as

$$F = F[(\sigma_{ij} - \alpha_{ij}), \xi, W^p] \tag{10}$$

where α_{ij} represents the location of continuously changing centre of the yield surface in the stress space. A particular form of α_{ij} may be expressed as $\alpha_{ij} = a\varepsilon_{ij}^p$, where a is a material parameter.

Using the principle of material invariance, it is possible to write eqn (10) as

$$F = F[(\sigma_i - a\varepsilon_{ij}^p), \xi, W^p] = F[L_1, L_2, L_3, \xi, W^p] \tag{11a}$$

where L_i $(i = 1, 2, 3)$ are the invariants of $(\sigma_{ij} - a\varepsilon_{ij}^p)$

$$L_1 = \mathrm{tr}\,(\sigma_{ij} - a\varepsilon_{ij}^p) = J_1 - aI_1^p$$
$$L_2 = \tfrac{1}{2}\mathrm{tr}\,(\sigma_{ij} - a\varepsilon_{ij}^p)^2 = J_2 - aK_1 + a^2 I_2^p$$
$$L_3 = \tfrac{1}{3}\mathrm{tr}\,(\sigma_{ij} - a\varepsilon_{ij}^p)^3 = J_3 + a^2 K_2 - aK_3 - a^3 I_3^p$$

A special case of eqn (11a) above can be written as

$$F = C_1 L_1^2 + C_2 L_2 - k^2 = 0 \tag{11b}$$

whose equivalent form from the general eqn (4) can be written as

$$F = b_0 + b_1 J_1^2 + b_2 J_1 I_1^p + b_3 (J_2^{1/2})^2 + b_4 K_1 + b_5 (I_1^p)^2 + b_6 I_2^p = 0 \tag{12a}$$

Here the coefficients b's are used for convenience; they represent α's relevant to terms of particular orders in the polynomial expansion, eqn (4). Equation (12a) can be expressed as

$$F = C_1[J_1^2 - 2aJ_1 I_1^p + a^2(I_1^p)^2] + 2C_2(J_2 - aK_1 + a^2 I_2^p) - k^2 = 0 \tag{12b}$$

Now, if we choose

$$C_1 = (c^2/9 - \tfrac{1}{2}) \qquad C_2 = \tfrac{3}{2} \qquad \text{and} \qquad p = J_1/3$$

we obtain

$$F = \tfrac{3}{2}[S_{ij} - aE_{ij}^p][S_{ij} - aE_{ij}^p] + c^2(p - aI_1/3)^2 - k^2 = 0 \tag{12c}$$

Here E_{ij}^p = deviatoric plastic strain tensor, and S_{ij} = deviatoric stress tensor. With $aE_{ij}^p = \alpha_{ij}$, $aI_1/3 = \beta/3$, this is the same as the yield surface proposed and used by Mroz (1967), Mroz et al. (1978), and Prevost (1978); their β is not the growth parameter used herein.

6.2 Orientation (Rotation)

In many conventional models, the yield surface is oriented symmetrically with respect to the J_1-axis, Fig. 10(a), in which case

$$F = F(S_{ij}, J_1) \tag{13}$$

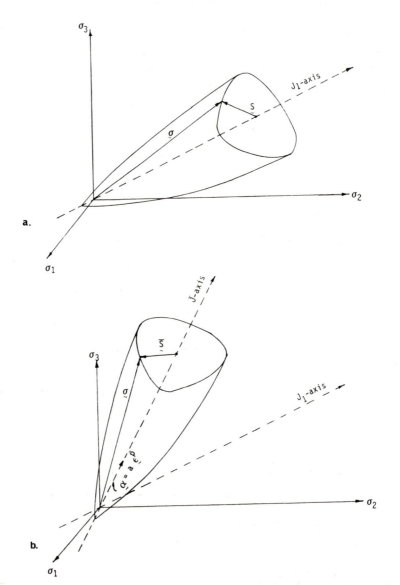

FIG. 10.   Rotation of yield surface: (a) J_1-axis orientation, (b) $\bar{J}$-axis orientation.

Now let us consider that the yield surface is oriented with respect to any axis, Fig. 10(b), given by unit tensor α_{ij}. In particular if $\alpha_{ij} = a\varepsilon_{ij}^p$, the yield surface may be expressed as

$$F = F(\bar{S}_{ij}, \bar{J}) \tag{14}$$

where

$$\bar{J} = \sigma_{ij} \cdot a\varepsilon_{ij}^p$$
$$\bar{S}_{ij} = \sigma_{ij} - a\varepsilon_{ij}^p \bar{J}$$

Using the principle of material invariance, eqn (14) can be written as

$$F(\bar{L}_1, \bar{L}_2, \bar{L}_3, \bar{J}) = 0 \tag{15a}$$

where $\bar{L}_i$ are the invariants of $\bar{S}_{ij}$ given by

$$\bar{L}_1 = \text{tr}(\bar{S}) = J_1 - aI_1^p \bar{J}^1$$
$$\bar{L}_2 = \tfrac{1}{2}\text{tr}(\bar{S})^2 = J_2 - aK_1\bar{J} + a^2 I_2^p \bar{J}^2$$
$$\bar{L}_3 = \tfrac{1}{3}\text{tr}(\bar{S})^3 = J_3 - aK_3\bar{J} + a^2 K_2\bar{J}^2 - a^3 I_3^p \bar{J}^3$$

A special case of eqn (15) can be written as

$$F = \bar{L}_2 - C^2 \bar{J}^2 = 0 \tag{15b}$$

whose equivalent form from the general eqn (4) can be expressed as

$$F = C_1 J_2 + C_2 K_1^2 + C_3 I_2^p K_1^2 \tag{15c}$$

If we set $C_1 = 2$, $C_2 = 2a^2 - c^2 a^2$, $C_3 = 2a^4$, eqn (15c) leads to

$$F = \bar{S}_{ij}\bar{S}_{ij} - c^2 \bar{J}^2 \tag{15d}$$

which is the same form as that proposed and used by Ghaboussi and Momen (1979).

6.3 Shape

The change in the shape of the yield surface can be achieved in a number of ways. For example, we can write eqn (5) as

$$J_1 J_3^a - \beta J_2^b = 0 \tag{16}$$

where $a = a$ (ζ or W^p) and $b = b$ (ζ or W^p). Then with the change in the parameter(s) with ζ or W^p, the shape of the yield surface will change during (plastic) straining. Alternatively, the procedure proposed by Ortiz and Popov (1983) can be used. Here the yield function is written as

$$F = f(J_i, I_k^p) - k\left(1 + \sum_{n=2}^{\infty} \rho_n \cos n\theta\right) = 0 \tag{17}$$

where ρ_n are scalar coefficients and θ is the angle that the stress tensor makes with the 'director' α_{ij} which defines the orientation of the distortion. If α_{ij} is chosen to be ε_{ij}^p, then

$$\cos\theta = \frac{\boldsymbol{\sigma}\boldsymbol{\varepsilon}^p}{|\boldsymbol{\sigma}||\boldsymbol{\varepsilon}^p|} = \frac{K_1}{2J_2^{1/2}I_2^{p\,1/2}} \tag{18}$$

and eqn (17) can be obtained from the general polynomial given in eqn (4).

7 KINEMATIC HARDENING WITH MODEL IN EQUATION (5)

Let us define

$$\bar{\sigma}_{ij} = \sigma_{ij} - a\varepsilon_{ij}^p \tag{19}$$

Then the invariants of $\bar{\sigma}_{ij}$ are given by

$$\bar{J}_1 = J_1 - aI_1^p$$
$$\bar{J}_2 = \tfrac{1}{2}(\sigma_{ij} - a\varepsilon_{ij}^p)(\sigma_{ij} - a\varepsilon_{ij}^p)$$
$$= J_2 - aK_1 + a^2 I_2^p$$
$$\bar{J}_{2D} = \tfrac{1}{2}(S_{ij} - aE_{ij}^p)(S_{ij} - aE_{ij}^p)$$
$$= J_{2D} - aK_{1D} + a^2 I_{2D}^p$$
$$\bar{J}_3 = \tfrac{1}{3}(\bar{\sigma}_{ik}\bar{\sigma}_{km}\bar{\sigma}_{mi})$$
$$= J_3 + a^2 K_2 - aK_3 - a^3 I_3^p$$

With these quantities, eqn (5) is written as

$$\bar{F} = \bar{J}_{2D} + \bar{\alpha}\bar{J}_1^2 - \bar{\beta}\bar{J}_1\bar{J}_3^{1/3} - \bar{\gamma}\bar{J}_1 - \bar{k}^2 = 0 \tag{20a}$$

In view of eqn (19) above, this function is capable of allowing for translation of the yield surface. Equation (20a) can now be written as

$$\bar{F} = (J_{2D} - aK_{1D} + a^2 I_{2D}^p) + \bar{\alpha}(J_1 - aI_1^p)^2 - \bar{\beta}(J_1 - aI_1^p)$$
$$\times (J_3 + a^2 K_2 - aK_3 - a^3 I_3^p)^{1/3} - \bar{\gamma}(J_1 - aI_1^p) - \bar{k}^2 = 0 \tag{20b}$$

Without the terms $a\varepsilon_{ij}^p$, eqn (20) will reduce to the isotropic hardening case, eqn (5). A schematic of the model in eqn (20) is shown in Fig. 11; here the yield surface translates between the initial surface and the ultimate surface (not shown in Fig. 11b).

An anisotropic hardening model capable of accounting for induced anisotropy, memory of maximum prestress and unloading/reloading effects can be formulated by using the translating surface $\bar{F}$ (eqn (20)) in

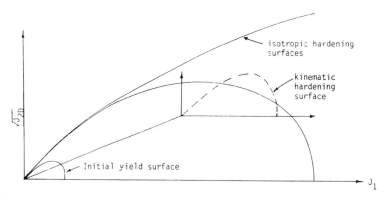

a.

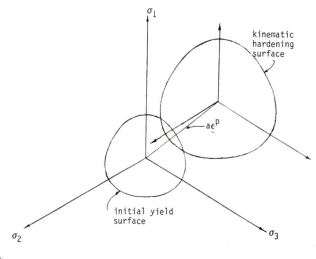

b.

FIG. 11.   Schematic representation of kinematic hardening surfaces: (a) on $J_1 - \sqrt{J_{2D}}$ space, (b) on octahedral plane.

conjunction with an isotropically expanding yield surface F (eqn (5)). $\bar{F}$ serves as a plastic potential surface that maintains its shape and size, but translates in the stress space. The location of $\bar{F}$ is governed by a translation rule specified in terms of ε_{ij}^p. F serves as a yield surface that isotropically expands (contracts) with the stress point during virgin loading. During unloading and reloading, while $\bar{F}$ translates with the stress point in the stress space, F remains fixed, serving as memory of maximum prestress until virgin loading is resumed.

The flow rule may be expressed as

$$\mathrm{d}\varepsilon_{ij}^p = \lambda \frac{\partial \bar{F}}{\partial \sigma_{ij}} \tag{21a}$$

During virgin loading

$$\lambda = \frac{-\dfrac{\partial F}{\partial \sigma_{rs}} \cdot \mathrm{d}\sigma_{rs}}{\dfrac{\partial F}{\partial \xi} \left(\dfrac{\partial \bar{F}}{\partial \sigma_{lm}} \dfrac{\partial \bar{F}}{\partial \sigma_{lm}} \right)^{1/2}} \tag{21b}$$

During unloading and reloading, an appropriate interpolation rule is specified for λ, depending on the relative position of the current state of stress in the stress space with respect to the prestress surface. Such an interpolation rule would provide for a smooth transition from the unload/reload portion to the virgin loading portion of the stress–strain response.

Although F is termed as an expanding surface in the foregoing description, in reality it is to provide a fixed field of surfaces in the stress space. In other words, the moving surface $\bar{F}$ travels in the fixed field of surfaces given by F and the description of loading, unloading and reloading is governed by the location of $\bar{F}$ with respect to the corresponding (fixed) surface defined by F. Thus the above model can be considered to be a single surface model, and can include isotropic and anisotropic hardening and nonassociative characteristics as special cases.

Example
The flow rule is given by

$$\mathrm{d}\varepsilon_{ij}^p = \lambda \frac{\partial \bar{F}}{\partial \sigma_{ij}} = \lambda \frac{\partial \bar{F}}{\partial \bar{\sigma}_{km}} \frac{\partial \bar{\sigma}_{km}}{\partial \sigma_{ij}} = \lambda \frac{\partial \bar{F}}{\partial \bar{\sigma}_{ij}} \tag{22}$$

Now, consider as an example, an initially isotropic material subjected to loading–unloading cycle(s) such that the plastic strain tensor at the end of the cycle is given by

$$\varepsilon_{ij}^p = \begin{pmatrix} \varepsilon_1^p & 0 & 0 \\ 0 & \varepsilon_2^p & 0 \\ 0 & 0 & \varepsilon_2^p \end{pmatrix} \tag{23}$$

Now, consider loading along a hydrostatic stress path. The use of eqn (21) for the hydrostatic loading leads to incremental plastic strains as

$$
\begin{aligned}
d\varepsilon_{ij}^p &= \left[\lambda \left(\frac{\partial \bar{F}}{\partial \bar{J}_1} + \frac{J_1}{3} \frac{\partial \bar{F}}{\partial \bar{J}_3} + \frac{J_1^2}{9} \right) \right] \delta_{ij} \\
&\quad + \left[\lambda \left(-a \frac{\partial \bar{F}}{\partial \bar{J}_2} - \frac{2a}{3} J_1 \frac{\partial \bar{F}}{\partial \bar{J}_3} \right) \right] \varepsilon_{ij}^p + \lambda a^2 \frac{\partial \bar{F}}{a \bar{J}_3} \varepsilon_{ik}^p \varepsilon_{kj}^p \\
&= \lambda g_1 \delta_{ij} + \lambda g_2 \varepsilon_{ij}^p + \lambda g_3 \varepsilon_{ik}^p \varepsilon_{kj}^p
\end{aligned}
\tag{24a}
$$

which leads to the increment of shear strain, $d\gamma^p$

$$
\begin{aligned}
d\gamma^p &= d\varepsilon_{11}^p - d\varepsilon_{22}^p \\
&= \lambda g_2 (\varepsilon_1^p - \varepsilon_2^p) + \lambda g_3 [(\varepsilon_1^p)^2 - (\varepsilon_2^p)^2] \\
&= [\lambda g_2 + \lambda g_3 (\varepsilon_1^p + \varepsilon_2^p)] \gamma^p
\end{aligned}
\tag{24b}
$$

Thus the proposed model will predict an increment of shear strain (in addition to volumetric strain) during hydrostatic loading from a condition represented by eqn (23). Note that if an isotropic hardening model had been employed, $d\gamma^p$ would have been zero.

8 CONCLUSIONS

A general procedure is proposed for constitutive modelling of (geological) materials. It is capable of allowing for change in the size of the initial yield surface leading to isotropic hardening and softening, and change in shape, orientation and location (translation) of the yield surface leading to general anisotropic hardening.

The isotropic hardening model that involves continuous yield surfaces is found to possess a number of advantages over the previous two-surface models. It is found to provide excellent simulation of the behaviour of a number of geological materials.

The proposed concept shows potential for development of constitutive models for a wide range of engineering materials, including soils and rocks.

ACKNOWLEDGEMENTS

A part of the investigations reported herein was supported by Grant No. CEE 8215344 from the National Science Foundation, Washington, DC.

66   C. S. DESAI, S. SOMASUNDARAM AND M. O. FARUQUE

M. O. Faruque contributed towards the development of the isotropic hardening model. Some of the concepts presented herein toward extension of the model are under investigation with the participation of the authors and their co-workers, M. Alawi, G. Franziskonis, M. Galagoda, Q. Hashmi, A. Muqtadir and M. R. Salami. We wish to acknowledge their participation, assistance and discussions.

REFERENCES

BAKER, R. and DESAI, C. S. (1982). Consequences of deviatoric normality in plasticity with isotropic strain hardening, *Int. J. Num. Analyt. Meth. in Geomech.*, **6**(3), 383–90.

BAKER, R. and DESAI, C. S. (1984). Induced anisotropy during plastic straining, *Int. J. Num. Analyt. Meth. in Geomech.*, **8**(2), 167–85.

BALTOV, A. and SAWCZUK, A. (1965). A rule for anisotropic hardening, *Acta Mech.*, **1**(2), 81–92.

DAFALIAS, Y. F. and POPOV, E. P. (1977). Cyclic loading for materials with a vanishing elastic region, *Nuclear Eng. & Design*, **41**(2), 173–92.

DESAI, C. S. (1980). A general basis for yield, failure and potential functions in plasticity, *Int. J. Num. Analyt. Meth. in Geomech.*, **4**, 361–75.

DESAI, C. S. and FARUQUE, M. O. (1983). A generalized basis for modelling plastic behavior of materials, *Proc. Int. Conf. on Constitutive Laws for Engineering Materials*, Univ. of Arizona, Tucson. Also in *Mechanics of Engineering Materials*, C. S. Desai & R. H. Gallagher (Eds), John Wiley & Sons, Chichester, 1984, pp. 211–30.

DESAI, C. S. and FARUQUE, M. O. (1984). Constitutive model for (geological) materials, *J. of Eng. Mech. Div.*, ASCE, **110**(9), 1391–1408.

DESAI, C. S. and SALAMI, M. R. A constitutive model for concrete (in preparation).

DESAI, C. S. and SIRIWARDANE, H. J. (1980). A concept of correction functions to account for non-associative characteristics of geologica media, *Int. J. Num. Analyt. Meth. in Geomech.*, **4**, 377–87.

DESAI, C. S. and SIRIWARDANE, H. J. (1984). *Constitutive laws for engineering materials*, Prentice-Hall, Englewood Cliffs.

DESAI, C. S., PHAN, H. V. and STURE, S. (1981). Procedure, selection and application of plasticity models for a soil, *Int. J. Num. Analyt. Meth. in Geomech.*, **5**(3), 295–311.

DESAI, C. S., SIRIWARDANE, H. J. and JANARDHANAM, R. (1982). *Interaction and load transfer through track support systems, Part 1 & 2*, Report DOT-OS-80013, Dept. of Transp., Office of Univ. Res., Washington, DC.

DIMAGGIO, F. L. and SANDLER, I. S. (1971). Material model for granular soils, *J. Eng. Mech. Div.*, ASCE, **97**(EM 3), 935–50.

FARUQUE, M. O. (1983). Development of a generalized constitutive model and its implementation in soil-structure interaction, Ph.D. Dissertation, Dept. of Civil Eng. & Eng. Mech., Univ. of Arizona, Tucson.

FARUQUE, M. O. and DESAI, C. S. Analysis and implementation of a general constitutive model for geological materials, *Int. J. Num. Analy. Meth. in Geomech.*, in press.

GHABOUSSI, J. and MOMEN, H. (1979). Plasticity model for cyclic behavior of sands, *Proc. 3rd Int. Conf. Num. Meth. Geomech.*, Aachen, W. Germany, pp. 423–34.

GREEN, A. E. and NAGHDI, P. M. (1965). A general theory of elastic-plastic continuum, *Arch. of Rat. Mech. & Analysis*, **18**(4), 251–81.

ISHLINSKI, A.-IU (1954). General theory of plasticity with linear strain hardening, *Ukr. Mat. Zh.*, **6**, 314.

LADE, P. V. (1977). Elastic-plastic stress–strain theory for cohesionless soil with curved yield surfaces, *Int. J. Solids and Struct.*, **13**, 1019–35.

MATSUOKA, H. and NAKAI, T. (1974). Stress-deformation and strength characteristics of soil under three different principal stresses, *Proc. Japan Soc. Civil Engrs.*, No. 232, pp. 59–70.

MOULD, J. C. (1979). Multiaxial testing and analytical constitutive characterization of granular materials, M.Sc. Thesis, Dept. of Civil Eng., Virginia Tech., Blacksburg.

MROZ, Z. (1967). On the description of anisotropic work-hardening, *J. Mech. and Physics of Solids*, **15**, 163–75.

MROZ, Z., NORRIS, V. A. and ZIENKIEWICZ, O. C. (1978). An anisotropic hardening model for soils and its application to cyclic loading, *Int. J. Num. Analyt. Meth. in Geomech.*, **2**, 203–21.

MUQTADIR, A. (1984). Three-dimensional nonlinear analysis of some soil-structure interaction problems, Ph.D. Thesis, Dept. of Civil Eng. and Eng. Mech., Univ. of Arizona, Tucson.

ORTIZ, M. and POPOV, E. P. (1983). Distortional hardening rules for metal plasticity, *J. of Eng. Mech., ASCE*, **104**(4), Aug. 1983, pp. 1042–57.

PRAGER, W. (1956). A new method of analyzing stresses and strains in work-hardening plastic solids, *J. Appl. Mech.*, **78**, 493–6.

PREVOST, J. H. (1977). Mathematical modelling of monotonic and cyclic undrained clay behavior, *Int. J. Num. Analyt. Meth. in Geomech.*, **1**, 196–216.

PREVOST, J. H. (1978). Plasticity theory for soil stress–strain behavior, *J. Eng. Mech. Div., ASCE*, **104**, 1177–94.

RIVLIN, R. S. and ERICKSEN, J. L. (1955). Stress-deformation relations for isotropic materials, *J. Rational Mech. Anal.*, **4**, 323–425.

SAMFORD, A. M. (1981). Constitutive models for an agricultural soil, M.Sc. Thesis, Dept. of Civil Eng., Virginia Tech., Blacksburg.

SCHEELE, F. and DESAI, C. S. (1983). *Laboratory behavior of Munich sand*, Annual Report, Dept. of Civil Eng. and Eng. Mech., Univ. of Arizona, Tucson.

SCHOFIELD, A. N. and WROTH, C. P. (1968). *Critical state soil mechanics*, McGraw-Hill, London.

SHRIVASTAVA, H. P., MROZ, Z. and DUBEY, R. N. (1973). Yield criterion and the hardening rule for a plastic solid, *Ziet. Angew. Math. Mech.*, **53**(10), 625–33.

STURE, S. and DESAI, C. S. (1979). Fluid cushion truly triaxial or multiaxial testing device, *J. of Geotech. Testing*, ASTM, **2**(1), 20–33.

ZIEGLER, H. (1919). A modification of Prager's hardening rule, *Quart. Appl. Math.*, **17**, 55–65.

Chapter 3

MULTI-LAMINATE REFLECTING SURFACE MODEL AND ITS APPLICATIONS

G. N. PANDE

Department of Civil Engineering,
University College of Swansea, UK

1 INTRODUCTION

Non-linearity of soil behaviour has been recognised by engineers for a long time. In the past, two major arguments against using complex soil models in design practice have been lack of analytical tools for solving practical problems and spatial variability of soil parameters and the associated difficulty of obtaining them. The situation is rapidly changing. Efficient solution techniques have been developed and advances in electronics enable the engineer to get a pretty good picture of the ground conditions. There is yet another motivation for attempting to characterise the non-linear behaviour of soils. Past experience with similar structures has been one of the main stays of soil mechanics. Recent activities in offshore, nuclear and large earth structures has meant that engineers have to design for situations for which little or no past experience is available. It is here that non-linear soil models have an important role to play.

There has been a proliferation of constitutive models in the last decade. Two different trends are noticed in the literature. Some researchers have tried to develop quite general models applicable to all types of soils and for all possible ranges of stresses while others have developed models for specific types of soils with limited range of applicability. The models in the former category tend to be generally more complex and involve a larger number of soil parameters, many of which may be rather obscure and devoid of any physical meaning. The argument given by the proponents of such models is that many of the parameters are constants for a specific type of soil. This approach of an all embracing constitutive model for soils, though academically elegant, is not really suitable for practical applications.

In recent years, a 'multi-laminate' framework for the development of constitutive relations of materials has been proposed. The first model belonging to this framework was called a 'multi-laminate model' and was developed for jointed rock masses (Zienkiewicz and Pande, 1977; Pande, 1980). Pande and Sharma (1980, 1981, 1983) developed 'multi-laminate models' for soils. Recently, Bazant and Oh (1982) have adopted the same framework for fracture analysis of concrete under the name 'microplane model'.

Multi-laminate models are elasto-plasticity based models and have the common drawback that on unloading the response is elastic. To overcome this drawback a 'reflecting' surface model has been proposed by Pande and Pietruszczak (1982) and used with success for prediction of liquefaction of sand layers by Shiomi et al. (1982).

This chapter gives a brief description of multi-laminate and reflecting surface models and unifies the two concepts into a single 'multi-laminate reflecting surface' model.

2   MULTI-LAMINATE FRAMEWORK

2.1 Introduction
The multi-laminate framework for the development of constitutive laws of soils pioneered by the author is based on the assumption that the key to soil behaviour lies in accurate and realistic description of laws for sliding and closing/separation of inter-granular boundaries of the soil skeleton. Phenomenological stress–strain relationships can be obtained by integrating the slippage/separation/closing on the inter-granular boundaries.

To obtain a physical model of soil, let us consider a solid block of arbitrary shape of homogeneous isotropic, linear elastic material, intersected by an infinite number of randomly orientated planes. These planes render the solid block into an assemblage of perfectly-fitting polyhedral blocks (Fig. 1). Let us further assume that, by some process, the boundaries of the microscopic polyhedral blocks are roughened, creating asperities which are elasto/visco-plastic in behaviour. The polyhedral blocks are now welded together without inducing any stress in the block.

The above description applies to a number of other engineering materials

FIG. 1.   Soil as an assemblage of polyhedral
blocks with roughened sides.

as well. It was originally proposed by Calladine (1971) for clays. Figure 2
shows a rheological analogue of the above physical model. A dashpot slider
unit is placed in series for each inter-granular boundary. The scale of the
problem being considered is, however, not grain size. It is such that the
inter-granular boundaries are infinite and are randomly oriented giving the
soil a uniform fabric. An infinite number of dashpot slider units represents
an infinite number of yield functions for the material, though all of them
may not be active at any time. The dashpot introduces time dependence in
the soil behaviour through a 'fluidity parameter'. If all inter-granular
boundaries have the same characteristics, the fluidity parameter for all the
dashpots is the same. Further, if the creep or time dependence is not of

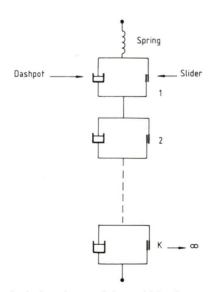

FIG. 2.   Rheological analogue of the multi-laminate model of soils.

interest in a particular problem, then the 'fluidity parameter' can assume any arbitrary value.

It is indeed possible to postulate asperities which are elasto/plastic instead of elasto/visco-plastic. The computational convenience of elasto/visco-plasticity is, however, essential if any practical problems are to be solved.

2.2 Critical State Model

The 'critical state model' or modified Cam-clay model is a comprehensive description of soil behaviour proposed and developed by the Soil Mechanics Group at the University of Cambridge (Roscoe *et al.* (1958), Schofield and Wroth (1968)). It assumes soil to be an elasto-plastic isotropic hardening material. Unlike metals where hardening is usually associated with deviatoric plastic strains, in the critical state soil model isotropic hardening is associated with volumetric plastic strains (ε_v^{vp}). The yield function, F, is written as a function of effective stress invariants. Representing total stresses by $\boldsymbol{\sigma}$ and pore pressure by p, the effective stresses ($\boldsymbol{\sigma}'$) can be written as

$$\boldsymbol{\sigma}' = \boldsymbol{\sigma} - \mathbf{m}p \qquad (1a)$$

where $\mathbf{m} = [1\ 1\ 1\ 0\ 0\ 0]^T$, and the yield function as

$$F = F(\sigma'_m, \bar{\sigma}, \theta, \varepsilon_v^{vp}) = 0 \qquad (1b)$$

where σ'_m (mean effective stress) $= \frac{1}{3}(\sigma'_1 + \sigma'_2 + \sigma'_3)$, σ'_1, σ'_2 and σ'_3 being effective principal stresses; $\bar{\sigma} = \sqrt{J_2}$, J_2 being the second invariant of deviatoric stresses given by

$$J_2 = \sqrt{\tfrac{1}{2}[(\sigma'_1 - \sigma'_2)^2 + (\sigma'_2 - \sigma'_3)^2 + (\sigma'_3 - \sigma'_1)^2]}$$

and θ is Lode's angle given by

$$\theta = \tfrac{1}{3}\sin^{-1}\left(-\frac{3\sqrt{3}}{2}\frac{J_3}{\bar{\sigma}^3}\right) \qquad -30° \le \theta \le 30°$$

where J_3 is the third invariant of deviatoric effective stress. θ is a measure of the relationship of the intermediate principal stress to the major and minor principal stresses. Thus $\theta = 30°$, $-30°$, and $0°$ represents triaxial compression, triaxial extension and simple shear conditions, respectively. In the context of triaxial compression tests, the stress invariants reduce to

$$\sigma'_m = \tfrac{1}{3}(\sigma'_1 + 2\sigma'_3)$$
$$\bar{\sigma} = \sigma'_1 - \sigma'_3$$
$$\theta = 30°$$

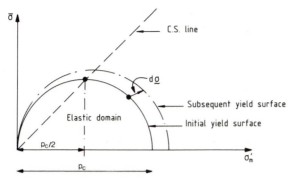

FIG. 3.   Critical state model in $\sigma'_m - \bar{\sigma}$ stress space.

and corresponding invariants of strain are

$$v = \varepsilon_1 + 2\varepsilon_3$$
$$\varepsilon = \tfrac{2}{3}(\varepsilon_1 - \varepsilon_3)$$

where ε_1 and ε_3 are the major and minor principal strains, respectively.

An important feature of the critical state model is that the soil at 'critical state' distorts or shears at constant volume. There is a unique value of stress ratio $(\bar{\sigma}/\sigma'_m) = M$ at the critical state condition which is related to the effective angle of friction ϕ' obtained in the triaxial compression tests. M is given by

$$M = \frac{6 \sin \phi'}{3 - \sin \phi'} \qquad (2)$$

The current yield function, F, is written as

$$F = \frac{4\bar{\sigma}^2}{M^2 p_c^2} + \frac{4(\sigma'_m - p_c/2)^2}{p_c^2} - 1 = 0 \qquad (3a)$$

where p_c is a hardening parameter related to the pre-consolidation pressure.

Equation (3) plots as an ellipse in $\bar{\sigma}$, $\bar{\sigma}_m$ stress space (Fig. 3) with the critical state line having a slope M. The stress states inside the elliptical yield surface represent elastic behaviour of the soil. Thus in this region

$$d\sigma = D_d \, d\varepsilon$$

where D_d is a matrix of elastic parameters obtained from drained tests.

The elastic bulk modulus (K) is given by

$$K = \frac{(1 + e)\sigma'_m}{\kappa} \qquad (3b)$$

where e is the void ratio and κ is the slope of the swelling and recompression lines (assumed identical) in $e - \ln \sigma'_m$ space.

Stress states on the yield surface, when $\sigma'_m > p_c/2$, are said to be 'wet' of critical while the stress states on the yield surface, when $\sigma'_m < p_c/2$, are said to be 'dry' of critical. On the 'wet' side shearing is associated with compressive plastic volumetric strains and hardening (expansion of the yield surface). On the other hand, on the 'dry' side shearing is associated with dilatational volumetric strains and softening.

The current value of p_c in eqn (3) is given by

$$p_c = p_{c0} e^{\chi \varepsilon_i^{vp}} \tag{4}$$

where p_{c0} is the initial value of p_c and

$$\chi = \frac{\lambda - \kappa}{1 + e} \tag{5}$$

λ being the slope of normal consolidation line in $e - \ln \sigma'_m$ space.

The elliptic shape of the yield surface on the wet side is generally accepted but on the dry side there is no unanimity among researchers. An alternative shape of the yield surface is shown in Fig. 4. A non-associated flow rule on the 'dry' side is often used.

2.3 Critical State Model in Multi-laminate Framework

Recalling the conceptual model of material behaviour described in Section 2.1, let us look in detail at the process of deformation at one of the boundaries of the microscopic polyhedral blocks (Fig. 5).

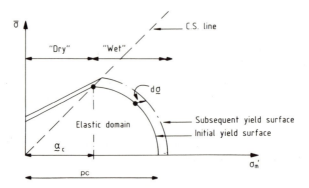

FIG. 4.   Critical state model modified on the 'dry' side.

It is possible to derive elastic parameters of the soil from the elastic normal and shear stiffnesses (k_n, k_s) of boundaries taking into account the soil grain size almost in a manner similar to that adopted by Gerrard (1982) and Pande and Gerrard (1983) for jointed rock masses. This approach, though academically elegant, is not of much use in practice. For elastic behaviour of soil, it is assumed that macroscopic behaviour is adequately represented by phenomenological laws and nothing is to be achieved by the multi-laminate framework.

For the process of plastic deformation, however, a distinct advantage accrues and we shall pursue this line. Assuming a certain thickness of the boundary formed by asperities it is reasonable to identify normal and shear plastic strains $(\varepsilon_n^{vp}, \varepsilon_s^{vp})$ associated with a particular boundary. The yield function for a boundary is written in terms of effective normal stress (σ_n'), shear stress (τ) and the plastic strains associated with that boundary. Thus

$$F = F(\tau, \sigma_n', \boldsymbol{\varepsilon}^{vp}) = 0 \qquad (6)$$

It is obvious that for a multi-laminate description of the critical state model, hardening should depend on the normal plastic strain (ε_n^{vp}) on the boundary under consideration. Therefore,

$$F = F(\tau, \sigma_n', \varepsilon_n^{vp}) = 0 \qquad (7)$$

2.3.1 Yield Function

In accordance with the critical state model, let us assume the existence of a critical state line such that when stress ratio (τ/σ_n') for a particular inter-granular boundary attains a critical value, M, shearing takes place without any change in the normal plastic strains on that boundary. For values of σ_n' less than $p_c/2$ dilation takes place (ride-up action on asperities) and for σ_n' greater than $p_c/2$ compaction takes place (due to crushing of asperities).

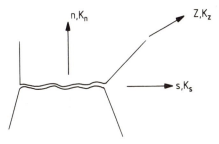

FIG. 5.   Local axes for a roughened boundary and corresponding elastic stiffnesses.

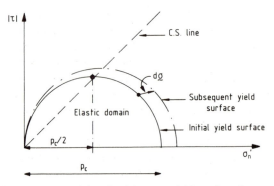

FIG. 6. Critical state model in $\sigma'_n - |\tau|$ space-yield surface for a typical inter-granular boundary.

Figure 6 shows the yield surface and the critical state line in $|\tau|$, σ'_n space. Subsequent yield surfaces depend on the normal plastic strains accumulated on the boundary under consideration. The yield function can now be written as

$$F = \frac{4\tau^2}{M^2 p_c^2} + \frac{4(\sigma'_n - p_c/2)^2}{p_c^2} - 1 = 0 \tag{8}$$

It is noted that eqn (8) is similar to eqn (3). However, there is an important difference in the significance of p_c. p_c is a hardening parameter and is relevant to the inter-granular boundary under consideration depending on the past loading history. The values of p_c on all boundaries are not the same unless the soil sample has been only subjected to a process of isotropic consolidation.

2.3.2 Hardening Law

When a soil sample is isotropically consolidated, volumetric strains take place. If these volumetric strains were resolved on the inter-granular boundaries, the normal strain on any boundary will be the same as the volumetric strain, i.e.

$$\varepsilon_v = (\varepsilon_n)_1 = (\varepsilon_n)_2 = (\varepsilon_n)_k \cdots = (\varepsilon_n)_\infty \tag{9}$$

where suffixes $1, 2, \ldots, k, \ldots, \infty$ refer to different inter-granular boundaries. However, if the sample is subjected to non-isotropic loading, normal strain on all the boundaries will not be the same. Now, as p_c is related to normal plastic strain (ε_n^{vp}), the sizes of yield surfaces would change from one boundary to the other. Thus there will be a continuous

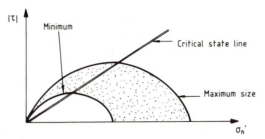

FIG. 7. A continuous spectrum of yield loci corresponding to an infinite number of boundaries of polyhedral blocks.

spectrum of yield surfaces as shown in Fig. 7. The expression for hardening of any inter-granular boundary is

$$p_c = p_{c0} e^{\chi \varepsilon_n^{vp}} \tag{10}$$

where p_{c0} and χ have the same meaning as defined in Section 2.2.

2.4 Complete Equations of Critical State Model in Multi-laminate Framework Using a Visco-plastic Algorithm

Details of the elasto/visco-plastic algorithm are discussed elsewhere. A brief description suitable for geotechnical engineers can be found in Naylor *et al.* (1983). Here only a very brief outline will be given for clarity and continuity.

In the theory of elasto/visco-plasticity, the plastic strains (called visco-plastic strains in this theory) take place with time. The total strains (ε) are composed of elastic strains (ε^e) and visco-plastic strains (ε^{vp}). Thus

$$\varepsilon = \varepsilon^e + \varepsilon^{vp} \tag{11}$$

The increments of effective stresses ($\Delta\sigma'$) are related to increments of elastic strains ($\Delta\varepsilon^e$) through an elastic drained modulus matrix (D_d), i.e.

$$\Delta\sigma' = D_d \Delta\varepsilon^e = D_d(\Delta\varepsilon - \Delta\varepsilon^{vp}) \tag{12}$$

In the critical state model, the D_d matrix is not constant as the drained bulk modulus is given by eqn (3b) and is dependent on σ'_m. The shear modulus, G, is usually assumed constant.

Normal and shear stresses on the ith inter-grain boundary are obtained via

$$\begin{bmatrix} \sigma'_n \\ \tau \end{bmatrix}_i = T_i \sigma' \tag{13}$$

where T_i represents a transformation matrix which is a function of the direction cosines (l_i, m_i, n_i) of a unit normal to the ith boundary.

The flow equation for the ith plane can be written as

$$\dot{\varepsilon}_i^{vp} = \gamma_i \langle \psi(F_i) \rangle \frac{\partial F_i}{\partial \boldsymbol{\sigma}'} \tag{14}$$

where $\langle \ \rangle$ are used to indicate that if $F \leq 0$, $\langle \psi(F) \rangle = 0$ and if $F > 0$, $\langle \psi(F) \rangle = \psi(F)$, $\dot{\varepsilon}^{vp}$ represents the rate of visco-plastic straining, γ_i is the fluidity parameter (usually adopted as equal to unity in computations if time dependence of plastic strains is not real). $\psi_i(F_i)$ represents a function of F_i such that $\psi_i(F_i)$ increases monotonically with F_i.

In most of soil mechanics computations $\psi_i(F_i)$ is assumed to be equal to F_i, i.e.

$$\psi_i(F_i) = F_i$$

Although the above formulation would permit use of different γ_i values for different inter-granular boundaries, there is hardly any justification to do so. We shall, therefore, assume

$$\gamma_1 = \gamma_2 = \cdots \gamma_k = \gamma_\infty = \gamma \tag{15}$$

and eqn (14) would be simply written as

$$\dot{\varepsilon}_i^{vp} = \gamma \langle F_i \rangle \frac{\partial F_i}{\partial \boldsymbol{\sigma}'} \tag{16}$$

The rheological analogue of Fig. 2 immediately suggests that macroscopic strains would be given by summation of contributions from all inter-granular boundaries. Therefore,

$$\dot{\boldsymbol{\varepsilon}}^{vp} = \sum_{i=1}^{k \to \infty} \gamma \langle F_i \rangle \frac{\partial F_i}{\partial \boldsymbol{\sigma}'} \tag{17}$$

The discrete summation in eqn (17) can be replaced by integration over the surface of a sphere of unit radius: any point on the surface representing the normal to the plane passing through the centre of the sphere. Thus,

$$\dot{\boldsymbol{\varepsilon}}^{vp} = \int_\Omega \gamma \langle (F) \rangle \frac{\partial F}{\partial \boldsymbol{\sigma}'} \, d\Omega \tag{18}$$

where $d\Omega$ represents an infinitesimal area on the surface of the unit sphere. Equations (17) and (18) demonstrate that a visco-plastic strain rate equation can be derived from the basic mechanism of sliding on the inter-granular boundaries, which is more fundamental in nature.

Equation (18) can be evaluated using a numerical integration rule (Abramowitz and Stegun, 1975; Bazant and Oh, 1982) for a function (g) varying over the surface of the sphere. For example,

$$\int_\Omega g \, d\Omega = 4\pi \sum_{j=1}^{j=r} W_j g(l_j, m_j, n_j) \tag{19}$$

where l_j, m_j and n_j represent the direction cosines of the normal to the jth sampling plane, W_j is the corresponding weight coefficient and r is the number of sampling planes.

A 26 point numerical integration rule has been used by Pande and Sharma (1983) for solving boundary value problems. Recently Bazant (1983) has proposed 42 and 50 point integration rules for modelling fracture in concrete through strain softening constitutive laws. Such high order integration rules have not been used in the context of the problems of soil mechanics and it may well be that they are not required. The orientation of the sampling planes as given by their direction cosines and weight coefficients for a 26 point ($r = 26$) numerical integration rule are given in Table 1.

For plane stress, plane strain or axi-symmetric situations, only 9 (and for three-dimensional problems 13) independent sampling planes are required to be considered as the remaining planes give values of τ^2 or $|\tau|$ and σ_n which are the same as those obtained on one of the sampling planes.

TABLE 1

DIRECTION COSINES AND WEIGHTS OF SAMPLING PLANES

Direction cosines			Weights W
l	m	n	
$\pm\sqrt{(1/3)}$	$\pm\sqrt{(1/3)}$	$\pm\sqrt{(1/3)}$	27/840
$\pm\sqrt{(1/2)}$	$\pm\sqrt{(1/2)}$	0	32/840
$\pm\sqrt{(1/2)}$	0	$\pm\sqrt{(1/2)}$	32/840
0	$\pm\sqrt{(1/2)}$	$\pm\sqrt{(1/2)}$	32/840
± 1	0	0	40/840
0	± 1	0	40/840
0	0	± 1	40/840

TABLE 2
SELECTED SAMPLING PLANES FOR PLANE STRESS, PLANE
STRAIN, AND AXISYMMETRIC CONDITIONS

Direction cosines			Weights W
l	m	n	
$\sqrt{(1/3)}$	$\sqrt{(1/3)}$	$\sqrt{(1/3)}$	108/840
$-\sqrt{(1/3)}$	$\sqrt{(1/3)}$	$\sqrt{(1/3)}$	108/840
$\sqrt{(1/2)}$	$\sqrt{(1/2)}$	0	64/840
$-\sqrt{(1/2)}$	$\sqrt{(1/2)}$	0	64/840
0	$\sqrt{(1/2)}$	$\sqrt{(1/2)}$	128/840
$\sqrt{(1/2)}$	0	$\sqrt{(1/2)}$	128/840
1	0	0	80/840
0	1	0	80/840
0	0	1	80/840

The direction cosines of these planes, together with adjusted values of weight coefficients are shown in Table 2. Equations (18) and (12) can be integrated using any of the standard time marching schemes.

2.5 Advantages of Multi-laminate Framework

The multi-laminate framework has the following advantages compared to the conventional formulation of constitutive laws in terms of stress invariants:

(i)   The multi-laminate framework has a sound physical basis and it is conceptually very appealing.

(ii)   As the description of sliding, closing/opening of inter-granular boundary is refined, a truer description of soil behaviour is obtained. Strain hardening/softening has to be related to normal and shear strains on a contact plane.

(iii)   As different boundaries undergo different histories of deformation, a multi-laminate framework allows one to account for rotation of principal stress axes in a rational manner. Initially isotropic material thus becomes anisotropic due to plastic flow. This is the most significant advantage and has been discussed in detail by Pande and Sharma (1983).

Simultaneous sliding/separation/closing on more than one boundary can take place giving rise to quite complex macroscopic behaviour though the description on one boundary remains relatively simple.

3   EXTENSION OF CRITICAL STATE MODEL FOR CYCLIC AND TRANSIENT LOADING

The critical state model, be it in a conventional invariant framework or multi-laminate framework, represents the behaviour of soil under monotonic loading. If an undrained soil sample was subjected to cyclic loads of say constant strain amplitude, the critical state model would predict that after the first cycle the soil behaves elastically. There will be no increase in the pore pressures and the soil sample could never fail in subsequent cycles. It has little resemblance to the observed behaviour of soils. Experiments (e.g. Matsui *et al.*, 1980; Taylor and Bacchus, 1969 and many others) show that in each cycle additional pore pressures are generated and amplitude of stress drops till finally the sample liquefies, i.e. effective stresses σ_1' and σ_3' are zero.

The fact that plastic strains appear to take place on unloading is directly in contradiction to the assumption of elastic behaviour for stress paths within the yield surface defined by the critical state model. Various modifications have been proposed to overcome this shortcoming of the critical state model. These range from introducing empirical relationships (Carter *et al.*, 1982) to kinematic hardening (Mroz *et al.*, 1979; Mroz and Norris, 1982; Prevost, 1978, 1980) and bounding surface plasticity (Dafalias and Herrmann, 1982).

A rather simple modification, viz. reflection of the yield surface on unloading/reloading, was suggested by Pande and Pietruszczak (1982), and used with success by Shiomi *et al.* (1982) to predict liquefaction of sand layers. The model was developed in the conventional space of stress invariants and thus ignored the influence of cyclic rotation of principal stress axes.

Here, we shall reformulate the reflecting surface model in the multi-laminate framework as discussed in Section 2 of this chapter.

4   REFLECTING SURFACE MODEL

4.1 Modelling Isotropic Consolidation Behaviour

Modelling the behaviour of soils under isotropic consolidation is the first step towards the general description. Fig. 8(a) shows a typical relationship between void ratio (e) and natural logarithm of isotropic pressure ($\ln p_c$). Starting from a point on the virgin consolidation line, an upward concave curve is obtained on unloading (branch AB in Fig. 8(a)). Reloading traces

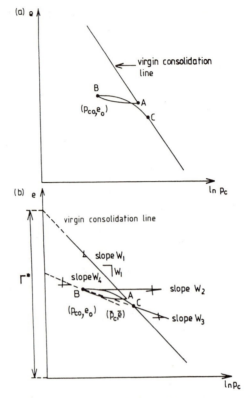

FIG. 8. (a) Typical $e - \log_e p_c$ isotropic consolidation curve; (b) Definition of symbols used.

the curve BC, the virgin consolidation line being tangential to it at a point C. A hysteretic loop is generated by the loading and unloading branches.

In the critical state model, unloading and reloading will be represented by the straight line AB without any hysteretic loop and no plastic strains will take place along this stress path. Clearly this is an approximation which is not suitable for modelling soils subjected to cyclic loading.

Here we shall discuss isotropic consolidation in three parts, viz. loading, unloading and reloading.

(a) *Loading:* Consider an analytical relationship between e and isotropic pressure (p_c) of the form

$$\mathrm{d}(\ln p_c) = -E_1[\Gamma - (e - e_0)]\,\mathrm{d}e + Z_1 \ln (p_c/p_{c0})\,|\mathrm{d}e| \qquad (20)$$

where E_1, Z_1 and Γ are constants and | | represents the absolute value. Equation (20) when integrated, represents a hyperbola passing through the point (p_{c0}, e_0) (see, for instance, the branch BC in Fig. 8(a)). Equation (20) can be rewritten as

$$\frac{d(\ln p_c)}{de} = -E_1[\Gamma - (e - e_0)] + Z_1 \ln\left(\frac{p_c}{p_{c0}}\right) \qquad (21a)$$

for $de < 0$

$$\frac{d(\ln p_c)}{de} = -E_1[\Gamma - (e - e_0)] - Z_1 \ln\left(\frac{p_c}{p_{c0}}\right) \qquad (21b)$$

for $de > 0$.

If parameters, E_1, Z_1 and Γ are suitably defined, it can be shown that eqn (21) generates a hysteretic loop, ABC as presented in Fig. 8(a). This is a very simple way to model non-linear behaviour and similar approaches have already been used in endochronic theories (Bazant *et al.*, 1982; Valanis and Read, 1982).

Let us now look in some detail at eqn (21). In order to determine the values of parameters E_1, Z_1 and Γ we impose the following conditions (see Fig. 8(b)).

(i) the initial slope of the hyperbola is equal to W_2, i.e.

$$\frac{d(\ln p_c)}{de}\bigg|_{\substack{p_c = p_{c0} \\ e = e_0}} = -\frac{1}{W_2} \qquad (22)$$

(ii) the loading branch of the hyperbola passes through the point $(\bar{p}_c, \bar{e})$ marked as C in Fig. 8(b). This is an intersection point of two straight lines: the virgin consolidation line and a straight line with the slope W_3 passing through p_{c0}, e_0.

(iii) at C the slope of the hyperbola is equal to the slope of the virgin consolidation line W_1, i.e.

$$\frac{d(\ln p_c)}{de}\bigg|_{\substack{p_c = \bar{p}_c \\ e = \bar{e}}} = -\frac{1}{W_1} \qquad (23)$$

In the normal soil mechanics terminology W_1 stands for the compression index and is denoted by λ, while W_2 stands for the swelling index denoted by κ. The need for departure from the standard terminology and notation will be apparent towards the end of this section.

To satisfy the first condition (i) we substitute eqn (22) in eqn (21). Thus,

$$E_1 \Gamma = \frac{1}{W_2} \tag{24}$$

Note, that according to eqn (24) both loading and unloading branches have the same initial slope W_2, since the second term in eqn (21) vanishes at $p_c = p_{c0}$.

The second condition requires the integration of eqn (21). We note that this is a non-homogeneous linear differential equation of the first order, which can easily be solved to give

$$\ln p_c = \mp \frac{E_1}{Z_1}\left(\Gamma \mp \frac{1}{Z_1}\right)\exp\left[\pm Z_1(e - e_0)\right]$$
$$+ \left\{\mp \frac{E_1}{Z_1}\left(e - e_0 - \Gamma \pm \frac{1}{Z_1}\right) + \ln p_{c0}\right\} \tag{25}$$

Now, condition (ii) imposed on the loading branch will provide the equation

$$\ln \bar{p}_c = -\frac{E_1}{Z_1}\left(\Gamma - \frac{1}{Z_1}\right)\exp\left[Z_1(\bar{e} - e_0)\right]$$
$$+ \left\{-\frac{E_1}{Z_1}\left(\bar{e} - e_0 - \Gamma + \frac{1}{Z_1}\right) + \ln p_{c0}\right\} \tag{26}$$

In order to determine the co-ordinates of the intersection point C (Fig. 8(b)), we shall write the equations of both of the straight lines, i.e.

$$e = e_0 - W_3 \ln\left(\frac{p_c}{p_{c0}}\right) \tag{27a}$$

$$e = \Gamma^* - W_1 \ln p_c \tag{27b}$$

Equation (27a) corresponds to the line passing through p_{c0}, e_0, whereas eqn (27b) describes the virgin consolidation line. The constant Γ^* is defined in Fig. 8(b) and denotes the value of e for $\ln p_c = 0$.

In view of eqns (27a) and (27b) the coordinates of the intersection point are computed as follows

$$\ln \bar{p}_c = \frac{1}{W_3 - W_1}(e_0 + W_3 \ln p_{c0} - \Gamma^*) \tag{28a}$$

$$\bar{e} = \Gamma^* - W_1 \ln \bar{p}_c \tag{28b}$$

Finally, the third condition (iii) applied to the loading branch of hyperbola eqn (25) will provide the equation

$$E_1 \left(\Gamma - \frac{1}{Z_1} \right) \exp \left[Z_1 (\bar{e} - e_0) \right] + \frac{E_1}{Z_1} = \frac{1}{W_1} \tag{29}$$

The system of three eqns (24), (26) and (29) can be solved for constants E_1, Z_1 and Γ in terms of W_1, W_2 and W_3 only. After some transformation we obtain

$$(\delta\Gamma + a - 1) \exp \left[a(\bar{e} - e_0) \right] \frac{1}{\Gamma} + (\bar{e} - e_0) - \delta\frac{W_2}{W_1} + \left(1 - \frac{W_2}{W_1} a \right) = 0 \tag{30}$$

$$E_1 = \frac{1}{W_2 \Gamma} \tag{31}$$

$$Z_1 = \frac{1}{\ln (\bar{p}_c/p_{c0})} \left[-\frac{1}{W_1} + E_1 (\Gamma + e_0 - \bar{e}) \right] \tag{32}$$

where

$$\delta = \frac{W_1 - W_2}{W_1 W_2 \ln (\bar{p}_c/p_{c0})} \qquad a = \frac{e_0 - \bar{e}}{W_2 \ln (\bar{p}_c/p_{c0})}$$

Thus, we have three explicit equations for Γ, E_1 and Z_1 which can easily be solved once the values of W_1, W_2, W_3 and Γ^* are known.

Numerical experiments show that the shape of predicted $e - \ln p_c$ curves is not very sensitive to parameter W_3. Conditions (ii) and (iii) therefore can be reformulated assuming $\bar{e} \to -\infty$ and $\ln \bar{p}_c \to \infty$. This implies that the slope of hyperbola approaches W_1 as $e \to -\infty$. From eqn (29) we have

$$\frac{E_1}{Z_1} = \frac{1}{W_1} \tag{33}$$

and from eqns (26) and (28b) we obtain

$$\Gamma = \left(1 - \frac{W_2}{W_1} \right)^{-1} \left[(\Gamma^* - e_0) - W_1 \ln p_{c0} \right] \tag{34}$$

It is, therefore, possible to evaluate E_1, Z_1 and Γ from eqns (24), (33) and (34).

(b) *Unloading:* For unloading we use again eqn (20) replacing e_0 and p_{c0} by the coordinates corresponding to the current unloading point (e_u, p_{cu}).

The parameters E_1, Z_1 and Γ remain unchanged. Equation (20) again represents a hyperbolic curve passing through the unloading point (e_u, p_{cu}) on the $e - \ln p_c$ plot. The initial slope, according to eqn (24), is equal to W_2 (i.e. κ-slope in the critical state model) and the subsequent deformation process is governed by eqn (20). With $\ln p_c$ decreasing the slope would tend to W_1 which is rather unrealistic. To remedy this situation it is proposed to limit the slope to W_4 (see Fig. 8(b)).

Thus,

$$\frac{d(\ln p_c)}{de} = -\frac{1}{W_4} \quad \text{for} \quad -E_1[\Gamma - (e - e_0)] - Z_1 \ln \left(\frac{p_c}{p_{c0}} \right) \le -\frac{1}{W_4} \quad (35)$$

and W_4 is the parameter which largely controls the shape and width of the hysteretic loop in an $e - \ln p_c$ plot.

(c) *Reloading:* Reloading is again described by eqn (20). Here e_0 and p_{c0} are replaced by the coordinates of the current reloading point, say e_{0r} and p_{cr}. The values of parameters E_1, Z_1 and Γ are to be recalculated imposing the conditions already discussed in (a). Equation (20) would now again plot as a hyperbolic curve.

4.2 Additivity Postulate and Hardening Rule

The total strains, according to this postulate of the theory of plasticity, are composed of elastic and plastic parts. It can be shown that this postulate holds good for void ratios as well. Thus,

$$de = de^e + de^{vp} \quad (36)$$

where de^e and de^{vp} represent the elastic and plastic increments of void ratio change.

Equation (20) proposed in Section 4.1 qualitatively describes the $e - \ln p_c$ relationship. To be able to propose a general hardening law within the framework of plasticity theory, we must distinguish between the elastic and plastic components of void ratio.

We now assume

$$W_1 = \lambda - \kappa$$
$$W_2 \to 0$$

where λ and κ are compression and swelling indices, respectively. W_1 now represents the slope of the $e^{vp} - \ln p_c$ plot. Equation (21) reduces to

$$\frac{\mathrm{d}p_c}{\mathrm{d}e^{vp}} = p_c\left[-E_1(\Gamma - (e^{vp} - e_0^{vp})) + Z_1 \ln\left(\frac{p_c}{p_{c0}}\right)\right] \qquad \text{if } \mathrm{d}e^{vp} < 0 \qquad (37\text{a})$$

$$\frac{\mathrm{d}p_c}{\mathrm{d}e^{vp}} = p_c\left[-E_1(\Gamma - (e^{vp} - e_0^{vp})) - Z_1 \ln\left(\frac{p_c}{p_{c0}}\right)\right] \qquad \text{if } \mathrm{d}e^{vp} > 0 \qquad (37\text{b})$$

which represents a hardening law.

The elastic increment of the void ratio ($\mathrm{d}e^e$) is related to κ as in the case of the critical state model through

$$\mathrm{d}e^e = -\kappa \frac{\mathrm{d}p_c}{p_c} \qquad (38)$$

and leads to an equation similar to (3b), i.e.

$$K = \frac{1+e}{\kappa} p_c \qquad (39)$$

defining the drained bulk modulus of the soil.

Before we end this section, a small note on the value of W_4. This constant is taken to be

$$W_4 = \frac{1-\beta}{\beta} \kappa \qquad (40)$$

where $0 < \beta < 1$ is a proportionality constant. It controls the 'openness' or width of hysteretic loops and has to be obtained from numerical experiments by matching the experimentally observed behaviour.

Figures 9(a) and 9(b) present the behaviour of saturated remoulded Kaolin (Banerjee and Stipho, 1978) as predicted by using the hardening rule of eqn (37) using two different values of β. It is noted that on cyclic isotropic consolidation the void ratio goes on progressively reducing. Obviously, in an undrained state, the soil would liquefy after some cycles.

4.3 Isotropic Consolidation and Hardening Rule in Multi-laminate Framework

Increments of void ratio are related to the increments of volumetric strain (ε_v) through the well known equation

$$\mathrm{d}\varepsilon_v = -\frac{\mathrm{d}e}{1+e} \qquad (41)$$

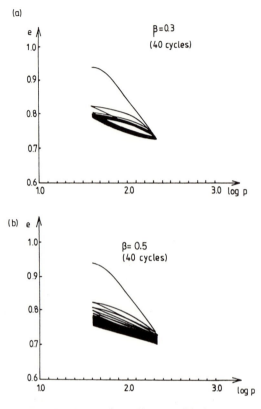

FIG. 9.   Isotropic cyclic consolidation.

Using the additivity postulate eqn (36), it is possible to write eqn (41) for plastic volumetric strains as well, i.e.

$$d\varepsilon_v^{vp} = -\frac{de^{vp}}{1+e^{vp}} \tag{42}$$

Reverting back to the multi-laminate model, it is suggested that plastic volumetric strain is the weighted sum of plastic strains in the normal direction (ε_n^{vp}) on sampling planes, i.e.

$$d\varepsilon_v^{vp} = \sum_{j=1}^{r} W_j (d\varepsilon_n^{vp})_j \tag{43}$$

Obviously in the process of isotropic consolidation

$$d\varepsilon_v^{vp} = (d\varepsilon_n^{vp})_1 = (d\varepsilon_n^{vp})_2 = \ldots(d\varepsilon^{vp})_n \tag{44}$$

and

$$\sum_{j=1}^{r} W_j = 1 \tag{45}$$

i.e. the normal plastic strain on each of the sampling planes is the same as volumetric plastic strain. However, as discussed earlier, this is not so for a general stress path. The hardening law of eqn (37) should now be written to represent hardening related to individual sampling planes.

The left hand side of eqn (37) can be written as

$$\frac{dp_c}{de^{vp}} = \frac{dp_c}{d\varepsilon_v^{vp}} \cdot \frac{d\varepsilon_v^{vp}}{de^{vp}} \tag{46}$$

which, using eqn (42), reduces to

$$\frac{dp_c}{de^{vp}} = -\left(\frac{1}{1+e^{vp}}\right) \cdot \frac{dp_c}{d\varepsilon_v^{vp}} \tag{47}$$

$$= -\frac{1}{(1+e^{vp})} \cdot \frac{dp_c}{d\varepsilon_n^{vp}} \cdot \frac{d\varepsilon_n^{vp}}{d\varepsilon_v^{vp}} \tag{48}$$

Substituting eqn (43) in (48) and (37a), the hardening law for the jth sampling plane can be written as

$$\begin{aligned}\left(\frac{dp_c}{de^{vp}}\right) &= -\left(\frac{1}{1+e^{vp}}\right)\frac{1}{W_j}\left(\frac{dp_c}{d\varepsilon_n^{vp}}\right) \\ &= p_c\left[-E_1(\Gamma - (e^{vp} - e_0^{vp})) + Z_1 \ln\left(\frac{p_c}{p_{c0}}\right)\right]\end{aligned} \tag{49}$$

Equation (49) can be rearranged to give

$$\left(\frac{dp_c}{d\varepsilon_n^{vp}}\right) = -W_j(1 + e^{vp})p_c\left[-E_1(\Gamma - (e^{vp} - e_0^{vp})) + Z_1 \ln\left(\frac{p_c}{p_{c0}}\right)\right] \tag{50}$$

Substituting for e^p after integrating eqn (42) we have,

$$\left(\frac{\mathrm{d}p_c}{\mathrm{d}\varepsilon_n^{vp}}\right) = -W_j(1 + e_0^{vp})\exp(-\varepsilon_n^{vp})p_c$$

$$\times \left[-E_1\{\Gamma - (1 + e_0^{vp})(\exp(-\varepsilon_n^{vp}) - 1)\} + RZ_1 \ln\left(\frac{p_c}{p_{c0}}\right)\right] \quad (51)$$

where $R = 1\cdot0$ if $\mathrm{d}e > 0$ and $R = -1$ if $\mathrm{d}e < 0$.

Equation (51) represents, finally, the hardening law for a sampling plane and enables the history of consolidation to be traced out for each individual plane in a general stress path.

Equation (51) looks complicated but in computer implementation poses no problem. It gives two different values of hardening moduli—one for loading and another for unloading. This enables hysteretic loops to be generated under cyclic loading programs.

5   COMPLETE EQUATIONS OF MULTI-LAMINATE REFLECTING SURFACE MODEL

In Section 4 a hardening law for inter-granular boundaries was discussed. To complete the formalism of the constitutive model, a flow rule is required to be established. First a few definitions and the terminology associated with the model are introduced.

Bounding surface: The concept of bounding surface has been introduced previously by Mroz (1967) in the context of metal plasticity and Dafalias and Popov (1975) in the context of soils. The bounding surface in the stress space represents the past history of loading. The actual state of stress always lies on or within the bounding surface. The hardening modulus associated with the bounding surface is related to the slope of the virgin consolidation line in the $e - \ln p_c$ plot.

Consolidation surface: A consolidation surface (CS) is associated with the current state of stress. In the model presented it is of the same geometric form as the bounding surface. Its equation is symbolised as $f_c = 0$.

Conjugate consolidation surface: A conjugate consolidation surface (CC) is a surface which is the mirror image of the consolidation surface. The reflection is adopted at $\sigma'_n =$ constant line passing through the current stress point. Its equation is symbolised as $f_{cc} = 0$.

Reflected surfaces: The consolidation surface and conjugate consolidation surface can be reflected in the stress space about a plane tangential to the respective surface at the current stress point. These surfaces are referred to as 'reflected consolidation surfaces' (RC) or 'reflected conjugate consolidation surfaces' (RCC) and their equations are symbolised as $f_c^R = 0$ and $f_{cc}^R = 0$, respectively.

Activation rule: Any of the five surfaces defined above can be 'active' loading surfaces. Which particular surface is actually active is defined by an 'activation' rule.

Plastic flow is always associated to the current loading surface. All the surfaces are defined in $|\tau| - \sigma'_n$ stress space for each of the sampling planes. Figure 10 shows diagrammatically the five surfaces. Depending upon which of the surfaces is the active loading surface, a flow rule associated to that surface is adopted. If the current stress situation is on the bounding surface, the consolidation surface coincides with the bounding surface and the model would reduce to a multi-laminate model.

5.1 Active Loading Surface and Flow Rule
To decide which loading surface is active, assume a system of Cartesian coordinates with the stress point as the origin and axes parallel to $|\tau|$ and σ'_n

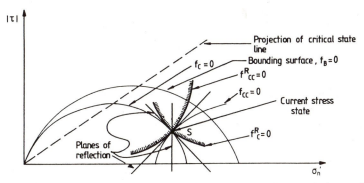

FIG. 10.   Various loading surfaces in $\sigma'_n - |\tau|$ stress space for a typical sampling plane.

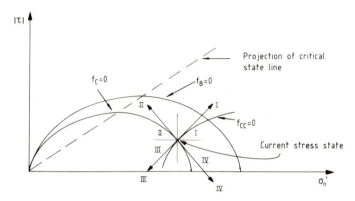

FIG. 11. Anticlockwise activation rule (roman numerals on flow vectors correspond to the stress increments in regions marked with like numbers).

axes (Fig. 11). Depending on which quadrant the elastic stress increment falls, the active loading surface is chosen. Table 3 below lists the various possibilities.

TABLE 3
ACTIVE LOADING SURFACE FOR STRESS INCREMENTS IN VARIOUS QUADRANTS

Quadrant	Stress increment	Active loading surface
I	$\lvert \dot{\tau} \rvert \geq 0$ $\dot{\sigma}'_n \geq 0$	Consolidation surface; $f_c = 0$
II	$\lvert \dot{\tau} \rvert > 0$ $\dot{\sigma}'_n < 0$	Conjugate consolidation surface; $f_{cc} = 0$; $\dot{\varepsilon}^{vp}_n$ dilatant
III	$\lvert \dot{\tau} \rvert < 0$ $\dot{\sigma}'_n < 0$	Reflected consolidation surface; $f_c^R = 0$; $\dot{\varepsilon}^{vp}_n$ dilatant
IV	$\lvert \dot{\tau} \rvert < 0$ $\dot{\sigma}'_n > 0$	Reflected conjugate consolidation surface; $f_{cc}^R = 0$

The above activation rule is a slight modification of the one used in the reflecting surface model of Pande and Pietruszczak (1982).

It is recognised that such activation rules would lead to discontinuities in the plastic strain flow vector but they are adopted here for simplicity of practical applications.

It is noted that different loading surfaces may be active for different sampling planes. This further illustrates the elegance of the multi-laminate framework.

Assuming that the current stress point is represented by $(\sigma_n'^*, |\tau|^*)$, the equation of the conjugate consolidation surface is written as

$$f_{cc} = \frac{4\tau^2}{M^2 p_c^2} + \frac{4(\sigma_n' - 2\sigma_n'^* + p_c)^2}{p_c^2} - 1 = 0 \tag{52}$$

One does not need ever to write the expressions for reflected surfaces as only gradients are needed in the visco-plastic formulation which can be obtained from consolidation and conjugate consolidation surfaces since

$$\frac{\partial f_c^R}{\partial \boldsymbol{\sigma}} = -\frac{\partial f_c}{\partial \boldsymbol{\sigma}}$$

and $\tag{53}$

$$\frac{\partial f_{cc}^R}{\partial \boldsymbol{\sigma}} = -\frac{\partial f_c}{\partial \boldsymbol{\sigma}}$$

Thus the evolution of only two surfaces (consolidation surface, $f_c = 0$ and bounding surface $f_b = 0$) needs to be traced. This is a significant advantage in computational implementation.

5.2 Hardening Rule when the Conjugate Consolidation Surface is the Active Loading Surface

Equation (51) was shown to give an appropriate hardening rule for cyclic isotropic consolidation. In this stress path consolidation and reflected consolidation surfaces are active loading surfaces. When the conjugate consolidation surface is active, dilatancy of the soil is associated with the expansion of the consolidation surface. A slight modification to eqn (51) enables this to be accounted for (eqn (54)).

$$\frac{dp_c}{d\varepsilon_n^{vp}} = -W_j(1 + e_0^{vp})e^{-\varepsilon_n^{vp}}R_1 p_c$$

$$\times \left[-E_1\{r - R_1(1 + e_0^{vp})(\exp(-\varepsilon_n^{vp}) - 1)\} + RZ_1 \ln\left(\frac{p_c}{p_{c0}}\right) \right] \tag{54}$$

where $R_1 = -1 \cdot 0$ if the conjugate consolidation surface or reflected conjugate consolidation surface is the active loading surface otherwise $R_1 = 1 \cdot 0$.

Admittedly R_1 has been chosen rather arbitrarily. Further numerical experiments will give clearer insight and are being carried out. However, eqn (54) is computationally convenient and, as shown in later sections, predicts the response of soils reasonably well.

6 QUALITATIVE RESPONSE OF THE MODEL

For a normally consolidated material, the consolidation and bounding surfaces coincide. These surfaces are also 'active' loading surfaces. An increment of stress such that $(\partial f_c/\partial \sigma')^T d\sigma' > 0$ leads to both consolidation and bounding surfaces expanding.

For overconsolidated material, the bounding surface and consolidation surfaces are different (Fig. 12). As discussed in Section 5 above, the current and subsequent positions of various surfaces for stress increments in each of the regions marked on Fig. 11 are shown in Fig. 13. It is noted that stress increments in Regions I and IV lead to contraction while stress increments

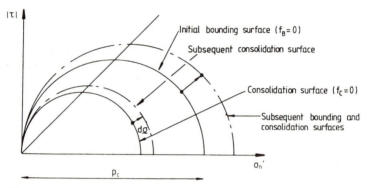

FIG. 12.   Position of consolidation and bounding surfaces for overconsolidated materials.

in Regions II and III lead to dilatancy. When the stress path lies in Zones I and IV, it may at some stage reach the bounding surface. In this situation the bounding surface becomes the active loading surface and the soil behaves as normally consolidated thereafter.

A feature of the model is that there is no elastic domain as such as assumed in classical plasticity.

7 NUMERICAL IMPLEMENTATION

Numerical implementation of the model is extremely simple. Unlike kinematic hardening models, evolution of only two surfaces, i.e.

consolidation and bounding surfaces, is required to be traced. Gradient vectors for any of the reflected surfaces are obtained simply by switching the signs of deviatoric and/or mean components. An elastic probe is made to identify the regions in which the stress path lies. (This is anyway an essential step in the visco-plastic algorithm). The hardening rule given by eqn (54) is quite convenient. However the parameters E_1, Γ and Z_1 have to be re-computed whenever there is reversed loading. This involves only solving three simultaneous equations (see Section 3).

8 NUMERICAL EXAMPLES

8.1 Numerical Examples of the Critical State Model in the Multi-laminate Framework

These have been presented by Pande and Sharma (1983) demonstrating that the response in a multi-laminate framework is the same as that of the standard critical state model for normally consolidated clays in monotonic loading for situations where no rotation of principal axes takes place. However, if rotation of principal stress axes takes place, the results of the two models are significantly different. This is illustrated by an example of a simple shear test.

A sample of clay has been consolidated to effective stresses of $\sigma_x = \sigma_z = -69 \cdot 44 \, \text{kN/m}^2$, $\sigma_y = -101 \, \text{kN/m}^2$ ($K_0 = 0 \cdot 69$). The sample is subjected to incremental shear strain in plane strain conditions. The volume of the sample is kept constant by maintaining the strain components ε_x, ε_y and ε_z all equal to zero by adjusting the components of stress. The sample is drained throughout. The following parameters for the clay have been adopted

Bulk modulus	$12\,000 \, \text{kN/m}^2$
Shear modulus	$4\,500 \, \text{kN/m}^2$
Hardening parameter	$13 \cdot 33$
ϕ'	$26°$

For the multi-laminate model, the consolidation process itself has to be simulated from the slurry state as the effective normal stresses on the 9 sampling planes will not be the same at the end of the consolidation phase. The current yield surfaces at the end of the consolidation phase for each of the sampling points are shown in Fig. 14. The numbers on this figure correspond to the sampling planes whose direction cosines are listed in

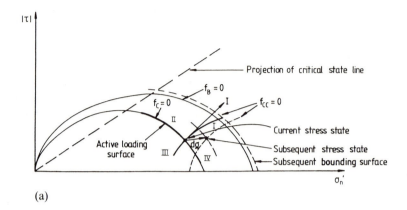

(a)

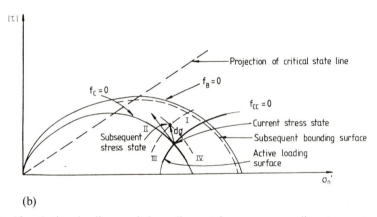

(b)

FIG. 13. Active loading and bounding surfaces corresponding to a stress increment in each of the four regions. (a) Stress increment in Region I; (b) Stress increment in Region II.

Table 2. The ratio of the least to the largest effective normal stress is 0·685, close to the K_0 value.

Figure 15(a) shows the variation of $t = (\sigma'_1 - \sigma'_3)/2$ (σ'_1, σ'_3 being the major and minor effective principal stresses) with shear strain (γ_{xy}) for the critical state as well as the multi-laminate model, the latter predicting finally a 7% lower failure stress. Figure 15(b) shows the variation of σ'_2/s (σ'_2 is the intermediate principal stress or σ'_z, $s = (\sigma'_1 + \sigma'_3)/2$) with γ_{xy}.

Figure 15(c) shows the variation of the angle through which principal

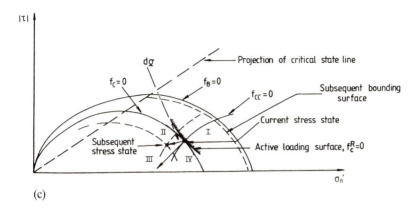

(c)

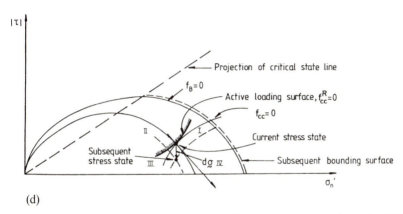

(d)

FIG. 13—*contd.* (c) Stress increment in Region III; (d) Stress increment in Region IV.

stress has rotated (α) with shear strain. It is noted that α approaches a value of 25° for the multi-laminate model, whereas the value for the critical state model is 45°. It is noted that on normally consolidated clays, response of the multi-laminate model is less stiff in comparison to the critical state model due to additional plastic strains taking place on rotation of the principal stress axes.

8.2 Numerical Examples of the Reflecting Surface Model

These have been presented by Pande and Pietruszczak (1982). The following example taken from this reference remains unaffected by the adoption of the multi-laminate framework as there is no rotation of principal stress axes involved.

One of the important tests of a model is prediction of the response in triaxial tests at different overconsolidation ratios.

Test data of Banerjee and Stipho (1978) on remoulded Kaolin have been chosen for comparison with the response predicted by the model. These tests were conducted on 3 in × 6 in size specimens under stress controlled conditions. Test results are available for OCR = 1, 1·2 and 2·0 for undrained conditions and will be used for comparison.

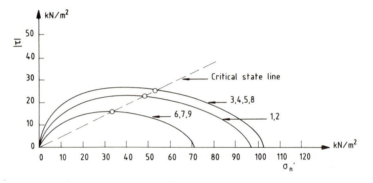

FIG. 14.   Initial yield surfaces associated with various sampling planes after K_0 consolidation.

Figure 16 shows the effective stress paths in p', q space followed by the test specimen. Both experimental and numerical results are presented. The data used for the model prediction are shown in the figure and are those proposed by Banerjee and Stipho (1978) except the parameter β. This parameter had to be chosen by numerical experiments as its identification involves matching of a complete loading, unloading and reloading loop in isotropic consolidation—information which is not available from the experimental tests of Banerjee and Stipho. Figure 17 shows the graph q vs ε_1 (axial strain) for the same tests. Agreement between test results and numerical prediction seems to be reasonable. It is noted that for OCR = 2 only the failure load was available and hence comparison of strains at lower values of q is not possible. Response of the model is stiffer than seen on the experiments—a feature common to all models based on the elliptical shape of the yield surfaces as used in the critical state model.

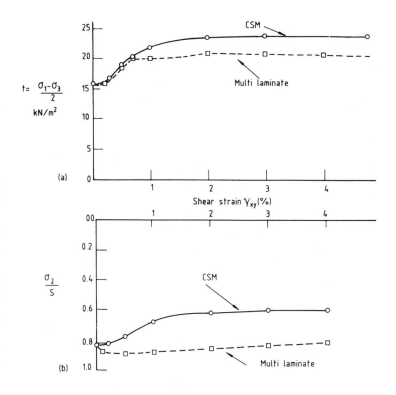

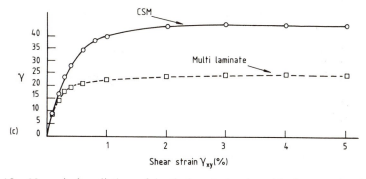

FIG. 15. Numerical predictions of simple shear tests using critical state and multi-laminate models.

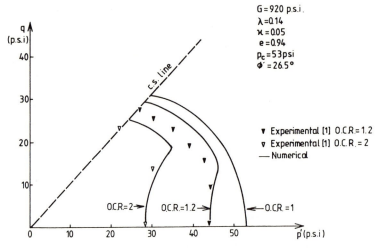

FIG. 16. Effective stress paths in an undrained triaxial test.

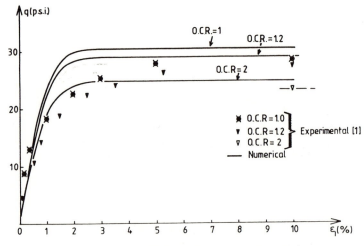

FIG. 17. q versus ε_1 graph for an undrained triaxial test.

9 CONCLUSIONS

A complete formulation of a multi-laminate reflecting surface model has been presented. The multi-laminate framework is very appealing from the point of view of the physical behaviour of soils. As the description of sliding/compacting/separation of inter-granular boundaries is refined, a more realistic model of soil behaviour is obtained. In the formulation presented, only volumetric hardening has been considered. It is easy to visualise shear hardening and thus combined hardening. Reflection of the loading surfaces in the stress space is a convenient way of modelling stress reversals. In bounding surface plasticity models an arbitrary interpolation rule for hardening moduli is used. A hardening modulus based on cyclic isotropic consolidation tests is proposed and incorporated in the reflecting surface model.

Research on the multi-laminate reflecting surface model is far from complete but it can be seen that it provides a sound basis for investigation of constitutive models for a wide variety of geomaterials. Evolution of only two surfaces is required to be traced in the model which gives a considerable computational advantage. There is discontinuity in the evolution of loading surfaces, i.e. the flow vector changes direction abruptly. This is a drawback but it leads to simplicity. The number of parameters required for the model is five; they are the same as those required for the critical state model.

The prediction of soil behaviour in closely monitored tests is the key to success and acceptance of a soil model. It is planned to make predictions of centrifuge model tests in static and dynamic conditions to prove the proposed model.

ACKNOWLEDGEMENTS

The author is grateful to Dr K. G. Sharma of the Indian Institute of Technology, Delhi and Dr St. Pietruszczak of McMaster University, Canada for their contributions to the continuing theme of research at the University College of Swansea.

REFERENCES

ABRAMOWITZ, M. and STEGUN, I. A. (1975) (Eds). *Handbook of Mathematical Functions*, Dover Publications, New York.
BANERJEE, P. K. and STIPHO, A. S. (1978). Associated and non-associated constitutive relations for undrained behaviour of isotropic clays, *Int. J. Num. Anal. Mech. Geomech.*, **2**, 35–6.

BAZANT, Z. P. (1983). *Mechanics of fracture and progressive cracking in concrete structures*, Report 83-2/428m, Centre for Concrete and Geomaterials, Northwestern University, Evanston, Illinois.

BAZANT, Z. P. and OH, B. H. (1982). *Efficient numerical integration on the surface of a sphere*, Report, Centre for Concrete and Geomaterials, Northwestern University, Evanston, Illinois.

BAZANT, Z. P., ANSAL, A. M. and KRISEK, R. J. (1982). Endochronic models for soils, in *Soil Mechanics—Transient and Cyclic Loads*, Chapter 15, John Wiley & Sons Ltd, Chichester.

CALLADINE, C. R. (1971). A microstructural view of the mechanical properties of saturated clay, *Geotechnique*, **21**, 391–415.

CARTER, J. P., BOOKER, J. R. and WROTH, C. P. (1982). A critical state soil model for cyclic loading, in *Soil Mechanics—Transient and Cyclic Loads*, Chapter 9, John Wiley & Sons Ltd, Chichester.

DAFALIAS, Y. F. and HERRMANN, L. R. (1982). Bounding Surface formulation of soil plasticity, in *Soil Mechanics—Transient and Cyclic Loads*, Chapter 10, John Wiley & Sons Ltd, Chichester.

DAFALIAS, Y. F. and POPOV, E. P. (1975). A model of nonlinearly hardening materials for complex loadings, *Acta Mechanica*, **21**, 173–92.

GERRARD, C. M. (1982). Joint compliances as a basis for rock mass properties and the design of support requirement, *Intl. J. Rock. Mech. Min. Sci. & Geomech. Abstr.*, **19**, 285–305.

MATSUI, T., OHARA, H. and ITO, T. (1980). Cyclic stress–strain history and shear characteristics of clay, *Jl. of Geotech. Dn.*, *A.S.C.E.*, **GT10**, 1101–20.

MROZ, Z. (1967). On the description of anisotropic work hardening, *J. Mech. Phys. Solids*, **15**, 163–75.

MROZ, Z. and NORRIS, V. A. (1982). Elasto-plastic constitutive model soils with application to cyclic loading, *Soil Mechanics—Transient and Cyclic Loads*, Chapter 8, J. Wiley & Sons, Chichester, 173–217.

MROZ, Z., NORRIS, V. A. and ZIENKIEWICZ, O. C. (1979). Application of an anisotropic hardening model in the analysis of the elasto-plastic deformation of soils, *Geotechnique*, **29**, 1–34.

NAYLOR, D. J., PANDE, G. N., SIMPSON, B. and TABB, R. (1983). *Finite Elements in Geotechnical Engineering*, Pineridge Press, Swansea.

PANDE, G. N. (1980). Numerical simulation of rock behaviour—problems and possibilities in *Num. Meths. in Geomechanics*, Ed. W. Wittke, Vol. 4, A. A. Balkema & Sons, Rotterdam, 1341–56.

PANDE, G. N. and GERRARD, C. M. (1983). The behaviour of jointed rock masses under various simple loading states, *Proc. 5th Intl. Cong. on Rock Mechanics*, Melbourne, F217–23.

PANDE, G. N. and PIETRUSZCZAK, ST. (1982). Reflecting surface model for soils, *Proc. of Int. Sym. on Num. Models in Geomechanics*, Zurich, A. A. Balkema, Rotterdam, 50–64.

PANDE, G. N. and SHARMA, K. G. (1980). A microstructural model for soils under cyclic loading, *Proc. Int. Symp. on Soils under Cyclic and Transient Loading*, Swansea, **1**, 451–62.

PANDE, G. N. and SHARMA, K. G. (1981). A multi-laminate model of clays—a numerical study of the influence of rotation of principal stress axes,

Implementation of Computer Procedures and Stress–Strain Laws in Geotechnical Engineering, Eds. C. S. Desai and S. K. Saxena, Vol. II, Acorn Press, Durham, NC, 575–90.

PANDE, G. N. and SHARMA, K. G. (1983). Multi-laminate model of clays—a numerical evaluation of the influence of rotation of principal stress axes, *Intl. J. Num. & Anal. Methods in Geomechs.*, **7**, 397–418.

PREVOST, J. H. (1978). Plasticity theory for soil stress–strain behaviour, *J. Eng. Mech. Div.*, *A.S.C.E.*, **104**(EM5), 1177–94.

PREVOST, J. H. (1980). Constitutive theory for soil, Proceedings, *NSF/NSERC North American Workshop on Plasticity and Generalised Stress–Strain Applications in Soil Engineering*, Montreal, Canada.

ROSCOE, K. H., SCHOFIELD, A. N. and WROTH, C. P. (1958). *Geotechnique*, **8**, 22–53.

SCHOFIELD, A. N. and WROTH, C. P. (1968). *Critical State Soil Mechanics*, McGraw-Hill, London.

SHIOMI, T., PIETRUSZCZAK, ST. and PANDE, G. N. (1982). A liquefaction study of sand layers using the reflecting surface model, *Proc. Int. Symp. Num. Models in Geomech.*, Zurich, A. A. Balkema, Rotterdam, 411–18.

TAYLOR, P. W. and BACCHUS, D. R. (1969). Dynamic cyclic strain tests on a clay, *Proc. 7th Int. Conf. on Soil Mech. Found. Eng.*, Mexico, **1**, 401–9.

VALANIS, K. C. and READ, H. E. (1982). A new endochronic plasticity model for soils, in *Soil Mechanics—Transient & Cyclic Loads*, Chapter 14, John Wiley & Sons Ltd, Chichester.

ZIENKIEWICZ, O. C. and PANDE, G. N. (1977). Time dependent multi-laminate of rocks—a numerical study of deformation and failure of rock masses, *Int. J. Num. Anal. Methods. Geomech.*, **1**, 219–47.

Chapter 4

BEHAVIOUR OF CLAY DURING CYCLIC LOADING

D. M. POTTS

*Department of Civil Engineering,
Imperial College of Science and Technology, London, UK*

1 INTRODUCTION

One of the basic problems in the design of platforms for offshore production of hydrocarbons is the requirement of foundation stability. A typical gravity structure for the northern North Sea may have a submerged weight of 2.6×10^5 tonnes; during a severe storm it will be subjected to transient horizontal wave forces of some 51×10^4 tonnes acting at 50 m above the foundation base, and causing an overturning moment of approximately 2.7×10^6 tonne metres. This combination of forces leads to loading conditions that are so far outside the range of 'normal' engineering experience that the use of classical, empirical bearing-capacity formulae (Terzaghi, Brinch Hansen, Mayerhof) becomes questionable. In addition, the problem of gravity structure foundation stability has a number of unusual features which are not taken into account by these classical formulae:

(i) The subsoil is layered, instead of homogeneous. When the foundation is clay, a very stiff overconsolidated layer often overlies softer normally consolidated material.

(ii) During the first months after installation of the gravity structure, a process of consolidation occurs, which changes the soil properties. After consolidation, the strength of a soil element depends on the local soil stresses, so that individual soil layers are no longer homogeneous as regards their stress–strain properties.

(iii) A storm causes cyclic loading of the subsoil, which again changes the stress–strain properties, and induces cumulative pore pressures which may take months to dissipate.

The problem of the foundation stability of a gravity structure is complicated even further by two facts: the inevitable scarcity of soil data for any particular location, and the fact that bearing-capacity formulae check only the stability against total failure, while it may well be that deformations (prior to failure) should be the limiting factor in foundation design.

An alternative to the bearing-capacity formulae is the finite element method, which allows both the stability and behaviour prior to failure to be investigated. The accuracy of the predictions from such analyses will, however, depend on the ability of the assumed constitutive law to accurately model the soil behaviour.

Whichever method of analysis is used, an essential component will be a model for the behaviour of soil under cyclic loading. This aspect of soil mechanics has not received much attention in the past, and the work that has been carried out has been mainly concerned with the behaviour of sand, as opposed to clay, for loading conditions similar to those imposed by earthquakes. As North Sea gravity structures are predominantly based on clay, and are subject to repeated loading from wave action, information on the cyclic behaviour of clay under realistic loading conditions is required. Such information is also required for other types of offshore foundations such as piles or anchors.

Recently a theoretical model (van Eekelen and Potts, 1977; 1978) has been developed which describes the behaviour of clay under quasi-static loading. Under monotonic loading the model provides a good description of both normally and overconsolidated clay behaviour. For repeated loading conditions, for example due to wave loading, the model provides a simple description of the 'fatigue' effects induced by cyclic loading, and of the relation between cyclic strains and cyclic stresses. This model has been incorporated into a finite element computer code and this provides an ideal tool for investigating the behaviour of offshore foundations.

In this chapter, the soil model is described and compared with experimental data. A simplified gravity structure foundation problem is then considered and its performance predicted using finite element analyses which incorporate the theoretical soil model.

2 STRESS AND STRAIN INVARIANTS

The soil model may be conveniently divided into two parts, namely the static and cyclic parts. The former describes the behaviour of clay under monotonic (i.e. 'static') loading conditions and the latter supplies additional information necessary for describing behaviour under repeated loading. The model assumes that the clay is an isotropic material and consequently all equations are defined in terms of stress and strain invariants. Values of the stress invariants p', J and the Lode angle θ have been adopted. These are defined as follows

$$p' = (\sigma_1' + \sigma_2' + \sigma_3')/3 \tag{1}$$

$$J^2 = 0.5 \text{ trace } \mathbf{s}^2 = \tfrac{1}{6}((\sigma_1' - \sigma_2')^2 + (\sigma_2' - \sigma_3')^2 + (\sigma_3' - \sigma_1')^2) \tag{2}$$

where $\mathbf{s}$ is the deviatoric tensor $\boldsymbol{\sigma}' - p'.\mathbf{1}$

$$\theta = -\tfrac{1}{3}\sin^{-1}(1.5\sqrt{3}\det \mathbf{s}/J^3) \tag{3}$$

where $\det \mathbf{s}$ is the determinant of the tensor $\mathbf{s}$. Alternatively

$$\theta = \tan^{-1}((2b - 1)/\sqrt{3}) \tag{4}$$

where

$$b = (\sigma_2' - \sigma_3')/(\sigma_1' - \sigma_3') \tag{5}$$

It should be noted that the choice of these invariants is not entirely arbitrary. The value of p' is a measure of the distance along the space diagonal of the current deviatoric plane from the origin in principal effective stress space. The value of J provides a measure of the distance of the current stress state from the space diagonal in the deviatoric plane and the magnitude of θ defines the orientation of the stress state within this plane. For example, the intersection of the Mohr–Coulomb failure criterion ($c' = 0$, ϕ') with a deviatoric plane is shown on Fig. 1. As the material is assumed to be isotropic, this produces a regular hexagon showing a sixfold symmetry and consequently attention may be restricted to only a sixth of the deviatoric plane such as zone A of Fig. 1. The distance of any stress state on this hexagon from the space diagonal, point '0', is given by $J/\sqrt{2}$ and the orientation by the value of the Lode angle 'θ'. It should be noted that θ ranges from $-30°$ (triaxial compression) to $+30°$ (triaxial extension). The

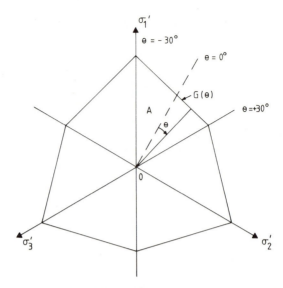

FIG. 1.   Intersection of the Mohr–Coulomb failure criterion with a deviatoric
plane.

Mohr–Coulomb failure condition may be written in terms of the three
invariants as follows

$$J = p' \cdot G(\theta) \tag{6}$$

where

$$G(\theta) = \frac{\sin \phi'}{\cos \theta + 1/\sqrt{3} \cdot \sin \theta \cdot \sin \phi'} \tag{7}$$

and expresses the variation in the deviatoric plane. ϕ' is the angle of
shearing resistance.

The following definitions of the volumetric (ε_{vol}) and deviatoric (E)
strain invariants have also been employed:

$$\varepsilon_{vol} = \varepsilon_1 + \varepsilon_2 + \varepsilon_3 \tag{8}$$

$$E^2 = 2/3((\varepsilon_1 - \varepsilon_2)^2 + (\varepsilon_2 - \varepsilon_3)^2 + (\varepsilon_3 - \varepsilon_1)^2) \tag{9}$$

The static and cyclic parts of the model will now be discussed in turn.

PART 1. STATIC BEHAVIOUR

3 CLAY UNDER STATIC LOADING

The static part of the soil model is based on critical state soil mechanics (Roscoe and Burland, 1968; Schofield and Wroth, 1968; van Eekelen and Potts, 1978) and it is assumed that the reader is familiar with this approach to modelling soil behaviour.

The consolidation characteristics of the soil are assumed to be adequately represented in $v - \log_e p'$ space by the virgin consolidation line

$$v = v_1 - \lambda . \log_e p' \qquad (10)$$

and the family of swelling lines

$$v = v_s - \kappa . \log_e p' \qquad (11)$$

where v = specific volume = $1 + e$, λ is the slope of the virgin consolidation line, κ is the slope of the swelling lines and v_1 is the virgin consolidation specific volume at unit pressure. λ, κ and v_1 are material properties. v_s is the specific volume at unit pressure on the current swelling line and is therefore not a material property. These lines are shown graphically on Fig. 2.

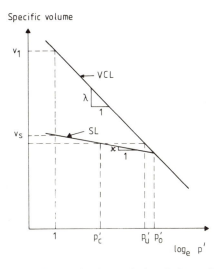

FIG. 2.   Consolidation/swelling behaviour of clay (VCL = virgin consolidation line, SL = typical swelling line).

Unlike the earlier critical state models, the present formulation uses two yield surfaces. The primary yield curve located vertically above each swelling line in J, p', θ and v space is given by

$$F_1 = S^2 - (2\Lambda - 1)\left[\left[\frac{p'(p_0'/p')^\Lambda + a}{p' + a}\right]^{1/\Lambda} - 1\right] = 0 \qquad (12)$$

where $\Lambda = 1 - \kappa/\lambda$, $a =$ the attraction, $S =$ the stress level $= J/((p' + a).G(\theta))$ and p_0' is the value of p' at the intersection of the current swelling line and the virgin consolidation line (see Fig. 2). For the present work, $G(\theta)$ has been assumed to be given by eqn (7) and therefore in the deviatoric plane the yield surface produces a regular hexagon. A sketch showing the primary yield surface above a swelling line is given on Fig. 3(a). It should be noted that the yield surface is bounded by the virgin consolidation line and the Mohr–Coulomb line (eqn (6)). Clearly a yield surface exists above each swelling line and these combine to produce the stable state boundary surface (SSBS) shown on Fig. 3(b). The intersection of an undrained plane ($v = $ constant) with this surface produces a curve of the form

$$F_u = S^2 - (2\Lambda - 1)\left[\left[\frac{p_u' + a}{p' + a}\right]^{1/\Lambda} - 1\right] = 0 \qquad (13)$$

where p_u' is the value of p' at the intersection of the undrained plane with the virgin consolidation line (see Fig. 2). In the present model, this curve forms the basis for the plastic potential corresponding to the primary yield curve. The plastic potential is assumed to be independent of the Lode angle θ having rotational symmetry about the space diagonal in effective stress space.

It is therefore obtained from eqn (13) by replacing the variable θ, used to evaluate S by the parameter $\theta(\sigma)$, the Lode angle at the point in stress space at which the plastic potential is to be employed to evaluate the plastic strain increments. Although replacing θ by $\theta(\sigma)$ does not change the value of F_u, it does change the value of the derivatives of F_u required to evaluate the strain increments. The plastic potential can therefore be written as

$$G_1 = S^2 - (2\Lambda - 1)\left[\left[\frac{p_u' + a}{p' + a}\right]^{1/\Lambda} - 1\right] = 0 \qquad (14)$$

where S is now given by $S = J/((p' + a)G(\theta(\sigma)))$. In terms of the nomenclature of classical plasticity, the primary yield surface and its plastic potential are non-associated.

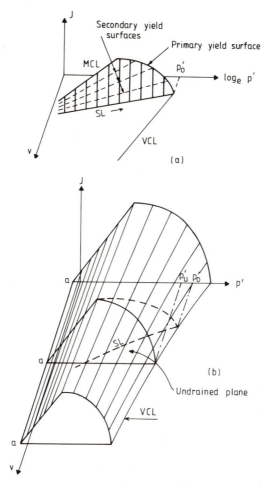

FIG. 3.   Yield curve (a) and stable-state boundary surface (b) for a particular value
of Lode's angle (θ).

The above primary yield surface and its plastic potential describe plastic
behaviour when the state of stress is on the stable state boundary surface
and to the right of the Mohr–Coulomb line. The material deforms at
constant volume when the stress state reaches the intersection of the curved
part of the state boundary surface and the Mohr–Coulomb line. This line
therefore represents the critical state line in $J - p'$ space. For stress states
below the SSBS, the present model assumes elasto-plastic behaviour with

the plastic part controlled by a secondary yield surface. This differs from the earlier critical state models, such as Modified Cam Clay (Roscoe and Burland, 1968), where only elastic behaviour occurs within the SSBS. This secondary yield surface takes the form of a hexagonal cone given by the following expression

$$F_2 = S - h = 0 \qquad (15)$$

where $S = J/((p' + a)G(\theta))$, $G(\theta)$ is given by eqn (7) and h is a hardening parameter related to the plastic strains by the following expression

$$h = I/(\alpha + I) \qquad (16)$$

where $dI = E(\dot{\varepsilon}_{p1})$ and the function E is defined by eqn (9). $\dot{\varepsilon}_{p1}$ are the plastic strains and α is a material constant. The plastic potential corresponding with this secondary yield surface is obtained from eqn (11) by replacing θ by the parameter $\theta(\sigma)$, the Lode angle at the point in stress space at which the plastic potential is to be employed to evaluate the plastic strain increments. The plastic potential therefore resembles a circular cone in principal stress space, with the space diagonal coinciding with the axis of symmetry of the cone. In mathematical terms, the plastic potential takes the form:

$$G_2 = S - h = 0 \qquad (17)$$

where $S = J/((p' + a)G(\theta(\sigma)))$.

So for stress paths which remain below or are directed below the stable boundary surface, the plastic behaviour is controlled by the secondary yield surface and its plastic potential. Once the stress state reaches the stable state boundary surface, control of the plastic behaviour is transferred to the primary yield surface and its plastic potential. It should be noted that at any time only one of the yield surfaces and its associated plastic potential is employed to evaluate soil behaviour. As a consequence of the secondary yield surface and its hardening law (see eqn (16)), a Mohr Coulomb cut-off is essentially applied to the SSBS. This is why such a cut-off was shown on Fig. 3 and it is impossible for the stress state to be outside this stable state boundary surface.

Soil behaviour under unloading and reloading of the mean effective stress p' is assumed to obey eqn (11) which gives the elastic bulk modulus K_E as:

$$K_E = v \cdot p'/\kappa \qquad (18)$$

This expression indicates that the elastic bulk modulus depends on the stress level p' and the specific volume v. In the earlier critical state models, shear strains were neglected; however, if the model is to be incorporated into an elasto-plastic finite element formulation, such an assumption produces problems when purely elastic behaviour is considered. One solution to this problem would be to define a constant value of Poissons ratio; however, if combined with eqn (18), a shear modulus G_E which varies with p' is found. If a stress loop is applied to an element of soil varying both p' and J, the above assumption would lead to the generation of net work and therefore violation of the second law of thermodynamics. To overcome this problem, a constant value of G_E in combination with eqn (18) has been employed.

It is worth noting at this stage the reason for adopting different shapes for the yield and plastic potential curves in the deviatoric plane. In a recent paper, Potts and Gens (1984), it is shown that the shape assumed for the plastic potential in the deviatoric plane in conjunction with the angle of dilation at failure determines the value of the Lode angle θ_f of the state of stress at failure in plane strain deformation. If a Mohr Coulomb hexagon (eqn (7)) is used for the shape of the plastic potential in the deviatoric plane, failure occurs at $\theta_f = -30°$ (triaxial compression) when the model is applied to plane strain problems. This is clearly unrealistic. The assumption that the plastic potential is a surface of revolution about the space diagonal results in a circle for the intersection with a deviatoric plane. For plane strain problems employing the present model (zero dilation at the critical state) this results in $\theta_f = 0°$ ($b_f = 0·5$) which is in better agreement with experiment. Potts and Gens (1984) discuss alternative shapes for the plastic potential in the deviatoric plane and show how any desired θ_f may be obtained. The present model may be easily adapted to account for alternative variations of both the yield and plastic potential curves in the deviatoric plane. Such changes are accommodated by simply changing the functions $G(\theta)$ and/or $G(\theta(\sigma))$ in eqns (12), (14), (15) and (17). In the finite element code several options are available for these expressions.

For undrained loading, the model predicts that at failure (i.e. the critical state) $S = 1$, $p'_f + a = ((1 - 1/2\Lambda)^\Lambda)(p'_u + a)$ and $J_f = (p'_f + a) . G(\theta)$. It can also be shown that the undrained strength C_u varies with the Lode angle at failure θ_f according to the following equation, $C_u = J_f . \cos(\theta_f)$. To completely specify the static part of the model values for the following parameters are required v_1, λ, κ, a (or c'), ϕ', G_E and α.

4   COMPARISON WITH EXPERIMENTAL DATA

A multi-sponsor research project on cyclic loading of clay, under offshore loading conditions, has been executed by four laboratories: The

Norwegian Geotechnical Institute, Fugro-Cesco, the Delft Soil Mechanics
Laboratories and the University of Nottingham. All tests were performed
on saturated samples of Drammen Clay. Apart from a number of static
(undrained) loading experiments, the bulk of the tests consisted of cyclic
triaxial and simple shear experiments, at constant stress or strain
amplitudes, on samples, with one of three different consolidation histories.
The results of the project, which was completed in October 1975, have been
summarised by Anderson (1976). The data from this research project are
employed to calibrate and verify the theoretical soil model.

The static part of the test project on Drammen Clay comprised triaxial
compression and simple shear tests. For the triaxial experiments, standard
equipment was used. The simple shear tests were performed with the NGI
apparatus, in which a cylindrical sample is enclosed by a reinforced rubber
membrane. The stress field in the sample is known to be inhomogeneous
(Lucks et al., 1972; Prevost and Hoeg, 1976), but this non-uniformity will
be ignored here. Furthermore, only the vertical normal stress $\sigma'_v = \sigma'_z$ and
the horizontal shear stress $\tau = \tau_{xz}$ are measured. It will be assumed that the
remaining shear stresses τ_{xy} and τ_{zy} are zero, and that the reinforced
membrane imposes a condition of no lateral strains $\varepsilon_x = \varepsilon_y = 0$. With these
assumptions, and with the soil model developed in the last section, it is
possible to compute the behaviour of a sample under simple shear as well as
under triaxial loading, provided the model parameters and the initial state
of the sample are known. In this respect, the following parameters are
adopted and are based on the test data available from the project:

$$v_1 = 2\cdot98 \qquad \lambda = 0\cdot26 \qquad \kappa = 0\cdot055 \qquad a = 2\cdot4\,\text{t/m}^2$$

$$\phi' = 31° \qquad G_E = 800\,\text{t/m}^2$$

The initial state of the sample follows from the consolidation procedure.
Without going into too much detail, it should be noted that the
preconsolidation pressure p'_0 was approximately $40\,\text{t/m}^2$, and that the
samples were unloaded to consolidation pressures p'_c of approximately 40,
10, or $4\,\text{t/m}^2$ for OCR $= 1$, 4 and 10. More precise values of p'_0, p'_c and the
undrained virgin pressures p'_u have been evaluated from the consolidation
procedures and the static model of the last section. For the simple shear
samples, it has been assumed that the coefficient of lateral earth pressure K_0
at the end of consolidation was equal to $0\cdot61$, $0\cdot97$ and $1\cdot22$ for OCR $= 1$, 4
and 10, respectively.

Figures 4 and 5 give computed and observed shear stresses and pore
pressures (u) as a function of horizontal shear strain γ, for simple shear, or

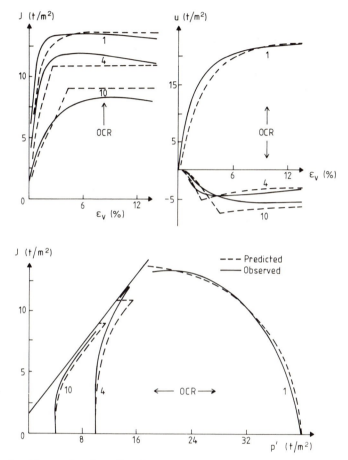

FIG. 4. Observed and predicted behaviour under static triaxial compression.

vertical strain ε_v, for triaxial compression (where the trivial contribution $\Delta\sigma_v/3 = \Delta p$ has been subtracted from the pore pressures). Predicted and observed stress paths are also shown.

The overall agreement for OCR = 1 is seen to be good, while for OCR = 4 and 10 it is reasonable, in view of the fact that the behaviour of overconsolidated clay is difficult to model. The slope discontinuities in the computed curves occur where the stress paths hit the cap of the SSBS, and are an artefact of the theory. They coincide with the point at which control transfers from the secondary to the primary yield surface. On the other

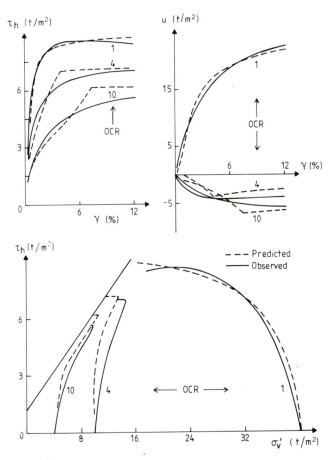

FIG. 5.   Observed and predicted behaviour under static simple shear. (τ_h = applied horizontal shear stress, σ'_v = vertical effective stress).

hand, the observed stress paths for overconsolidated clays indeed show a tendency to bend back near failure.

It should also be noted that the experimental stress paths for simple shear do not quite reach the Mohr–Coulomb (or critical state) line. The reason for this may be that these tests were stopped too early; at the end of the test, the second strain invariant ($E = \gamma$) had only reached 14 %, as against 24 % in the case of triaxial compression (where $E = \sqrt{3}\varepsilon_v$). Alternatively, one might assume that the stress ratio $K = \sigma'_h/\sigma'_v$ is less than unity at failure. The present flow rules give $K = 1$ and $\theta_f = 0$ at the end of the test. As noted in the previous section, alternative values of θ_f and therefore K may be obtained by modifying the shape of the plastic potential in the deviatoric plane, $G(\theta)$ (see also Potts and Gens (1984)).

To summarise, the static part of the soil model presented in the preceding section gives a reasonable fit to the test data for static undrained loading and presents a simple and consistent picture of the static behaviour of clay. In the following sections of this chapter it will be used as a framework in which to describe the effects of cyclic loading.

PART 2. CYCLIC BEHAVIOUR

5 CYCLIC LOADING TESTS

The part of the soil model for cyclic behaviour of clay is based on cyclic loading data obtained in the research project on Drammen Clay (Anderson, 1976). Most tests were performed under undrained conditions, with one-way or two-way stress, or strain-controlled cyclic loading. In the simple shear tests, a cyclic horizontal force (or displacement) was applied to the top of the sample, while in the triaxial tests, the vertical stress or strain was varied, keeping the cell pressure constant.

As regards the variation of the loading intensity with time, the tests may be divided into four distinct categories:

(a) constant stress amplitude tests (undrained),
(b) constant strain amplitude tests (undrained),
(c) storm-loading tests, in which batches of cycles were applied, each batch having a different stress amplitude (undrained),
(d) intermittent loading tests in which batches of undrained cycles were applied, separated by rest periods during which excess pore-water pressures were allowed to dissipate. These tests were intended to simulate intermittent stormy and calm sea periods.

The majority of the tests performed were, in fact, constant stress amplitude tests. All tests were carried out with a loading frequency of 0·1 Hz, corresponding to a wave period of 10 s. The tests were terminated when the strain amplitude (γ_c for simple shear and ε_{vc} for triaxial tests) reached 3 %, or when 2000 (simple shear) or 5000 (triaxial) cycles had been applied. The samples were then slowly sheared to failure, in order to investigate the effect of cyclic loading on the undrained static strength of the clay. Most of the triaxial tests were conducted on isotropically consolidated samples, but a few tests were also performed on samples having an anisotropic consolidation history and hence inbuilt permanent shear stress.

6   SOIL BEHAVIOUR UNDER REPEATED LOADING

Before discussing the theoretical model in detail, a short qualitative account of soil behaviour will be presented. Figure 6 shows a cross-section of the stable-state boundary surface (SSBS) for a particular (undrained) value of specific volume v, for triaxial compression. Consider a sample with initial conditions represented by Point A (normally consolidated), subject

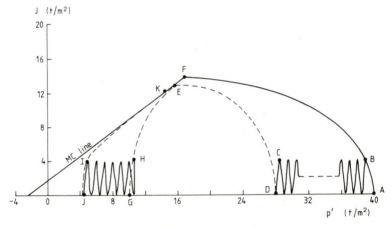

FIG. 6.   Typical behaviour of clay in undrained cyclic loading.

to triaxial compression cycles of constant-stress amplitude. The first quarter cycle is similar to static loading, and the sample's stress state moves along the SSBS from Point A to Point B, while a pore water pressure similar to that developed in a static test is generated.† With subsequent loading cycles, the state of effective stress moves from Point B to Point C. This means that extra pore water pressures are generated during cyclic loading,

---

† Since the rate of loading in this quarter cycle is much higher than in the static test, there may be some delay before the full 'static' pore pressure is measured. There may also be some rate effect on the pore pressure generated.

causing the effective stress p' to be reduced. If cyclic loading is stopped at Point D and and a static test performed on the sample, then a stress path DE is followed. Point E represents the soil strength after cyclic loading, and this strength is less than the original static strength represented by Point F.

A similar behaviour is also found for overconsolidated clays. If a sample initially at Point G on Fig. 6 is subjected to triaxial compression cycles, the first quarter cycle gives a stress path GH similar to that found for a static test. With repeated loading, positive pore water pressures are generated, and the stress path HI is followed. If at Point J cyclic loading is terminated and a static test JK performed, it is again found that the soil strength is lower than the original strength represented by Point F. It can therefore be

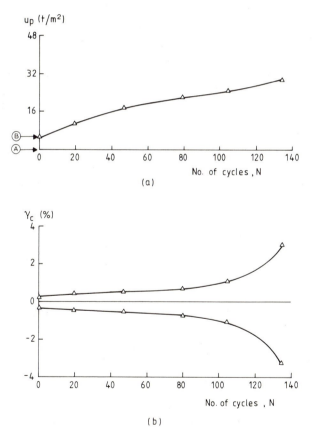

FIG. 7.   Observed variation of permanent pore pressure and strain amplitude with a number of cycles in a simple shear test. (OCR = 1, constant stress amplitude).

concluded that, in both normally consolidated and overconsolidated clays, cyclic loading generates positive pore water pressures and causes a reduction in soil strength.

If cyclic loading is continued past Points C or I, the stress state continues to move to the left on Fig. 6, until the MC line is reached. On approaching this line, the shear strains recorded in the test become large and cause the tests to be terminated. It seems, therefore, that failure under repeated loading may be said to occur when the MC line is reached, or, in terms of the generalised soil model presented in Section 3, when the effective stress path intersects the Mohr Coulomb cone.

By way of example, Fig. 7 shows results from a typical simple shear test at constant stress amplitude on a sample with OCR = 1. On Fig. 7(a), the permanent pore pressure u_p is plotted against the number of cycles N. This u_p does not include variations within each cycle, but represents the mean level of the pore pressure. The initial rise AB may be associated with the first quarter cycle and will be called u_{st} because it is similar to the pore pressure developed in a static test. The subsequent steady increase of u_p with N is purely a result of the repeated loading; this part of the pore pressure will be called u^*, so that $u_p = u_{st} + u^*$.

Figure 7(b) shows that the cyclic shear strain γ_c also increases with the number of cycles N. It should be noted that, while the pore pressure increase at a fairly constant rate, the rise in strain amplitude accelerates as N increases. Finally, after the cyclic test, the static failure strength was found to have been reduced to $7.6\,\text{t/m}^2$, as compared with $8.5\,\text{t/m}^2$ for a virgin sample with OCR = 1.

7 A SINGLE PARAMETER MODEL FOR THE EFFECTS OF CYCLIC LOADING

Before starting a quantitative analysis of the cyclic test data, a theoretical framework has to be defined. In this respect, it should be noted that considerable scatter existed in the test data and this makes a close fit between theory and experiment impossible. It was also intended to use the model in finite element calculations for offshore structures. As a typical design storm may consist of up to 4000 waves, the model must be such that 'blocks' of cycles can be applied in the analyses. This prohibits the use of a theoretical model which requires that each cycle of loading be treated incrementally. For the above reasons, the soil response to cyclic loading was modelled by using a single state parameter k, called 'fatigue'. The assumptions implicit in such a model have been fully discussed by van Eekelen (1977, 1980) and van Eekelen and Potts (1977, 1978). The positive pore pressure u^* generated by cyclic loading has been identified with the fatigue parameter k, and it can be shown that the following information is required:

(i) The pore pressure relation: this expresses how the increase of the fatigue ($k = u^*$) increases with continued cyclic loading, and is given by a relationship of the form

$$du^*/dN = Q(u^*, \tau_c) > 0 \qquad (19)$$

where τ_c represents the cyclic stress amplitude.

(ii) The cyclic stress strain relation: this relates the cyclic strain amplitude with the cyclic stress amplitude and the fatigue ($k = u^*$), and is of the form

$$\gamma_c = F(u^*, \tau_c) \qquad (20)$$

where γ_c represents the cyclic strain amplitude.

(iii) The effect of cyclic loading on the static behaviour: as mentioned in the previous section, cyclic loading leads to a reduction in undrained strength and must therefore modify some or all of the parameters defining the static part of the soil model.

The model is extended to cover different types of loading and different initial soil conditions by redefining τ_c and γ_c as generalised, invariant stress and strain amplitudes, and by suitably normalising τ_c with respect to the initial state of consolidation. The functions $F(u^*, \tau_c)$ and $Q(u^*, \tau_c)$ and the effects of cyclic loading on the static part of the model have been found from the experimental data and are discussed below.

8 THE PORE PRESSURE RELATION

It was shown by van Eekelen and Potts (1978) that a linear variation of u^* with the number of cycles N was a good approximation to the data obtained from cyclic tests with constant stress amplitude. This linear variation of u^* with N implies that the function Q in eqn (19) may be written as $Q(\tau_c)$, so that Miner's rule (Miner, 1945) applies and the ordering of the cycles in a stress controlled test is not important. This means that the cumulative effect of stress cycles of different intensities may be obtained by linear superposition and is independent of the order in which individual cycles occur.

In order to allow for different types of cyclic loading, and for different initial soil conditions, τ_c in $Q(\tau_c)$ must be replaced by a generalised invariant stress amplitude W, which is suitably normalised.

For simplicity it is assumed that it is possible to define two 'extreme phases' of the stress cycle (e.g. under the trough and crest of a wave), with stress tensors $\boldsymbol{\sigma}_1'$ and $\boldsymbol{\sigma}_2'$, and replace τ_c by the second invariant J_c of the stress amplitude $0.5(\boldsymbol{\sigma}_2' - \boldsymbol{\sigma}_1')$, normalised by a weighted average of the failure strengths at the two extremes of the cycle.

$$W = \frac{J_c}{\langle J_f \rangle} \quad \text{with} \quad \langle J_f \rangle = \frac{J(\boldsymbol{\sigma}_1') \cdot J_{f1} + J(\boldsymbol{\sigma}_2') \cdot J_{f2}}{J(\boldsymbol{\sigma}_1') + J(\boldsymbol{\sigma}_2')} \quad (21)$$

J_{f1} and J_{f2} are the static failure values of J (for a sample with the same water content) taken for the Lode angles at the two extremes of the cycle. The stress amplitude W can be considered as the degree of strength mobilisation by cyclic loading. It should be noted that W depends on the stress amplitude and, through J_f, on the water content of the clay; for a given water content, it does not depend on the overconsolidation ratio, or on the value of u.

A detailed examination of the test data for Drammen clay resulted in the following expression for $Q(W)$.

$$\mathrm{d}u^*/\mathrm{d}N = Q(W)$$
$$Q(W) = A \exp(W/B) \qquad \text{for } W > C \qquad (22)$$
$$Q(W) = 0 \qquad\qquad \text{for } W \leq C$$

where for Drammen clay, $A = 4.54 \times 10^{-5}\,\mathrm{t/m^2}$, $B = 0.073$ and $C = 0.2$. The cut-off at $W = C$ means that, for lower values of the normalised stress amplitude W, the soil behaves 'elastically' and generates no permanent pore pressure.

9   THE CYCLIC STRESS STRAIN RELATION

As regards the cyclic stress–strain behaviour, the nature of the available data did not justify the construction of a detailed elasto-plastic model, including damping. It was possible, however, to derive a more restricted correlation between stress amplitude and strain amplitude (see eqn (20)):

$$E_c = \alpha_c \cdot \frac{S_c}{\sqrt{(1 - S_1)(1 - S_2)}} \qquad (23)$$

where E_c is the second invariant of the double amplitude of strain and is obtained from eqn (9) by replacing ε by $0 \cdot 5(\varepsilon_1 - \varepsilon_2)$, S_1 and S_2 the stress levels (S) at the two extremes of the cycle, α_c a material constant and S_c a normalised cyclic stress amplitude given by:

$$S_c = \frac{J_c}{\langle J_{mc} \rangle} \qquad \langle J_{mc} \rangle = \frac{J(\sigma'_1) . J_1^{mc} + J(\sigma'_2) . J_2^{mc}}{J(\sigma'_1) + J(\sigma'_2)} \qquad (24)$$

where the values of J^{mc} at the extremes of the cycle are evaluated using the following equation

$$J^{mc} = (p' + a) . G(\theta)$$

where $G(\theta)$ is given by eqn (7).

Consequently, the fatigue parameter u^* enters the stress–strain relation, eqn (23), through the dependence of S_1, S_2 and S_c on mean effective stress, p'.

According to eqn (23), E_c goes to infinity when S_1 or S_2 approaches unity, i.e. when the state of effective stress approaches the Mohr Coulomb cone $S = 1$. This is in agreement with experiment.

It should be noted that eqn (23) represents an empirical description of strain amplitudes in cyclic tests on homogeneous samples of clay under uniform and proportional loading. It is a scalar relation, which has to be translated into a tensorial stress–strain law before it can be used in a foundation analysis. In the finite element code this has been done by assuming that the cyclic stress–strain law is non-linear elastic, with a shear modulus given by $G_c = \langle J_{mc} \rangle . \sqrt{(1 - S_1)(1 - S_2)}/\alpha_c$.

10 STRENGTH REDUCTION BY CYCLIC LOADING

As noted above, if a static test is performed after cyclic loading has been terminated, it is found in most cases that cyclic loading has caused some reduction in soil strength. In the present model this strength decrease is associated with the fatigue, u^*.

As noted in Section 3, the static strength before cyclic loading is given by

$$J_f = \beta(p'_u + a) \qquad (25)$$

where $\beta = (1 - 1/(2\Lambda))^\Lambda G(\theta)$. Noting that $p'_u/p' = (p'_0/p')^\Lambda$, which is derived from eqns (10) and (11), this may be rewritten as

$$J_f = \beta(p'^{\Lambda}_0 . p'^{1-\Lambda}_c + a) \qquad (26)$$

where p'_0 and p'_c are the preconsolidation and consolidation pressure, respectively. The static strength after cyclic loading was initially assumed to be given by the above equations but with p'_c replaced by $p'_c - u^*$, namely

$$J_{fc} = \beta(p_0'^\Lambda \cdot (p'_c - u^*)^{1-\Lambda} + a) = \beta\left(p'_u\left(1 - \frac{u^*}{p'_c}\right)^{\kappa/\lambda} + a\right) \qquad (27)$$

This equation implies that the strength, after repeated loading, of a sample with consolidation pressure p'_c is equal to the original static strength of a sample (on the same swelling line) with consolidation pressure $p'_c - u^*$. The strength decrease may also be interpreted in terms of the static soil model: eqn (27) may be rewritten by substituting for p'_u from eqn (10):

$$J_{fc} = \beta\left(\exp\left[\frac{v_1 + \Delta v_1 - v}{\lambda}\right] + a\right) \qquad (28)$$

where $\Delta v_1 = \kappa \cdot \log_e(1 - u^*/p'_c) \leq 0$.

Hence cyclic loading has reduced the parameter v_1 of the static model by an amount which depends on the value of u^*/p'_c. This reduction of v_1 means that the virgin consolidation line has shifted. The other parameters of the static model are unaffected by cyclic loading.

Comparison with the test data indicates that eqn (28) tends to overestimate the strength reduction. An improved correlation is obtained by replacing κ in eqn (28) by a somewhat smaller number κ_1; the decrease of v_1 would be correspondingly less and

$$\Delta v_1 = \kappa_1 \cdot \log_e(1 - u^*/p'_c) \leq 0 \qquad (29)$$

However, the introduction of κ_1 adds an extra parameter to the model and for conservative predictions it may be adequate to assume $\kappa_1 = \kappa$. Such an assumption is adopted in the remainder of this chapter.

11 APPLICATIONS OF THE MODEL

The two basic relations, eqns (22) and (23) may be used to compute the results of tests with variable stress amplitudes. Figures 8 and 9 give computed and observed behaviour in two-way simple shear, for a storm loading test and for a test in which the strain amplitude was kept constant. Agreement between theory and experiment is reasonable, being within the general accuracy of the test data.

Consideration is now given to the case of 'intermittent' loading, where clay samples are subjected to series of cycles, separated by drainage periods

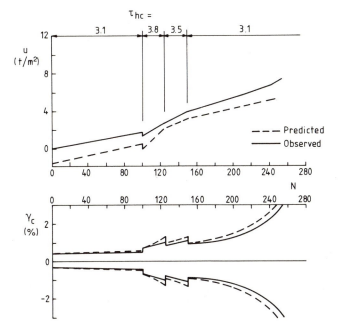

FIG. 8. Simple shear storm-loading test, OCR 4. (τ_{hc} is in t/m^2.)

during which the pore pressures dissipate. Point A on Fig. 10 represents a slightly overconsolidated sample of clay, with initial undrained strength $J_f = \beta(p'_{uA} + a)$. Undrained cyclic loading moves the sample to Point C, and shifts the virgin consolidation line (VCL) to the position of the dashed line on Fig. 10. The reduced strength of the sample is given by $J_{fc} = \beta(p'_{ua} + a)$, with p'_{ua} the new value of the undrained virgin pressure. Subsequent drainage moves the sample along the swelling line from C to D, and its strength increases to $\beta(p'_{ud} + a)$. As u_{st} on Fig. 10 is positive, one finds $p'_{ud} > p'_{uA}$, so that the sample strength at Point D is higher than it was at Point A. If an identical series of undrained cycles are now applied, smaller cumulative pore pressures and cyclic strains than before are generated; the new value u_{st} will also be smaller, because the sample has become more overconsolidated. This implies, however, that the gain in strength after a second drainage period will be lower than after the first drainage period. With further intermittent loading and draining, the sample becomes even stronger, pore pressures and cyclic strains become smaller, and the sample becomes progressively more overconsolidated.

D. M. POTTS

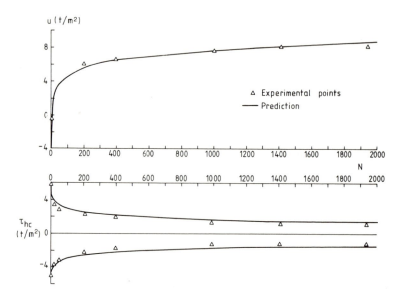

FIG. 9.   Simple shear constant-strain amplitude test, OCR = 4.

Eventually, an equilibrium state is reached in which $u_{st} = 0$. It should be noted that the above arguments are based on the assumption $\kappa_1 = \kappa$.

For a heavily overconsolidated sample of clay, the situation is reversed. In this case u_{st} is negative, and after drainage a net strength reduction results; a new series of cycles will cause higher pore pressures u^*, and larger cyclic strains. On the other hand, the sample has become slightly less overconsolidated, and on the application of a further batch of cycles the new (negative) value of u_{st} will be smaller and consequently the loss of strength after a second drainage period will be less than after the first. Again, an equilibrium state with $u_{st} = 0$ may finally be reached if failure due to cyclic loading does not intervene.

Predictions for 'intermittent' one-way triaxial loading are presented on Figs 11 and 12, for a normally consolidated sample and for a sample with OCR = 4, respectively. In both cases five batches of 1000 cycles of constant stress-amplitude were applied, with drainage periods of sufficient length to enable all excess pore pressures to dissipate. The effects mentioned above are clearly visible: for the normally consolidated sample, pore pressures and cyclic strains decrease, whereas for the OCR = 4 sample they increase. Unfortunately, there are no reliable test data against which these

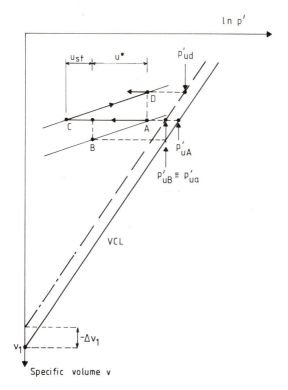

FIG. 10. Behaviour of a lightly overconsolidated clay sample under 'intermittent' loading.

predictions may be quantitatively compared. Limited experimental results from 'intermittent' simple shear tests are, however, in agreement with the above predictions.

If intermittent loading is continued indefinitely, and failure due to cyclic loading does not occur, an equilibrium state (where $u_{st} = 0$) will be reached in which no further change of undrained strength occurs. In principle, the equilibrium state (where $u_{st} = 0$ for the given value of J_c) may be derived from the static part of the model. However, in practice, it may be better to assume that, for any value of J_c, u_{st} is positive, zero or negative, depending on whether the mean effective stress p' after drainage is larger than, equal to, or smaller than the current value of p'_f, the mean effective stress at undrained failure. Since the mean effective stress after drainage is equal to the consolidation pressure p'_c, the above assumption implies that in the

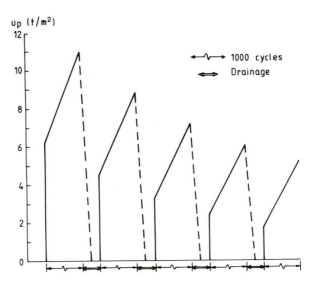

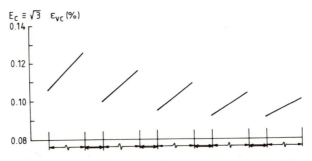

Fig. 11.   Prediction for 'intermittent' loading on a normally consolidated triaxial sample (stress amplitude $J_c = 0.35 J_f$).

equilibrium state $p'_f = p'_c$ and the ultimate undrained static strength after drainage is given by

$$J_f^{ult} = (p'_c + a) \cdot G(\theta) \qquad (30)$$

Using eqn (26) for the initial undrained strength of the clay prior to any cyclic loading, one obtains the following approximate estimate for the ratio of ultimate to initial undrained strength

$$\frac{J_f^{ult}}{J_f^{init}} = \left[1 - \frac{1}{2\Lambda}\right]^{-\Lambda} \frac{(p'_c + a)}{(p'_c(p'_0/p'_c)^\Lambda + a)} \qquad (31)$$

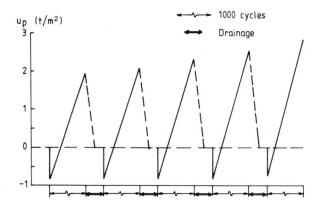

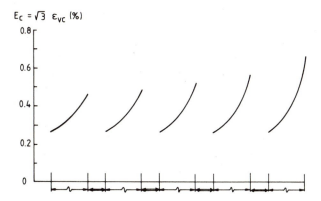

FIG. 12.   Prediction for 'intermittent' loading on overconsolidated triaxial sample, OCR = 4 (stress amplitude $J_c = 0.3J_f$).

For Drammen clay ($\Lambda = 0.79$, $a = 2.4\,\text{t/m}^2$ and $p_0' = 40\,\text{t/m}^2$) this ratio becomes 2·2, 0·85 and 0·53 for OCR = 1, 4 and 10, respectively.

It should be noted that, in the case of an offshore gravity platform, the relevant values of J_f^{init}, p_0' and p_c' for eqn (31) are those obtaining after consolidation of the clay under the dead weight of the structure.

It should be noted that the present theoretical model contains one inconsistency. The rate of pore pressure generation du^*/dN remains finite at all times. After each batch of cycles the pore pressure u^* drains away, and if intermittent loading is continued indefinitely this implies that the volume of a clay element will continue to decrease indefinitely. This inconsistency may be removed by assuming that eqn (22) which gives du^*/dN, does not apply when the water content of the clay has been changed drastically by repeated loading and drainage periods. In other words, one or more of the parameters A, B and C in eqn (22) could depend on the changing water content of the clay. However, the tests on which this theory is based do not allow any conclusions on this point.

To summarise, the model indicated that the effect of drainage periods on the behaviour of clay under cyclic loading is such, that a normally consolidated or lightly overconsolidated clay is likely to become stronger and more resilient to repeated loading, while a medium to heavily overconsolidated clay is likely to become weaker and less resilient to repeated loading.

These results have a direct impact on the behaviour of gravity-structure foundations. If such a structure is based on a clay initially in a normally or lightly overconsolidated clay, then if it survives the first severe storm, it is likely to survive further similar storms. If, on the other hand, the gravity structure is founded on heavily overconsolidated clay, the soil strength may deteriorate in the long run, and there is no guarantee that, having survived the first storm, it will survive the next. Sufficient safety may be obtained however, if the design strength of the clay is reduced according to eqn (31). In addition, the strength reduction due to cyclic loading within a single storm should be taken into account, as described in Section 9. Stability in the short term using the undrained shear strength prior to platform installation should also be considered.

12   GRAVITY STRUCTURE SUBJECTED TO STORM LOADING

As noted in the introduction to this chapter, the theoretical model has been implemented into a finite element code. As an example of the use of this program, some results of an investigation into the behaviour of a hypothetical offshore gravity structure foundation will be presented. The finite element mesh employed is shown on Fig. 13 and consists of 174 eight noded isoparametric elements. Plane strain conditions were assumed and loading conditions simulating the dead weight of the structure and storm loading were applied to the finite elements modelling the foundation base. In this respect the submerged unit weight of the structure was taken as $2 \cdot 6 \times 10^5$ tonnes and the hypothetical design storm is given in Table 1.

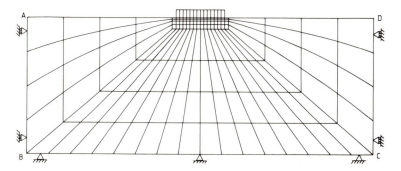

FIG. 13.   Finite element mesh for analyses of hypothetical gravity structure.

The soil was assumed to be clay and the parameters necessary to define the theoretical model were assigned the following values:

$$v_1 = 3.57 \qquad \lambda = 0.26 \qquad \kappa = 0.05 \qquad \phi' = 30°$$
$$\alpha = \alpha_c = 0.0048 \qquad A = 4.45 \times 10^{-5} \, \text{t/m}^2$$
$$B = 0.073 \qquad C = 0.2 \qquad \text{and} \qquad \kappa_1 = 0.05$$

The profiles of undrained strength in triaxial compression ($C_u = J_f \cos -30°$) and overconsolidation ratio (OCR) are given on Fig. 14. The coefficient of earth pressure at rest (K_0) is assumed to be given by

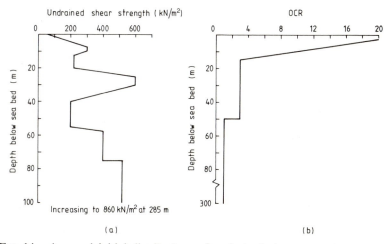

FIG. 14.   Assumed initial distributions of undrained shear strength (C_{u0}) and OCR.

TABLE 1

DESIGN STORM

Wave number	Horizontal force H/H_{max}	Moment M/M_{max}	Number of waves
$1 \rightarrow 1\,650$	0·39	0·39	1 650
$1\,651 \rightarrow 1\,750$	0·53	0·53	100
$1\,751 \rightarrow 1\,800$	0·59	0·59	50
$1\,801 \rightarrow 1\,850$	0·66	0·66	50
$1\,851 \rightarrow 1\,888$	0·75	0·75	38
$1\,889 \rightarrow 1\,913$	0·81	0·81	25
$1\,914 \rightarrow 1\,925$	0·88	0·88	12
$1\,926 \rightarrow 1\,929$	0·93	0·93	4
$1\,930$	1·0	1·0	1
$1\,931 \rightarrow 1\,934$	0·93	0·93	4
$1\,935 \rightarrow 1\,946$	0·88	0·88	12
$1\,947 \rightarrow 1\,971$	0·81	0·81	25
$1\,972 \rightarrow 2\,008$	0·75	0·75	37
$2\,009 \rightarrow 2\,058$	0·66	0·66	50
$2\,059 \rightarrow 2\,108$	0·59	0·59	50
$2\,109 \rightarrow 2\,208$	0·53	0·53	100
$2\,209 \rightarrow 3\,858$	0·39	0·39	1 650

$H_{max} = 5\cdot1 \times 10^4$ tonnes.
$M_{max} = 2\cdot7 \times 10^6$ tonne m.

$K_0 = (1 - \sin \phi')\text{OCR}^{\sin \phi'}$. It should be noted that it is not possible to satisfy the above distributions of C_u, OCR and K_0 simultaneously. The procedure adopted for the present study was, therefore, to use the OCR values to obtain a K_0 distribution and to adopt this and the C_u distribution given on Fig. 14 to obtain the distribution of the hardening parameter, p'_0. In this respect, a saturated bulk unit weight of 21 kN/m³ has been assumed.

The elastic shear modulus G_E was assumed to vary with depth and to be given by the expression $G_E = 20 \times p'_0$ kN/m². The results of two analyses will be considered briefly as lack of space prevents any detailed or further discussion. In the first analysis, the design storm is applied immediately after platform installation, whereas in the second, full consolidation is allowed to occur after platform installation and prior to applying the storm. In all other respects the analyses are identical. These two cases were chosen to represent the extreme situations in which the design storm occurs either immediately after installation or after a period of relatively calm weather.

Before considering the behaviour under storm loading it is of interest to

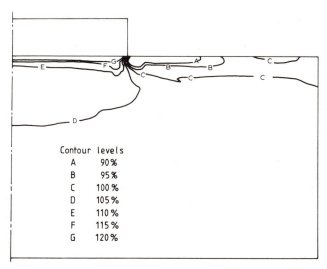

FIG. 15. Contours of normalised undrained shear strength C_u/C_{u0} (in %) after platform installation and consolidation but prior to storm loading.

consider the behaviour during platform installation. Both analyses predict a vertical settlement of the platform of 0·36 m on undrained installation. For the second analysis in which the excess pore water pressures generated on installation are allowed to dissipate, further settlement occurs and reaches a value of 1·3 m after full consolidation. On installation positive excess porewater pressures occur under the platform, whereas zones of negative excess pore pressure are predicted in the soil adjacent to the structure and near the soil surface. These arise as a consequence of the soil having a high OCR which gives rise to dilation on shearing and to the small increase in mean total stress outside the loaded area. Dissipation of these excess porewater pressures results in a change in undrained strength (C_u) and this is shown on Fig. 15 where contours of C_u/C_{u0} are given. C_u represents the current undrained strength in triaxial compression ($\theta = -30°$) and C_{u0} the initial value prior to the installation of the platform. An increase in strength occurs beneath the platform whereas a reduction is predicted adjacent to it. As will be noted later, these zones of weaker material at the edges of the platform have a marked effect on the platform behaviour under storm loading.

Displacements predicted during the storm for both analyses are given in Table 2. The cyclic displacement of the underside of the gravity structure

D. M. POTTS

TABLE 2
MOVEMENT OF GRAVITY STRUCTURE DURING STORM LOADING

	Cyclic displacement amplitudes of GS			
	Centre of base		Edge of base	
	Horizontal amplitude $(\times 10^{-2}\,m)$	Vertical amplitude $(\times 10^{-2}\,m)$	Horizontal amplitude $(\times 10^{-2}\,m)$	Vertical amplitude $(\times 10^{-2}\,m)$
Analysis 1 (no consolidation after installation)				
'BIG' wave				
(middle of storm)	$\pm 19\cdot3$	$\pm 0\cdot0$	$\pm 19\cdot3$	$\pm 6\cdot3$
Last wave	$\pm 5\cdot2$	$\pm 0\cdot0$	$\pm 5\cdot2$	$\pm 2\cdot2$
Analysis 2 (with consolidation after installation)				
'BIG' wave				
(middle of storm)	$\pm 21\cdot6$	$\pm 0\cdot0$	$\pm 21\cdot6$	$\pm 5\cdot7$
Last wave	$\pm 5\cdot8$	$\pm 0\cdot0$	$\pm 5\cdot8$	$\pm 1\cdot8$

base for the largest and the last wave of the storm are given. A comparison of these predictions indicates that the horizontal movements are larger and the vertical movements smaller in the second analysis. This is consistent with the soil strength changes which occur as a result of the consolidation and have been discussed above.

Contours of normalised undrained shear strengths, C_u/C_{u0}, associated with conditions at the end of the storm are given on Fig. 16 for both analyses. C_{u0} is again the undrained shear strength existing in the soil prior to platform installation. For the first analyses a reduction in strength is predicted and the limited depth of soil affected should be noted. For the second analysis, consolidation after platform installation causes a change in strength as noted above. The contours presented on Fig. 16 indicate that the storm loading does not cause the strength beneath the platform to reduce below the initial value, C_{u0}, prior to installation. A reduction in strength from the higher values existing after the consolidation stage has, however, occurred. It should be noted that contours of C_u/C_{u0} greater than 100% are not indicated on this figure. Figure 16 also indicates that storm loading does not cause any further significant weakening of the soil adjacent to the platform.

Contours of stress level, τ_m/C_{uc}, under the crest of the largest wave of the

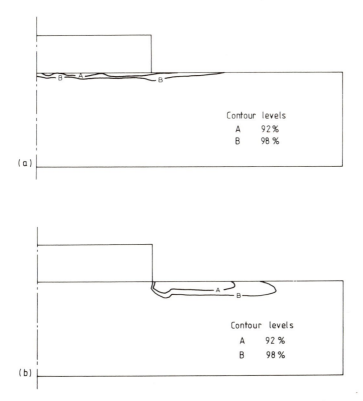

FIG. 16. Contours of normalised undrained shear strength C_u/C_{u0} (in %) after storm loading. (a) No consolidation after installation. (b) With consolidation after installation.

storm are given on Fig. 17 for both analyses. τ_m is the maximum shear stress (i.e. radius of the Mohrs circle of stress) and C_{uc} is the current value of the undrained shear strength. These contours give some indication of the degree of strength mobilisation. In both analyses high stress levels are mobilised immediately below the base of the platform. However, there are significant differences in the pattern of the contours. In particular, the stress levels are higher for the second analysis (consolidation allowed after installation) and there are zones of soil immediately below the base of the platform which have failed, $\tau_m/C_{uc} = 1$. This would imply that the factor of safety against horizontal sliding may be less than for the first analysis in which no consolidation was allowed.

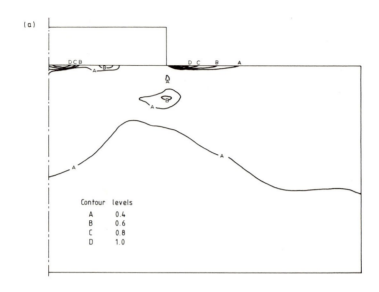

(a)

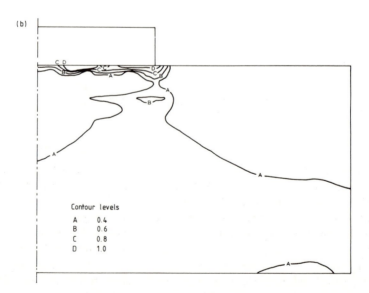

(b)

FIG. 17. Contours of stress level, $\tau_m C_{uc}$, under the crest of the largest wave of the storm. (a) No consolidation after installation. (b) With consolidation after installation.

The results from these two analyses indicate that consolidation after platform installation does not necessarily increase stability under subsequent storm loading or reduce the horizontal movements of the platform. The zones of weaker soil adjacent to the edge of the platform which result from dissipation of the negative excess porewater pressures appear to have a dominant influence on subsequent behaviour. The results also imply that any provision of drainage in the soil under the base of the structure to speed up consolidation may not have the desired effect of increasing platform stability under storm loading.

13   CONCLUDING REMARKS

In this chapter a theoretical model for clay behaviour under static and cyclic loading has been described. The static part of the model requires 7 basic parameters: v_1, λ, κ, a (or c'), ϕ', G_E and α. The cyclic loading is described in terms of a single fatigue parameter, i.e. the porewater pressure u^* generated by cyclic loading, and requires five basic parameters: A, B, C, α_c and κ_1. These may be reduced by assuming $\kappa_1 = \kappa$ and $\alpha_c = \alpha$. The model is capable of predicting the pore pressure build-up, degradation in cyclic stiffness and reduction in undrained strength during cyclic loading. In this respect, the type of cyclic loading relevant to offshore foundations has been considered. Comparison with test data indicates that the model provides both realistic and adequate predictions.

The model has been used to investigate the long term effects of a series of undrained cycles separated by drainage periods. The model is incomplete in that it does not include creep, permanent strains, or damping. It is of a rather empirical nature: it describes cyclic loading effects, without explaining them in terms of more fundamental material laws.

The cyclic data on which the present model is based show a large degree of scatter. Nevertheless, these data are among the best and most comprehensive available at present, and they clearly indicate a number of consistent 'average' trends. The details of the model that has been derived from these trends may be changed in the future, as more or better data become available; such improvement will be facilitated by the fact that the present model forms a consistent framework, into which more accurate data may be incorporated without changing the structure of the model.

The combination of the soil model with the finite element method provides an extremely powerful tool. Not only does it allow both stability and deformations to be assessed, but it also provides valuable insight into mechanisms of behaviour which lead to a greater understanding of the problem. Application to the hypothetical gravity structure foundation problem highlights the potential of this combination for investigating real engineering problems.

REFERENCES

ANDERSON, K. H. (1976). Behaviour of clay subjected to undrained cyclic loading. *Proc. Conf. Behaviour of Offshore Structures, Trondheim 7*, pp. 392–403.

VAN EEKELEN, H. A. M. (1977). Single-parameter module for progressive weakening of soil by cyclic loading. *Geotechnique*, **27**(3), 357–68.

VAN EEKELEN, H. A. M. (1980). Fatigue models for cyclic degradation of soils. *Soils under Cyclic and Transient Loading*, (Eds) G. N. Pande and O. C. Zienkiewicz, A. A. Balkema, Rotterdam.

VAN EEKELEN, H. A. M. and POTTS, D. M. (1977). Clay behaviour under cyclic loading. *Proc. Dynamical Methods in Soil and Rock Mechanics, Karlsruhe 2: 'Plastic and long term effects in Soils'*, (Ed.) G. Gudehus, A. A. Balkema, Rotterdam.

VAN EEKELEN, H. A. M. and POTTS, D. M. (1978). The behaviour of Drammen Clay under cyclic loading. *Geotechnique*, **28**(2) 173–96.

LUCKS, S. A., CHRISTIAN, J. I., BRANDOW, G. E. and HOEG, K. (1972). Stress conditions in NGI simple shear test. *Jnl. Soil Mech. Fdn Div. Am. Soc. Civ. Engrs*, **98**, 155–60.

MINER, M. A. (1945). Cumulative damage in fatigue. *Trans. ASME*, **67**, A159–64.

POTTS, D. M. and GENS, A. (1984). The effect of the plastic potential in boundary value problems involving plane strain deformation. *Int. Jnl. Num. Anal. Meth. in Geomechanics*, **8**(3), 259–86.

PREVOST, J. H. and HOEG, K. (1976). Reanalysis of simple shear soil testing. *Can. Geotechnical Jnl.*, **13**, 418–29.

ROSCOE, K. H. and BURLAND, J. B. (1968). On the generalized stress–strain behaviour of 'wet' clay. *Engineering Plasticity*, (Eds) J. Heymen and F. A. Leckie, Cambridge University Press, Cambridge.

SCHOFIELD, A. and WROTH, C. P. (1968). *Critical State Soil Mechanics*, McGraw-Hill, New York.

Chapter 5

ON MODELLING OF CYCLIC BEHAVIOUR OF SOILS

S. Pietruszczak

Department of Civil Engineering and Engineering Mechanics, McMaster University, Hamilton, Ontario, Canada

and

H. B. Poorooshasb

Department of Civil Engineering, Concordia University, Montreal, Quebec, Canada

1   INTRODUCTION

A realistic and meaningful solution of a geotechnical problem depends to a large extent on the choice of an appropriate constitutive law specifying the behaviour of soil. Consequently, in the recent years a great deal of effort has been devoted to the research in that area. At present there are at least 40 different constitutive concepts published in the literature. Those concepts are either of micromechanical or phenomenological nature. In the latter category the existing formulations are founded on nonlinear elasticity, hypoelasticity, endochronic theory and, finally, the theory of plasticity.

Although a variety of concepts exist, none of them is at present fully satisfactory. They all fail to predict properly several important aspects of soil behaviour (see Pande and Pietruszczak (1984)) and further research in the area is required, giving special attention to simulation of complex loading histories such as cyclic loading, for instance.

In general, it seems doubtful that any phenomenological description will ever represent the true nature of soil adequately, with all its complexities. In that sense a successful constitutive concept would be the one which is mathematically consistent and capable of appropriate simulation of several fundamental aspects of soil behaviour which have already been recognised (at least qualitatively) through laboratory investigations. Some of those aspects are briefly reviewed in the following section.

Simulation of monotonic loading histories under static conditions presents at the moment little difficulty. In fact, any isotropic hardening model for instance, based on the theory of plasticity, can be expected to give quite satisfactory results in solving certain types of boundary-value problems. However, for time-dependent loads and, in particular, for cyclic loading histories, when hysteretic phenomena are of great importance, a more accurate description of mechanical behaviour is required. In Section 3, several constitutive concepts based on the plasticity theory are briefly reviewed. Both isotropic and anisotropic types of hardening rules are discussed and the question of material memory in the context of particular loading events is analysed. Besides this brief review, a detailed mathematical formulation of a recently proposed model by Poorooshasb and Pietruszczak (1985), is presented. The chapter is concluded by discussing the performance of various constitutive concepts under cyclic loading conditions.

In general, the objective of the entire chapter is to indicate to the reader the need for a more accurate description of the inelastic behaviour of soils and to expose him to several mathematical formulations available at present.

2 BEHAVIOUR OF SANDS AND CLAYS UNDER CYCLIC LOADING

There has been a large volume of material published on the behaviour of both sands and clays under cyclic loading conditions. A detailed review of laboratory investigations is presented in the reference by Wood (1982). Most of the published results come from tests in either triaxial or simple shear apparatus, although several true triaxial tests were also performed (see Yamada and Ishihara (1981)).

As already emphasised by some authors, many quantitative aspects of those results remain very problematic. The response of the material proved to be very sensitive to the methods of sample preparation, to the rate of testing, etc. Even for monotonic loading, the results are often influenced by the testing procedure. In fact, unless special precautions are taken, the sample tends to deform non-uniformly. Consequently, it does not truly represent the material behaviour and such a simplified interpretation may often yield misleading conclusions. For good quality triaxial testing, measurements of both the pore pressures and deformations should be made in the central deforming region of the sample, which unfortunately still presents serious technical difficulty. It seems, therefore, that at the present time a detailed quantitative simulation of certain aspects of soil response to cyclic loading is meaningless. It applies to factors like number of cycles to failure or number of cycles to produce liquefaction, etc., which to a large extent are influenced by the testing procedure. On the other hand, there are certain aspects of soil behaviour which, in a qualitative sense at least, can be accepted as typical for a given soil. Some of those aspects will be discussed further, later in this section. Consequently, any advanced constitutive concept should not only be formulated consistently but should also be able to simulate those aspects properly.

It is not the authors' intention here to discuss the testing procedures nor to give an up-to-date review of experimental investigations reported in the literature. The present section is aimed only at indicating some typical features of both sands and clays response in standard cyclic loading configurations.

(i) Response of Sands to Cyclic Loading
Figure 1 shows typical results of a stress-controlled drained triaxial test on loose sand, as reported by Tatsuoka and Ishihara (1974). During the testing, both triaxial compression and extension with constant amplitude were repetitively applied.

Figure 1(a) presents the volume changes against the applied stress ratio.* In the course of cyclic loading, the sand densifies and volumetric compression occurs at a progressively decreasing rate. As far as shear strains are concerned (Fig. 1(b)) the hysteresis exhibited in the first cycle is the greatest. Subsequently, the shear strain amplitude decreases gradually as the cycles proceed. Deformations stabilise after approximately nine cycles.

The behaviour of the same material in a two-way (compression-extension) strain-controlled cyclic program is presented in Fig. 2.

Again (Fig. 2(a)), a progressive densification of sand can be observed with a gradually decreasing rate. It is now important to notice that the

---

* Here p' is the effective mean principle stress and q represents deviatoric stress $(p' = -(\sigma'_1 + 2\sigma'_2)/3, \ q = \sigma'_2 - \sigma'_1)$.

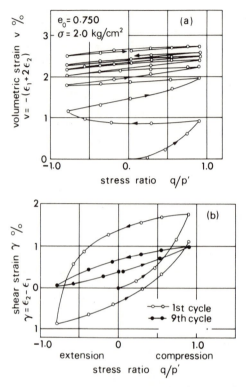

FIG. 1.   Drained cyclic test on a loose sand sample with a medium amplitude of stress ratio (after Tatsuoka and Ishihara (1974)).

stress ratio increases its amplitude as constant amplitude of strain is repetitively applied. Although, as seen from Fig. 2(b), the strain amplitude γ could not have been strictly maintained during the test, the above conclusion is consistent with what is usually observed in this type of experiment. Again, deformations tend to stabilise after a number of cycles.

Concluding briefly the above observations, it is evident that in drained tests with constant stress amplitude, the amplitude of resultant strain *decreases* gradually as the cycles proceed, whereas in constant strain amplitude tests, the stress amplitude tends to *increase* progressively.

The response of loose sand in undrained triaxial testing is presented in Figs 3 and 4. Figure 3 shows typical results of a two-way stress controlled (constant stress amplitude) cyclic test. During the test the pore pressure progressively builds up causing the effective stress path to migrate towards

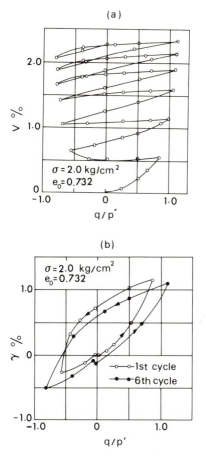

FIG. 2. Measured performances of sand in a drained constant strain amplitude test (after Tatsuoka and Ishihara (1974)).

the origin (Fig. 3(a)). Initially, the pore pressures are generated successively in both compression and extension domains. After a number of cycles, a phenomena called cyclic mobility occurs in which, during the loading phase, negative pore pressure develops due to dilatancy of the material, followed by a subsequent build-up during the unloading phase. For a loose sample the state of cyclic mobility leads to a complete liquefaction of the sample.

In an analogous strain-controlled test (Fig. 4(a)), the response is qualitatively similar with the exception that cyclic mobility effects are now

(a)

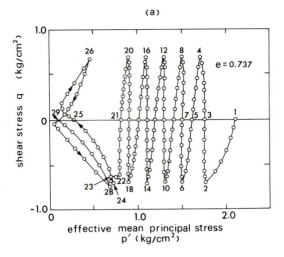

(b)

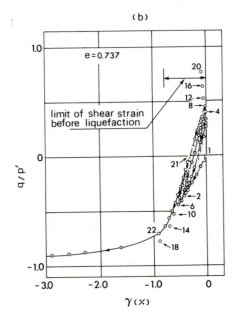

FIG. 3. Response of a loose sand in an undrained stress-controlled cyclic test
(after Ishihara *et al.* (1975)).

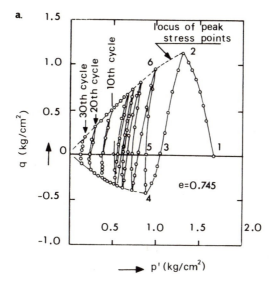

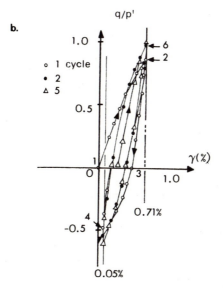

FIG. 4. Response of a loose sand in an undrained strain-controlled cyclic test (after Ishihara *et al.* (1975)).

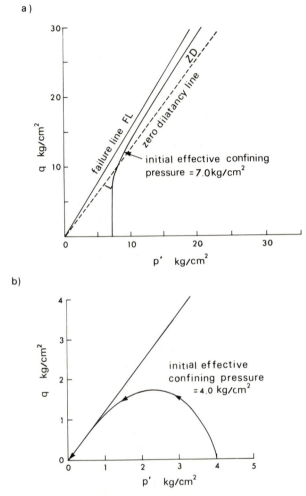

a)

b)

FIG. 5.   Response of a very dense (after Baladi and Rohani (1979)) and a very loose
(after Castro (1969)) sand in a monotonic undrained triaxial test.

practically excluded. This is due to progressive *reduction* in stress
amplitude which from the very beginning accompanies the generation of
pore pressure. This is again a very typical observation common for most
experiments of strain-controlled type. For a loose sand, the migration of
the effective stress path remains progressive (although the rate may
decrease) and leads eventually to liquefaction.

At this stage it again should be emphasised that several quantitative aspects of these results might be doubtful for the reasons explained earlier in this section. In addition, for undrained testing the effect of membrane penetration becomes important since it reduces the measured pore pressure. Consequently, the observed resistance to liquefaction may be significantly overestimated.

The above presented results can be considered as typical for a loose sand. Obviously, the response of sand to cyclic loading will be considerably affected by the degree of initial compaction and the past load history (Ishihara and Okada, 1978). In general, the more dense the sand, the more prominent the dilatancy effects are. Figure 5 presents two extreme reactions in monotonic undrained testing for a dense and a very loose sand, respectively. For a dense material, one can clearly separate (in effective stress space) a failure surface (i.e. peak strength envelope) from a zero dilatancy surface. Below the latter surface, material compacts and upon exceeding it, tends to dilate (even if the response is stable). Consequently, the dense material will develop significant negative pore pressures which will clearly tend to prevent liquefaction. On the other hand, a very loose sand will show no tendency to dilate and in extreme cases, it may liquefy even during a single load cycle (Fig. 5(b)).

For the range of void ratios encountered in practical situations, there will be a clear distinction between both surfaces. With increasing void ratio the zero dilatancy surface will gradually approach the failure surface.

The existence of the zero dilatancy surface has serious implication on the material response in both drained and undrained cyclic tests. In drained tests, cycling above this surface will lead to dilatancy which might have certain destabilising effects on deformation; below this state-compaction will occur with progressive stiffening. For loading under undrained conditions, one could speculate about the existence of a certain characteristic state located between both surfaces. Then (see Fig. 6), small stress amplitudes will develop positive pore pressure and will eventually lead to liquefaction (loose sand). Cycles with stress amplitudes approaching this characteristic state will cause cyclic mobility effects and finally above this state, dilatancy will lead to significant negative pore pressures which will rapidly stabilise the deformation.

(ii) Response of Clays to Cyclic Loading
There is a considerable number of test results on the behaviour of clays under cyclic loading available in the literature. Experimental evidence is even more extensive than for sands. Again, it is not the authors' intention

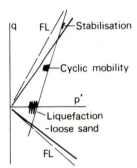

FIG. 6. Different reactions of sand to an undrained cyclic loading program (after Wood (1982)).

here to present a detailed discussion of these results but to indicate certain aspects of clay response which can be considered as typical. This might help in assessing the value of some constitutive concepts discussed further in this chapter. For a more detailed review, the reader is referred to Wood (1982).

Typical behaviour of clay in undrained monotonic triaxial compression test is presented in Fig. 7. For a normally consolidated clay, a progressive build-up of the pore pressure is observed and the mean effective stress is gradually reduced. On the other hand, for a highly overconsolidated material negative pore pressure develops (due to plastic dilatancy) and the effective stress path migrates away from the origin. The failure takes place either on the Critical State line (for normally consolidated samples) or the failure envelope which is situated above this line (overconsolidated

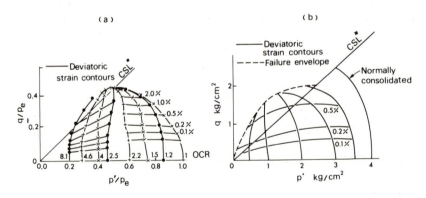

*CSL = critical state line

FIG. 7. Undrained tests on overconsolidated clay (after Wroth and Loudon (1967) and Mitchell (1970)).

samples). Samples with OCR (i.e. the overconsolidation ratio) of about 2 exhibit almost no change in effective pressure.

This type of behaviour has again great implications in response to cyclic loading. Figure 8 presents typical results of an undrained stress-controlled triaxial compression test as reported by Sangrey *et al.* (1969). The build-up of pore water pressure leads to migration of the effective stress path towards the stress origin until after a number of cycles a stable state, shown by the closed stress loop 'n–m', is reached. If the stress amplitude is now changed, a qualitatively similar response might be expected. Changes in amplitude, however, will affect the location of the stable state. Figure 9(a) presents the locus of the points representing the stress peaks of the stabilised hysteresis loops. The point of intersection of this locus with the critical state envelope represents the upper limit of applied stress amplitudes which will lead to a stable state. Any repeated loading above this stress level will eventually cause *failure* of the sample.

In Fig. 9(b) the loci of stress peak points for steady-state cycles are presented for samples starting with different overconsolidation ratios (OCR) but the same maximum consolidation stress. Slope of the steady-state line indicates the direction of the migration of effective stress path. It is evident that for OCR = 2 almost no variation of pore pressure occurs, whereas for OCR = 4 an increase in mean effective stress takes place.

Again, for overconsolidated material with OCR > 2, amplitudes

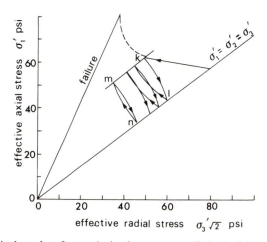

FIG. 8.   Typical results of an undrained stress controlled triaxial compression test on clay (after Sangrey *et al.* (1969)).

(a)

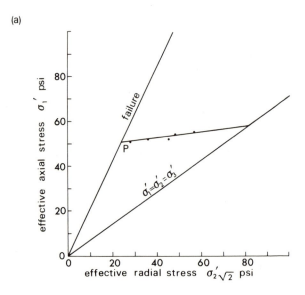

(b)

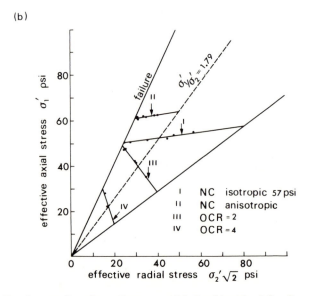

FIG. 9.   Steady-state lines for various consolidation histories (after Sangrey *et al.* (1969)).

reaching the failure envelope before the steady-state is approached will lead
to failure of the sample (an upper limit on stress amplitude is approximately
the point of intersection of the steady-state locus with the Critical State
line).

In general, for both normally consolidated and overconsolidated clay,
the migration of the effective stress path is largely controlled by the
behaviour in the first few cycles.

Typical results of constant strain amplitude triaxial test are presented in
Figs 10, 11 and 12. The tests (reported by Taylor and Bacchus (1969)) were
performed on halloysite at the frequency of 0·2 Hz and involved strain-
cycles passing from compression to extension. The tests can be classified as
fast (especially for higher amplitudes) and therefore cannot be regarded as

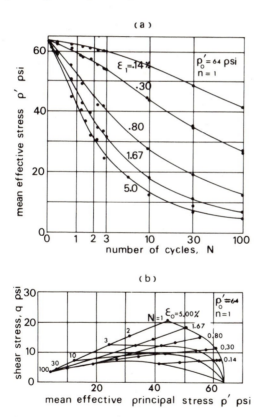

FIG. 10.   Undrained strain-controlled test on normally consolidated halloysite
(after Taylor and Bacchus (1969)); (b) envelopes of peak deviatoric stress.

a fully reliable guide for study of the material behaviour; nevertheless, they provide a sufficient illustration of all general trends.

For normally consolidated material, application of constant strain amplitude generates a progressive increase in pore pressure which decreases the mean effective stress (Fig. 10(a)). At the same time the stress amplitude

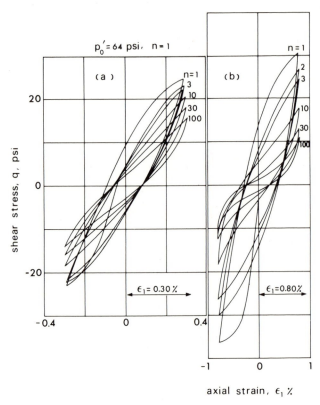

FIG. 11. Stress–strain loops corresponding to $\varepsilon_1 = 0.3\%$ and $\varepsilon_1 = 0.8\%$ (after Taylor and Bacchus (1969)).

that can be attained *declines* (Fig. 10(b)). Figure 11(a) presents deviator stress–axial strain response for strain amplitude $\varepsilon_1 = 0.30\%$. Surprisingly, the authors obtained rather symmetric hysteresis loops with the same amplitudes being reached in both compression and extension, however, a progressive reduction in those amplitudes is evident. For higher strain amplitudes (Fig. 11(b)), the stress–strain loops (after a number of cycles) show an initial reduction in stiffness followed by a subsequent increase (the 'S'-shape). Although a similar response was observed in some tests on sand (Castro, 1969), the present results might be affected by the high rate of straining and any specific conclusions in that respect could be misleading.

For an overconsolidated material, the response will again be influenced by both the strain amplitude and overconsolidation ratio. With both parameters increasing, the plastic dilatancy effects will be more prominent. Taylor and Bacchus (1969) present the results only for a relatively large strain amplitude $\varepsilon_1 = 1\cdot67\%$. For OCR $= 8$, Fig. 12, the mean effective stress initially increases. Consequently, the response of the material is

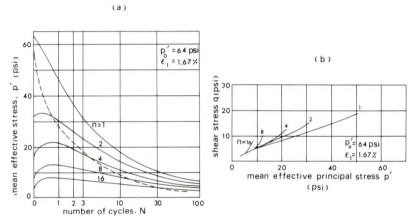

FIG. 12.   Undrained strain-controlled tests on overconsolidated halloysite (after Taylor and Bacchus (1969)); (b) envelopes of peak deviatoric stress.

stiffer and the stress amplitude also increases. In subsequent cycles a very slow progressive reduction in mean effective stress is observed and the stress path slowly migrates back towards the origin.

The effective stress path for static tests to failure after cyclic loading resemble the monotonic paths for overconsolidated samples. In general, as reported by Taylor and Bacchus (1969), the failure criterion appears to remain unaltered by the cyclic loading. A similar conclusion has been reached by several other investigators as well.

Both strain and stress controlled tests on soil, as discussed above, cover various aspects of material response to cyclic loading. A good constitutive concept should now be able to predict those general trends properly.

3   ON MODELLING OF SOIL BEHAVIOUR

The existing phenomenological concepts describing the behaviour of soil are based on different fundamental theories. Those include nonlinear elasticity, hypoelasticity, so-called endochronic theory, and finally the theory of plasticity.

The simplest of all are nonlinear elasticity models in which elastic moduli are assumed as nonlinear function of stress. Although sometimes numerically effective, those concepts are quite unrealistic from the physical point of view. Soils clearly exhibit irreversible deformations and this fact cannot remain unaccounted for. With respect to several formulations there are serious arguments against their validity. In fact, some concepts (for example, the most popular one due to Duncan and Chang (1970)) are not conservative since energy is continuously extracted from the material when subjecting it to any simple stress cycle (Zytynski *et al.*, 1980).

The hypoelastic approach displays also certain disadvantages. Although several formulations within this category are consistent in a mechanical sense, they may predict an unrealistic material response for some loading paths, in particular for cyclic loading conditions (Mroz, 1980). This is the result of loading–unloading criteria used in hypoelasticity which are defined by the sign of the stress work rate.

In the past decade several endochronic and endochronic-plasticity models have been developed, the latter based on plasticity without the yield surface. The original work of Valanis (1971) on metals has been extended by Bazant and Bhat (1976) and Bazant and Krizek (1975) to include soil behaviour. Again, there are a number of arguments and counter arguments for the validity of this class of models. In general, the existing formulations are very complex and involve a large number of material parameters. Both factors are likely to discourage practising engineers from using them, at least for some time to come.

It seems, therefore, that among the existing formulations those based on the theory of plasticity are at present of advantage. The theory has a considerable flexibility to enable modelling of the complex behaviour of different types of soil. It also proves to be very convenient in incorporating the memory rules of particular loading events, the fact of a great importance in modelling the behaviour under fluctuating load.

The present section will be aimed at discussing several elastoplastic formulations. In subsequent paragraphs a brief review of both isotropic and anisotropic hardening rules will be given followed by a mathematical formulation of a two-surface model for sand recently proposed by the present authors.

3.1 Elastoplastic Isotropic Hardening Concepts

The above constitutive concepts are based on the assumption that the material is initially isotropic and exhibits isotropic hardening (or softening) depending on the variation of one or several scalar parameters such as relative density, deviatoric plastic strain or plastic work. In fact, the applicability of such models is limited to monotonic loading histories since during unloading only elastic changes are assumed to occur.

The most popular concept within this category is the Critical State model. Here, the evolution of the yield surface is assumed to depend on irreversible void ratio variation $\dot{e}^p$ which is directly related to plastic volumetric strain: $\dot{e}^p = -(1 + e)\operatorname{tr}\dot{\boldsymbol{\varepsilon}}^p$. The yield condition is expressed in terms of effective stress $\boldsymbol{\sigma}'$ and e^p which is formally regarded as a hardening (or softening) parameter

$$F(\boldsymbol{\sigma}', e^p) = 0 \tag{1}$$

Usually, the associated flow rule is assumed

$$\dot{\boldsymbol{\varepsilon}}^p = \dot{\lambda}\,\frac{\partial F}{\partial \boldsymbol{\sigma}'} \tag{2}$$

which together with the consistency condition

$$\left(\frac{\partial F}{\partial \boldsymbol{\sigma}'}\right)^{\mathrm{T}} \dot{\boldsymbol{\sigma}}' + \frac{\partial F}{\partial e^p}\,\dot{e}^p = 0 \tag{3}$$

provides the expression for $\dot{\lambda}$

$$\dot{\lambda} = \left(\frac{\partial F}{\partial \boldsymbol{\sigma}'}\right)^{\mathrm{T}} \dot{\boldsymbol{\sigma}}'/H \tag{4}$$

where

$$H = \frac{\partial F}{\partial e^p}\,(1 + e)\operatorname{tr}\frac{\partial F}{\partial \boldsymbol{\sigma}'} \tag{5}$$

and H represents the hardening modulus. If $\partial F/\partial e^p > 0$, then the sign of H is determined by the value of $\operatorname{tr}\partial F/\partial \boldsymbol{\sigma}'$, which, in general, might be positive, negative or equal zero. Experimental evidence suggests that normally consolidated clays tend to compact prior to failure and when failure is actually approached volumetric deformations become negligible. To satisfy this, it is sufficient to define $F(\boldsymbol{\sigma}', e^p) = 0$ in such a way that $\operatorname{tr}\partial F/\partial \boldsymbol{\sigma}'$ would vanish along the failure surface. Then, any convex yield surface of a closed form will consequently predict compaction below the failure surface with $H > 0$ (i.e. stable response) and dilatancy ($\operatorname{tr}\partial F/\partial \boldsymbol{\sigma}' < 0$ and thus

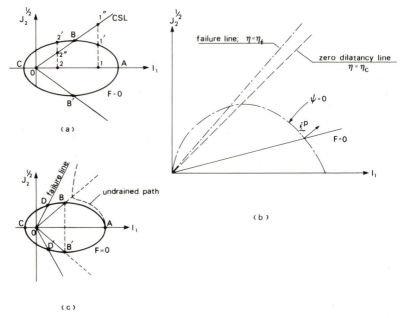

FIG. 13.   Meridional cross-section of the yield surface. (a) Volumetric hardening $F(\sigma', e^p) = 0$; (b) deviatoric hardening $F(\sigma', \varepsilon_d^p) = 0$; (c) combined hardening $F(\sigma', \kappa) = 0$.

tr $\dot{\varepsilon}^p < 0$) for stress states exceeding this surface. In the latter case, there will be $H < 0$ from eqn (5) and the material will exhibit an unstable response (strain softening). A typical meridional cross-section of the yield surface is presented in Fig. 13(a).* Here, the failure condition is approximated by a straight line, referred to as a Critical State line ($H = 0$ and tr $\dot{\varepsilon}^p = 0$).

Several different forms of the yield condition known as Cam-clay model, cap model, etc., have been used so far. From a numerical point of view probably the most convenient is a simple elliptical shape. In general, however, there is little physical justification for adopting either of those shapes.

The Critical State concept was in fact intended to model the monotonic response of normally consolidated clays. For overconsolidated material the predictions are poor and for sands the concept is virtually not applicable.

* In Fig. 13, I_1 is the first invariant of the effective stress tensor and J_2 represents the second invariant of the stress deviator.

An alternative description for simulating sand behaviour is the one in which deviatoric plastic strain is assumed to act as a hardening parameter. Then the function

$$F(\boldsymbol{\sigma}', \varepsilon_d^p) = 0 \tag{6}$$

where

$$\varepsilon_d^p = [2/3(\text{dev } \dot{\boldsymbol{\varepsilon}}^p)^{\text{T}} \text{dev } \dot{\boldsymbol{\varepsilon}}^p]^{1/2} \tag{7}$$

represents the yield condition. Assuming, in general, a non-associated flow rule

$$\dot{\boldsymbol{\varepsilon}}^p = \dot{\lambda} \frac{\partial \psi}{\partial \boldsymbol{\sigma}'} \tag{8}$$

and satisfying consistency condition

$$\left(\frac{\partial F}{\partial \boldsymbol{\sigma}'}\right)^{\text{T}} \dot{\boldsymbol{\sigma}}' + \frac{\partial F}{\partial \varepsilon_d^p} \dot{\varepsilon}_d^p = 0 \tag{9}$$

we obtain

$$H = -\frac{\partial F}{\partial \varepsilon_d^p}\left[2/3\left(\text{dev } \frac{\partial \psi}{\partial \boldsymbol{\sigma}'}\right)^{\text{T}} \text{dev } \frac{\partial \psi}{\partial \boldsymbol{\sigma}'}\right]^{1/2} \tag{10}$$

The value of the hardening modulus would now be largely controlled by $\partial F/\partial \varepsilon_d^p$. Both strain hardening and strain softening effects can be included. In general, $\partial F/\partial \varepsilon_d^p$ should tend to zero when the stress point approaches the failure surface. At the same time plastic deformations are controlled by the shape of the plastic potential surface. In Fig. 13(b), both the yield and failure condition are conveniently approximated by the straight lines (in the meridional plane). In particular, the shape of the plastic potential is such that the states for which there is no plastic volume deformation (represented by the zero dilatancy line) are separated from the failure condition. In this case, the material is allowed to dilate prior to failure, a fact which is commonly observed in dense sands and overconsolidated clays.

In general, both the volumetric and deviatoric components of plastic strain can act simultaneously as a combined hardening parameter. In this way, for instance, the applicability of the Critical State concept can be extended to both overconsolidated clays and dense sands (Nova and Wood, 1979; Wilde, 1977). In such a formulation, the yield surface has the form

$$F(\boldsymbol{\sigma}', \kappa) = 0 \tag{11}$$

where the rate of the combined hardening parameter κ is expressed as

$$\dot{\kappa} = \beta[2/3(\text{dev } \dot{\boldsymbol{\varepsilon}}^p)^T \text{dev } \dot{\boldsymbol{\varepsilon}}^p]^{1/2} + (1+e)\,\text{tr } \dot{\boldsymbol{\varepsilon}}^p \tag{12}$$

The first term in eqn (12) represents the deviatoric strain and the second corresponds to irreversible density variation. β is a positive material constant. Using the associated flow rule (2) and satisfying the consistency condition, we arrive at the expression for hardening modulus

$$H = \left(-\frac{\partial F}{\partial \kappa}\right)\left\{\beta\left[2/3\left(\text{dev }\frac{\partial F}{\partial \boldsymbol{\sigma}'}\right)^T \text{dev }\frac{\partial F}{\partial \boldsymbol{\sigma}'}\right]^{1/2} + (1+e)\,\text{tr }\frac{\partial F}{\partial \boldsymbol{\sigma}'}\right\} \tag{13}$$

With the present sign convention, the consistency condition requires $\partial F/\partial \kappa < 0$, and thus according to eqn (13) the hardening modulus remains positive when

$$\text{tr }\frac{\partial F}{\partial \boldsymbol{\sigma}'} > -\frac{\beta}{(1+e)}\left[2/3\left(\text{dev }\frac{\partial F}{\partial \boldsymbol{\sigma}'}\right)^T \text{dev }\frac{\partial F}{\partial \boldsymbol{\sigma}'}\right]^{1/2} \tag{14}$$

Consequently, the failure line (as defined by $H = 0$) deviates from the zero dilatancy line (Fig. 13(c)) and the separation between both surfaces is now controlled by the parameter β. For $\beta = 0$ the original Critical State concept is obtained.

Introduction of a combined hardening parameter κ, as defined by eqn (12), significantly extends the range of applicability of the Critical State concept. Now the predictions of both drained and undrained responses of overconsolidated material under monotonic load are much more realistic.

Finally, in another category of constitutive concepts the multi yield-loci theories of soil deformation are implemented (Poorooshasb and Young, 1982). In most of the existing formulations the mode of yielding is assumed to be governed by two different mechanisms; the first responsible for plastic volumetric strains only and the other for plastic distortions. Thus, both hardening parameters act independently of each other.

Assume that N families of yield function $f_n = 0$ and the plastic potential $\psi_n = 0$ are incorporated in the proposed mode. Let $f_m \in f_n$ $(n = 1, 2, \ldots, N)$ be expressed in a general form

$$f_m(\boldsymbol{\sigma}', e^p, \varepsilon_d^p) = 0 \tag{15}$$

and let

$$\psi_m(\boldsymbol{\sigma}') = 0 \tag{16}$$

represent the corresponding plastic potential. The yielding due to f_m will take place if

$$f_m = 0 \quad \text{and} \quad \left(\frac{\partial f_m}{\partial \boldsymbol{\sigma}'}\right)^{\text{T}} \dot{\boldsymbol{\sigma}}' > 0 \tag{17}$$

When both eqns (17) are satisfied f_m is said to have been activated and makes a contribution to the total plastic rate of a magnitude equal

$$\dot{\boldsymbol{\varepsilon}}^p_{(m)} = \dot{\lambda}_m \frac{\partial \psi_m}{\partial \boldsymbol{\sigma}'} \tag{18}$$

If the contribution from all the activated yield surfaces are added, then

$$\dot{\boldsymbol{\varepsilon}}^p = \sum_n \dot{\lambda}_n \frac{\partial \psi_n}{\partial \boldsymbol{\sigma}'} \tag{19}$$

where the summation includes only those n's for which eqn (17) is satisfied.

Figure 14 presents a graphical representation of the families of yield function $f_n = 0$ (after Poorooshasb and Young (1982)). The surface $f_1 = 0$ is assumed to be independent of ε_d^p, whereas $f_2 = 0$ is independent of e^p. Hardening functions for both surfaces can be deducted from eqns (5) and (10), respectively. This particular concept is intended to describe the behaviour of normally consolidated clays; there are, however, several concepts applicable for sands as well (Baker et al., 1980).

In general, the combined hardening parameter κ or multi yield-loci theories are intended to improve the accuracy of predictions based on a single hardening parameter. Nevertheless, all the constitutive concepts discussed above, in their present form, are applicable only for monotonic

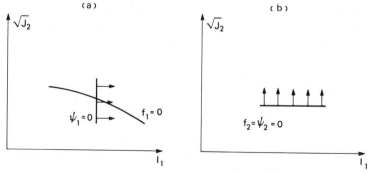

FIG. 14. Constitutive model proposed by Poorooshasb and Young (1982).

loading conditions. They all assume purely elastic behaviour for a stress path penetrating the interior of the yield surface. Consequently, neither of the cyclic loading effects, as indicated in the previous section, can be modelled properly.

3.2 Modelling of Cyclic Behaviour; Combined Isotropic-Kinematic Hardening Rules

In order to model the behaviour of soils under fluctuating load properly the constitutive concept should take into account the effects of reverse plastic flow as observed during unloading of the sample. Those effects significantly influence the soil response, which is an evident conclusion from Section 2.

A very convenient way of formulating such a general constitutive concept is to extend some of the isotropic-hardening descriptions (as discussed in the previous paragraph) to include the aspect of reverse plastic flow. Since this goal can be achieved in different ways it is no wonder that a variety of such generalisations has been proposed so far (Dafalias and Herrmann, 1982; Ghaboussi and Momen, 1979; Lade, 1977; Mroz and Pietruszczak, 1983; Mroz et al., 1978; Pande and Pietruszczak, 1982; Poorooshasb and Pietruszczak, 1985; Prevost, 1978).

Many of the existing formulations utilise the isotropic-hardening surface as a so-called bounding surface which reflects the isotropic properties of the material. The concept of bounding surface was developed by Krieg (1975) and Dafalias and Popov (1975, 1977); its definition, however, is used in an entirely different context in several of the present formulations (Mroz and Pietruszczak, 1983). The use of an isotropic bounding surface implies that the effects of textural anisotropy (as attributed to the preferred orientation of soil particles) remain unaccounted for. For some materials those effects are not very prominent (Mitchell, 1970; Quigley and Thomson, 1966) and such a simplification might be justified. At the same time, however, the so-called residual stress anisotropy resulting from inhomogeneity of deformation on the microscale develops within the material. Those effects are usually quite significant and they should be properly taken into account (Pietruszczak and Mroz, 1983).

Therefore, among the variety of existing formulations, the concepts of a combined isotropic-kinematic hardening type seem to be of advantage over those assuming complete isotropy. The latter, although mathematically simpler, are, in general, less convincing from the physical point of view.

Another important aspect of a more general material model is its capacity to memorise particular loading events. It is logical to expect that the events of certain intensity can only be erased from material memory by the events of larger intensity, otherwise they should influence the material response. The concept of a discrete material memory is discussed in more details by Mroz and Norris (1982). In general, the multi-level memory rules will certainly complicate the formulation. At the same time, however, such a formulation will be far more realistic.

As already indicated, several different generalisations of the concepts discussed in Section 3.1 have been proposed. Among the formulations maintaining e^p as the isotropic hardening parameter and thus adopting the Critical State concept as a base for generalisation those due to Dafalias and Herrmann (1982), Carter *et al.* (1982) and Mroz *et al.* (1978) are noticeable. In the concepts of Dafalias and Herrmann (1982) and Carter *et al.* (1982), soil is assumed to exhibit full isotropy on both loading and unloading. At the same time, the concept of Carter *et al.* (1982) is of a semi-empirical nature as long as the stress path penetrates the interior of the isotropic hardening surface. Concepts of Mroz *et al.* (1978, 1981) are of a combined isotropic-kinematic character. A multi-surface description with a discrete multi-level memory rule (Mroz and Norris, 1982) and a simplified two surface-version have been proposed so far.

In general, the above mentioned formulations are applicable for clays only since they all use exclusively the volumetric type of isotropic hardening. Consequently, those formulations in which the plastic distortion governs isotropic hardening will be applicable for sands, whereas those using the combined parameter κ (as defined by eqn (12)) are expected to simulate the behaviour of both sands and clays. Again, several different generalisations to the isotropic concepts have been proposed. Ghaboussi and Momen (1979), for instance, founded their combined isotropic-kinematic concept on ε_d^p, whereas Nova and Hueckel (1982) use a combined parameter κ together with a 'paraelastic' (i.e., path-independent between suitably defined stress reversal points) description for stress-reversals.

In the present paragraph two alternative concepts to those proposed by Ghaboussi and Momen (1979) and Nova and Hueckel (1982) will be reviewed. Both constitute a direct extension of isotropic formulations from Section 3.1 with either deviatoric (ε_d^p) or combined volumetric-deviatoric (κ) type of hardening. The concepts were chosen because of the first author's involvement in their formulation but no particular significance should be attached to this fact. First, the basic assumptions of a general constitutive model for soils (applicable to both clays and sands) with a multi-level memory rule will be presented followed by a more detailed discussion of a generalised two-surface model for sand as recently proposed by Poorooshasb and Pietruszczak (1985).

Both concepts are of an isotropic-kinematic nature and both can simulate many aspects of soil response to a fluctuating load as discussed in Section 2. Although the performance of neither of them is not yet entirely satisfactory (neither is it for any of the existing formulations), they both represent a step forward towards a more realistic modelling of soil behaviour.

(i) *A Multi Surface Hardening Model with Anisotropic Hardening Rule*
The details of this concept are provided in Mroz and Pietruszczak (1983) and here only the basic assumptions will be reviewed.

In a mechanical sense, one of the major differences between clays and sands lies in the definition of the state of initial consolidation. Whereas for clays, the applied consolidation pressure p_c defines uniquely the void ratio e; for granular materials any degree of compaction may in fact be attained by the appropriate deposition of grains under gravity forces (for instance, by pouring sand from a hopper). Consequently, for a dense material the required consolidation pressure corresponding to a given void ratio may be very high as compared to actual values of the mean pressure and may not be attained at all during the testing.

In the present formulation, the initial densification process is described by the isotropic hardening surface

$$F_c(\boldsymbol{\sigma}', \kappa) = 0 \qquad (20)$$

where κ is defined by eqn (12).

For a granular material this surface (called a *configuration* surface) reflects the degree of initial compaction and both its size and the shape are assumed to depend on initial density. In general, for a loose granular material the current stress state usually remains in the vicinity of this surface and such a material is regarded as lightly overconsolidated (Fig. 15(a)). On the other hand, for a dense material the stress states corresponding to the configuration surface may be several orders of magnitude larger than those encountered in actual testing (Fig. 15(b)). Therefore, the material behaves as heavily overconsolidated.

For clay-like materials, $\beta = 0$ is assumed in eqn (12) and the isotropic-hardening surface (now referred to as a *consolidation* surface) is of the form

$$F_c(\boldsymbol{\sigma}', e^p) = 0 \qquad (21)$$

and is regarded as being constituted in a natural way by the initial consolidation process.

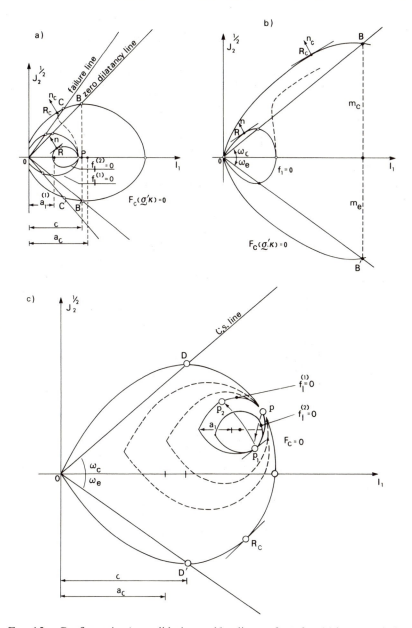

FIG. 15.   Configuration/consolidation and loading surfaces for: (a) loose sand, (b) dense sand, and (c) clay.

Thus, within the present formulation the major difference between the treatment of clay and sand-like materials lies in appropriate specification of the consolidation/configuration surface.

As long as the stress point remains on this surface the material undergoes isotropic (density or combined) hardening. The associated flow rule is assumed and the hardening modulus is expressed by eqns (5) or (13), respectively.

For all stress paths within the configuration/consolidation surface, it is postulated that the domain of elastic response is of an infinitesimal size and consequently a plastic strain increment occurs for any stress increment. To make a distinction between particular loading events, the concept of an *active loading* and a *stress-reversal* surface is introduced. The actual stress state always corresponds to the active loading surface $f_\ell^{(i)}(\sigma' - \alpha, \kappa) = 0$ for the ith loading event, whereas the stress-reversal surface $f_r^{(i-1)} = 0$ represents the maximum prestress from the past loading history.

Consider, for instance, an initial loading process OP consisting of a hydrostatic pressure, Fig. 15(a). If the mean stress increases, the active loading surface $f_\ell^{(1)}(\sigma' - \alpha, \kappa) = 0$ expands progressively. This, in fact applies to all stress paths for which $(\partial f_\ell^{(1)}/\partial \sigma')^T \dot{\sigma}' > 0$. However, when the stress increment from P is directed into the interior of the surface $f_\ell^{(1)} = 0$, this surface becomes a stress-reversal surface and a new loading surface $f_\ell^{(2)} = 0$ is created, being tangential at P to the $f_r^{(1)} = f_\ell^{(1)} = 0$. The surface $f_\ell^{(2)} = 0$ expands and translates, so that the stress point always satisfies its equation. This second loading event continues for any stress path directed into the exterior of $f_\ell^{(2)} = 0$ and terminates when $f_\ell^{(2)} = f_r^{(1)} = 0$, that is when the active loading surface and the stress-reversal surface coincide. At this stage, the above loading history is erased from the material memory.

Figure 15(c) illustrates a similar evolution of active loading surfaces for the load history $P-P_1-P_2$ in which the stress point is initially located on the consolidation surface $F_c(\sigma', e^p) = 0$.

The plastic strain rate along any stress path is generated by the associated flow rule (2), regarding the current active loading surface as the yield surface. The normalised hardening modulus K, defined as

$$K = H\left[\left(\frac{\partial f_\ell}{\partial \sigma'}\right)^T \frac{\partial f_\ell}{\partial \sigma'}\right]^{-1} \tag{22}$$

is assumed to vary between its initial large value $K = K_0$ for a vanishing size of the loading surface and the value $K = K_c$ corresponding to the configuration/consolidation surface and described by eqns (13) or (5) and

(22), respectively. The variation of the hardening modulus is postulated in the form

$$K = K_c + (K_0 - K_c)\left(\frac{a_\ell}{a_c}\right)^\zeta \tag{23}$$

or, since $K_0 \gg K_c$

$$K \simeq K_c + K_0 \left(\frac{a_\ell}{a_c}\right)^\zeta \tag{24}$$

where ζ is a constant and both a_ℓ and a_c are regarded as size parameters corresponding to the active loading and the configuration/consolidation surface, respectively. The value of K_c is determined at the 'conjugate' point R_c which has the same direction of the exterior normal as that at the instantaneous stress point R on the active loading surface (Fig. 15(a)).

In general terms, the above concept is now completely defined, provided the elastic portion of the strain rate is suitably accounted for.

All the mathematical details of the present description are given in Mroz and Pietruszczak (1983). In particular, the proposed form of eqn (20) and the formulation for updating the subsequent loading surface, etc., are extensively discussed in the above reference and will not be repeated here.

In general, the present formulation constitutes a direct extension of the multi-surface hardening concept as originally proposed by Mroz (1967). This concept was first adopted (Mroz et al., 1981) to describe the behaviour of clays under cyclic loading and subsequently extended to include the response of granular materials (Mroz and Pietruszczak, 1983).

The above formulation displays a multi-level memory structure implying that loading events of a given intensity can only be erased from the material memory by events of a larger intensity. Several simplified versions (like, for instance, a two-surface model), more convenient for numerical implementation have also been proposed (see Mroz and Norris, 1982; Pietruszczak and Mroz, 1980).

(ii) A Generalised Two-Surface Model for Sand
For convenience let the state of stress be specified by its three principal values σ_i ($i = 1, 2, 3$)* and define the stress space by an orthogonal cartesian

_____

* All stresses are effective. The 'prime' index (dropped now for convenience) is used later in a different context.

system of coordinates whose axes are labelled Σ_i ($i = 1, 2, 3$). It is postulated that:

(i)   a bounding surface is a cone having its apex at the origin and its axis coinciding with the diagonal of the stress space Σ_i,

(ii) a yield surface is a cone of similar shape to that of the bounding surface with its apex at the origin of the stress space, Fig. 16. Now, Σ_i' represent a new set of axes such that their space diagonal coincides with the axes of the yield cone.

If parameters P, Q and θ (Lode's angle) are defined through the set of relations

$$P = \frac{1}{\sqrt{3}} p \tag{25}$$

$$Q = [(\sigma_1 - p/3)^2 + (\sigma_2 - p/3)^2 + (\sigma_3 - p/3)^2]^{1/2} \tag{26}$$

and

$$\theta = \tan^{-1}(\sqrt{3}(\sigma_3 - \sigma_2)/(2\sigma_1 - \sigma_2 - \sigma_3)) \tag{27}$$

where $p = \sigma_1 + \sigma_2 + \sigma_3$ and θ is defined for that sector of Σ_i space for which $\Sigma_2 \leq \Sigma_3$ and $\Sigma_2 \leq \Sigma_1$, then the equation of the bounding surface may be represented by

$$F(\sigma_i, \varepsilon^p_{\text{history}}) = Q - \eta P g(\theta) = 0 \tag{28}$$

The parameter η records the history of plastic distortion ε^p (hereafter referred to as $\varepsilon^p_{\text{history}}$) and may be represented by*

$$\eta = \eta(\varepsilon^p_{\text{history}}) \tag{29}$$

To appreciate the meaning of this parameter reference may be made to Fig. 17. Figure 17(a) shows the stress ratio (Q/P) versus the total plastic distortion as encountered in a P-constant conventional triaxial test involving both compression and extension programs. Curve OA is a stress ratio–strain curve in compression. OB represents the same curve, had the sample been subjected to an extension loading program only. Curves OB' and OA' represent the mirror images of OB and OA about the Q/P axis.

During the loading, unloading and reloading process—represented by 0–1, 1–3 and 3–5 segments on Fig. 17(a), the parameter η traces a unique

---

* According to eqns (25) and (26) the plastic distortion $\dot{\varepsilon}^p$ is defined as $\dot{\varepsilon}^p = \sqrt{\frac{3}{2}}\dot{\varepsilon}^p_d$ where $\dot{\varepsilon}^p_d$ is specified by eqn (7).

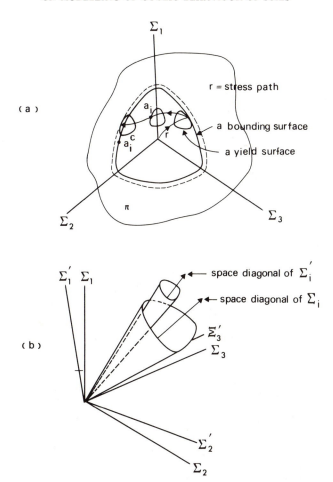

FIG. 16. Bounding and yield surface in the principal stress space. (a) Intersection of bounding and yield surface with a π plane; (b) global Σ_i and local Σ_i' systems of references.

curve in the η-$\varepsilon^p_{\text{history}}$ coordinate system as shown in Fig. 17(b). Thus, according to eqn (28), the bounding surface expands or contracts as $\varepsilon^p_{\text{history}}$ increases or decreases.

It should be noted that the present concept constitutes an extension of the isotropic formulation as discussed in Section 3.1 (eqn (6)). The bounding surface again reflects the isotropic properties of the material and its evolution is directly related to plastic distortions.

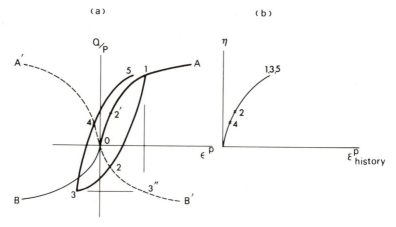

FIG. 17.   Expansion and contraction criterion for the bounding surface.

The yield surface has a form similar to eqn (28) according to the second postulate (ii). If parameters P', Q' and θ' are defined to have precisely the same forms as eqns (25), (26) and (27) with the exception that they are measured in the Σ'_i system of reference, then for the yield surface we have

$$f(\sigma'_i) = Q' - \alpha P' g(\theta') = 0 \qquad (30)$$

where α is now assumed to be a constant.

The yield surface is allowed to translate and rotate within the bounding surface and its kinematics are guided by a particular stress vector referred to as the conjugate stress vector located on the bounding surface. The intersection of this stress vector and the π plane passing through the current stress point is known as the conjugate stress point. Referring to Fig. 16(a), if a_i is the current state of stress located on the current yield surface then its conjugate is defined by a^c_i on the bounding surface so that $\theta = \theta'$, where θ' is the local Lode parameter (in Σ'_i system) and θ is the Lode parameter corresponding to the conjugate point on the bounding surface (and measured in Σ_i system).

The mode of translation and rotation of the yield surface is governed by the following two rules.

—The axis of the yield surface (which coincides with space diagonal of Σ'_i) moves parallel to a plane containing the stress vector and the conjugate stress vector; i.e. the plane $0\sigma_i\sigma^c_i$ passing through the origin, point σ_i and point σ^c_i.

—The rotation of the yield surface is such that the Lode parameter corresponding to the set of stress points common to the plane $0\sigma_i\sigma_i^c$ and the new yield surface (the yield surface resulting from the incremental change in stress point σ_i) remains equal to the Lode parameter of the conjugate stress vector σ_i^c.

In addition to the above two requirements, the new yield surface must, of course, satisfy a consistency condition, i.e., the new yield surface must contain the new stress point $\sigma_i + \dot{\sigma}_i \mathrm{d}t'$. The detailed mathematical formulation governing the kinematics of the yield surface is provided in the original paper by Poorooshasb and Pietruszczak (1985).

According to Poorooshasb et al. (1966/67) for the conventional triaxial compression tests, the plastic potential may be represented by a relationship in the form

$$\psi = P\bar{\psi}(M) - P_0 = 0 \tag{31}$$

where M is an auxiliary parameter defined by $M = Q/P$ and P_0 is a suitably chosen constant.

A generalisation of eqn (31) assumes the form

$$\psi = P'\bar{\psi}[M'/g(\theta')] - P'_0 = 0 \tag{32}$$

where M' is an auxiliary parameter defined by $M' = Q'/P'$ and function $g(\theta')$ is identical to $g(\theta)$ of eqn (28). During a virgin loading process the stress point is located on the bounding surface and $\dot{\varepsilon}^p = \dot{\varepsilon}^p_{\text{history}}$. Therefore the consistency condition reads

$$\frac{\partial F}{\partial \sigma_i}\dot{\sigma}_i + \frac{\partial F}{\partial \eta}\frac{\mathrm{d}\eta}{\mathrm{d}\varepsilon^p}\dot{\varepsilon}^p = 0 \tag{33}$$

The direction and magnitude of the plastic flow is governed by the equation

$$\dot{\varepsilon}_i'^p = \lambda \frac{\partial \psi}{\partial \sigma_i'}$$

where $\dot{\varepsilon}_i'^p$ are the components of the plastic strain rate vector measured in the Σ_i' system of reference. But

$$\dot{\varepsilon}_i^p = a_{ij}\dot{\varepsilon}_j'^p = a_{ij}\lambda \frac{\partial \psi}{\partial \sigma_j'} \tag{34}$$

from which the rate of plastic distortion $\dot{\varepsilon}^p$ may be evaluated:

$$\dot{\varepsilon}^p = \sqrt{\tfrac{2}{3}}\lambda\beta \tag{35}$$

The a_{ij} are the direction cosines of the axes Σ_i with respect to axes Σ_i' and the scalar β is defined by the equation

$$\beta = \left[\left(a_{1i} \frac{\partial \psi}{\partial \sigma_i'} \right)^2 + \left(a_{2i} \frac{\partial \psi}{\partial \sigma_i'} \right)^2 + \left(a_{3i} \frac{\partial \psi}{\partial \sigma_i'} \right)^2 \right.$$
$$\left. - a_{1i}a_{2j} \frac{\partial \psi}{\partial \sigma_i'} \frac{\partial \psi}{\partial \sigma_j'} - a_{2i}a_{3j} \frac{\partial \psi}{\partial \sigma_i'} \frac{\partial \psi}{\partial \sigma_j'} - a_{3i}a_{1j} \frac{\partial \psi}{\partial \sigma_i'} \frac{\partial \psi}{\partial \sigma_j'} \right]^{1/2} \tag{36}$$

Substitution of eqn (35) in (33) results in the expression for λ:

$$\lambda = \frac{\partial F}{\partial \sigma_i} \dot{\sigma}_i \left/ \left(-\sqrt{\frac{2}{3}} \frac{\partial F}{\partial \eta} \frac{d\eta}{d\varepsilon^p} \beta \right) \right. \tag{37}$$

Denoting the denominator of eqn (37) by H, the plastic hardening modulus, and noting that $\partial F/\partial \eta = -Pg(\theta)$ from eqn (28) yields

$$\lambda = \frac{\partial F}{\partial \sigma_i} \dot{\sigma}_i / H \tag{38}$$

where

$$H = \sqrt{\tfrac{2}{3}} P g(\theta) \frac{d\eta}{d\varepsilon^p} \beta \tag{39}$$

Substitution for λ from eqn (38) into eqn (34) yields

$$\dot{\varepsilon}_i^p = \frac{a_{i\kappa} \dfrac{\partial \psi}{\partial \sigma_\kappa'} \dfrac{\partial F}{\partial \sigma_j}}{H} \dot{\sigma}_j$$

$$\dot{\varepsilon}_i^p = P_{ij}\dot{\sigma}_j \tag{40}$$

where for convenience $a_{i\kappa}(\partial \psi/\partial \sigma_\kappa')(\partial F/\partial \sigma_j)/H$ has been denoted by P_{ij}.

The total strain rates are given by

$$\dot{\varepsilon}_i = C_{ij}\dot{\sigma}_j \tag{41}$$

where $C_{ij} = E_{ij} + P_{ij}$ and E_{ij} is the tensor of elastic moduli.

In certain applications it is required to express the stress rates in terms of the total strain rates. From eqn (41) such an evaluation is possible since

$$\dot{\sigma}_j = C_{ij}^{-1}\dot{\varepsilon}_i \tag{42}$$

where C_{ij}^{-1} is the inverse of the matrix C_{ij}.

For the stress reversal program involving the evolution of the yield surface $f = 0$ the plastic strain rates are given by the non-associated flow rule

$$\dot{\varepsilon}_i^p = h \frac{\partial \psi}{\partial \sigma_i} \frac{\partial f}{\partial \sigma_j} \dot{\sigma}_j \tag{43}$$

where h is a hardening parameter: the inverse of the plastic hardening modulus H as defined by eqn (38).

The magnitude of the parameter h is dependent on the position of the stress vector within the bounding surface, i.e., its relation to the conjugate stress vector and a datum stress vector σ_i^d. The vector σ_i^d is located on the bounding surface and is coplanar with the stress vector σ_i and the conjugate stress vector σ_i^c.

Let the spatial angle between the stress vector and the conjugate stress vector be δ and denote the angle between the datum and the conjugate stress vector (both of which are on the bounding surface) by δ_0. Then a general expression for h is

$$h = h(\delta, \delta_0) \tag{44}$$

Equation (44) must satisfy two criteria. First when $\delta \approx \delta_0$, i.e., when stress reversal initiates from a state near the bounding surface $h \approx h^d$. The value of h^d is usually very small and it may be assumed to be equal to zero. In this way the transition from elastic to elastic-plastic behaviour for samples subjected to reversed loading near the bounding surface would be quite smooth. Secondly, as $\delta \to 0$, i.e., the loading approaches to states corresponding to the bounding surface $h \to h^c$. That is the hardening parameter associated with the actual stress point and its conjugate (which are now approaching each other) must tend towards the same value.

The complete stress–strain rate relation is in the form

$$\dot{\varepsilon}_i = C_{ij}^R \dot{\sigma}_j \tag{45}$$

where

$$C_{ij}^R = E_{ij} + h a_{i\kappa} a_{j\ell} \frac{\partial \psi}{\partial \sigma_\kappa'} \frac{\partial f}{\partial \sigma_\ell'} \tag{46}$$

By analogy with eqn (42) the relation between stress and strain rates may be stated as

$$\dot{\sigma}_j = [C_{ij}^R]^{-1} \dot{\varepsilon}_i \tag{47}$$

where $[C_{ij}^R]^{-1}$ is the inverse of the matrix C_{ij}^R.

In order to identify the model, the following material parameters have to be evaluated.

(i)   The form of function $\eta = \eta(\varepsilon^p_{\text{history}})$, eqn (29). For a loose sand a hyperbolic relationship appears to be appropriate:

$$\eta = \eta_f \frac{\varepsilon^p}{A + \varepsilon^p} \tag{48}$$

where for convenience the subscript 'history' has been dropped. The parameter η_f is a constant depending on the strength of the sand and numerically is equal to $2\sqrt{2} \sin \phi_f/(3 - \sin \phi_f)$ where ϕ_f is the angle of friction of the sand at failure. Coefficient A, the isotropic hardening parameter, is a constant of a magnitude to be determined later.

(ii)   Elastic moduli E and v (or equivalently G and K where G is the elastic shear modulus and K is the elastic bulk modulus).

(iii) Parameters identifying the failure condition η_f and the so-called zero dilatancy line in the stress space η_c.

(iv)   The form of function $h(\delta, \delta_0)$, eqn (44). It is proposed that

$$h = h^c(1 - \delta/\delta_0)^\mu \tag{49}$$

where μ is a positive constant and h^c is the hardening parameter associated with the conjugate stress point.

Equation (30) requires the existence of a small elastic domain during any loading program. Consequently, the shear modulus G may be evaluated from the initial portion of the stress–strain curve of, e.g., P-constant test,

$$G = \frac{1}{2} \frac{\partial Q}{\partial \varepsilon} \bigg|_{Q=0} \tag{50}$$

The bulk modulus can be determined from $K = 2G(1 + v)/(3(1 - 2v))$. Both K and G can be assumed as constant or they both may depend on effective pressure,†

---

† If both moduli are pressure sensitive there is a coupling effect between volumetric and deviatoric terms of stress and strain rates due to $G = G(p)$. If this coupling is neglected, the energy dissipation would result for a closed circuit stress path (Mroz and Norris, 1982; Zytynski et al., 1980).

Parameter A is evaluated from equation

$$A = \eta_f P/(2G) \tag{51}$$

Finally, the value of the kinematic hardening parameter μ must be determined by a process of trial and error using any reverse-compression curves.

4   ON PERFORMANCE OF SOME CONSTITUTIVE CONCEPTS UNDER CYCLIC LOADING CONDITIONS

In the following, we shall restrict ourselves to the performance of the multi-surface hardening concept and two-surface model for sand as discussed in Section 3.1 although some comments regarding other concepts mentioned in that section will also be made. The multi-surface hardening concept, though applicable for both sands and clays, has been extensively tested for clays only (Mroz et al., 1979, 1981). The simulation of sand response has been mainly contained to monotonic programs (Mroz and Pietruszczak, 1983).

In the reference by Mroz et al. (1981), a number of numerical tests simulating the undrained response of clay under cyclic loading have been performed. Some of those results are presented in Fig. 18. Figure 18(a) shows the effective stress paths as obtained in an undrained stress-controlled triaxial compression test on a normally consolidated clay. The applied stress amplitudes were not sufficient to cause failure and in each case the deformation stabilised after a number of cycles. As expected, the changes in stress amplitude affected the location of the stable state. The locus of stress-peak points for steady-state is defined by the line AC.

For overconsolidated material, Fig. 18(b), the effective stress path migrates initially to the right and subsequently reverses towards the origin. Again, the line AC defines steady-state conditions for different stress amplitudes.

In a qualitative sense the above predictions seem very encouraging as they agree quite well with the experimental evidence (Sangrey et al., 1969).

Unfortunately, the multi-surface concept has not been extensively tested under strain-controlled regimes. It seems that in this case the conclusions would be less optimistic.

In a quantitative sense the numerical results for such programs are very sensitive to the value of elastic shear modulus, which affects considerably the corresponding stress amplitudes. Consequently, both the rate of pore

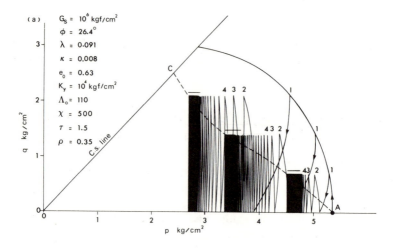

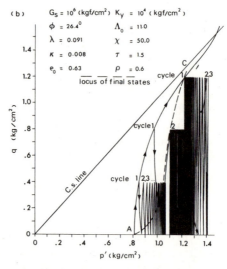

FIG. 18. Effective stress paths for an undrained stress-controlled cyclic test (numerical predictions after Mroz *et al.* (1981)). (a) Normally consolidated clay; (b) overconsolidated clay (OCR = 6·5).

pressure generation and the location of stable-state (if any) remain affected as well.

In general, most of the Critical State based concepts underestimate very much the deviatoric strains generated under undrained conditions (Pande and Pietruszczak, 1984). It also applies to the multi-surface concept. As a result, the hysteresis loop cannot be simulated with sufficient accuracy. Moreover, most of these concepts predict an initial increase in stress amplitude followed, in some cases (Pande and Pietruszczak, 1984), by subsequent reduction. Experimentally (see Section 2) the stress amplitudes progressively decline.

Figure 19 shows the predictions of a two-way strain controlled undrained test for a semi-empirical concept by Carter *et al.* (1982) based on the Critical State theory. The numerical response is, in general, far from being satisfactory.

The inability to deal successfully with strain-controlled programs, which is common to many constitutive concepts, is very evident from Fig. 20. The figure presents a $\bar{G}$–γ plot, where γ denotes the deviatoric strain amplitude and $\bar{G}$ represents the apparent shear modulus of the soil after a finite number (adopted as 10) of deviatoric strain cycles. Definition of $\bar{G}$ is provided in Fig. 20(a). In Fig. 20(b), $\bar{G}$ is normalised with respect to the initial shear modulus G_0 and plotted against the logarithm of strain amplitude γ. Both experimental results and numerical predictions are shown (after the reference by Pande and Pietruszczak (1984)). Experiments indicate that the apparent shear modulus decreases as the amplitude of shear straining is increased. For most soils, with strain amplitudes of 1 %,

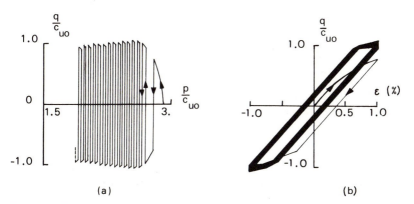

FIG. 19.   Prediction for a two-way strain-controlled triaxial test (after Carter *et al.* (1982)).

(a)

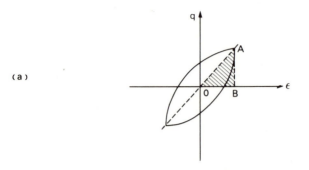

Apparent shear modulus = $\frac{1}{3}$ × slope of OA

(b)

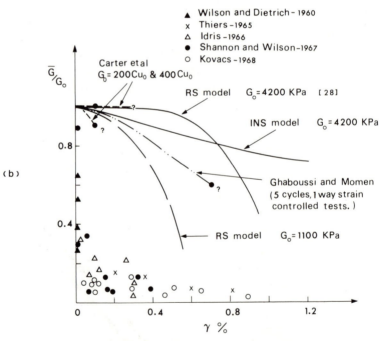

FIG. 20. $\bar{G}/G_0$ versus γ plot for various models and experiments on saturated clays (see Pande and Pietruszczak (1984) for detailed references). (a) Definition of apparent shear modulus.

the apparent shear modulus drastically reduces to some 20–10 % of the initial monotonic value (G_0). It is evident from this figure that several constitutive models produce $\bar{G}$–γ plots of quite the wrong type. It indicates that these concepts do not generate enough plastic strain at low amplitudes of shaking. It applies to the multi-surface concept (marked on the figure as INS-model) as well.

The two-surface model, as described in paragraph 3(ii), was intended to simulate the behaviour of sand. The performance of this model in various test configurations is presented in subsequent figures. Since the concept is quite recent no extensive testing has been performed as yet. Nevertheless, the currently available results give certainly some indication of its ability. Figures 21 and 22 present the predictions of a monotonic undrained test

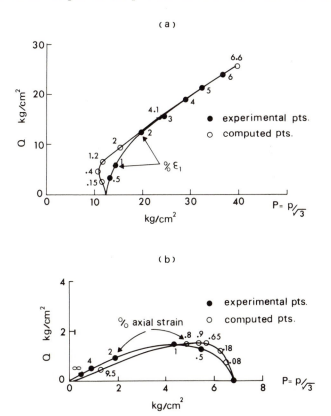

FIG. 21.   Predictions for a monotonic undrained triaxial test (after Poorooshasb and Pietruszczak (1985)) on (a) dense sand, (b) very loose sand.

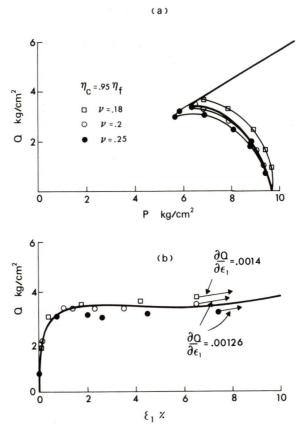

FIG. 22.   Loose sand; predictions for a monotonic undrained triaxial test (after Poorooshasb and Pietruszczak, 1985).

on a very loose, loose and dense sand, respectively. The predictions are compared with experimental results by Castro (1969) (Fig. 21(b)), Townsend and Mulilis (1976) (Fig. 22) and Baladi and Rohani (1979) (Fig. 21(a)).

For a very loose sand, the undrained constraint leads to a complete liquefaction of the sample during the test. Numerical prediction indicates the same phenomenon.

In a loose sample (Fig. 22) initial build-up of pore pressure is observed, followed by subsequent decline. The plastic dilatancy effects are not very prominent, however, and the sample fails soon after exhibiting the

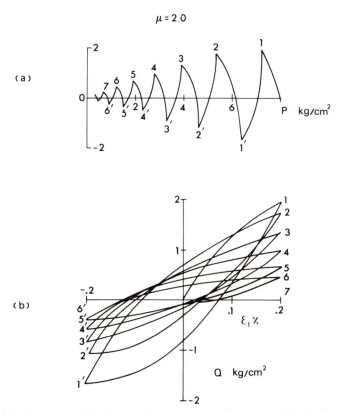

FIG. 23. Numerical predictions for a two-way strain-controlled undrained cyclic test on a loose sand (after Poorooshasb and Pietruszczak, 1985).

transition in behaviour. Again, numerical predictions indicate fairly good agreements. Finally, the dense sand (Fig. 21(a)) tends to dilate from the beginning and consequently develops significant negative pore pressures. Within the applied range of stresses the sample does not fail. Both experimental and numerical results display the same trend in behaviour.

In general, the above shown predictions are very encouraging and it is evident that the model covers a very wide spectrum of material response.

Figure 23 presents qualitatively (no comparison with experimental data is made) the numerical simulation of a two-way strain controlled cyclic test (axial strain amplitude 0·2 %). Values of the material parameters correspond to a loose sand from Fig. 22. The cyclic loading process causes a gradual build-up of pore pressure and the effective stress path migrates towards the origin. The pore pressure generation takes place during both loading and unloading, and is accompanied by a progressive reduction in stress amplitude. In general, the resulting stress amplitudes in compression exceed those in extension. After a number of cycles the effective pressure reduces to zero and the sample liquefies.

Note, that for a loose material the model permits liquefaction in a single cycle (very loose sand, Fig. 21(b)) or after a number of cycles (loose sand, Fig. 23). On the other hand, dense sand (Fig. 21(a)) because of plastic dilatancy effects, would have practically never liquefied under similar loading conditions.

Finally, Fig. 24 shows the results of a two-way stress controlled cyclic test. The amplitude of Q was selected as equal to $1.2 \, \text{kg/cm}^2$ in the compression domain and $-0.9 \, \text{kg/cm}^2$ for the extension portion. The sample, again a loose sand of similar mechanical properties to that represented in Fig. 22, liquefies after about six cycles by necking, i.e. in the extension mode.

In general, many aspects of the above predicted behaviour are widely

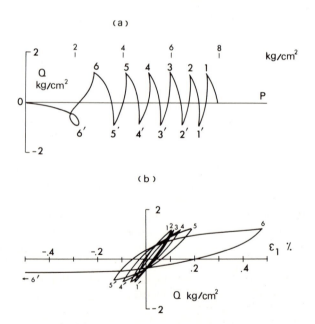

FIG. 24.   Loose sand subjected to a stress controlled cyclic test (after Poorooshasb and Pietruszczak, 1985).

supported by experimental evidence (see Section 2). In that sense, the results from Figs 23 and 24, though purely qualitative, are again very encouraging.

5 CONCLUSIONS

For many reasons an objective evaluation of various constitutive concepts based on their performance under cyclic loading seems to be very difficult (if not impossible) at the moment. Firstly, for most of the existing formulations the material published on their performance is very fragmentary. Also, the concepts in themselves are continually being modified and updated to improve the performance. At the same time, as indicated in Section 2, the experimental data are not fully reliable since they proved to be very sensitive to the methods of sample preparation, to the rate of testing, etc. Consequently, although several attempts at assessing different constitutive concepts have been made recently (Gudehus *et al.*, in press; Pande and Pietruszczak, 1984) they should all be regarded with some caution.

In the present Chapter an attempt to provide a brief survey of developments in the area of constitutive modelling has been made with a view of stimulating further research on this topic. The potential values of applying kinematic hardening to soil has been emphasised. Using this approach, considerable success has been achieved in stimulating qualitative aspects of soil response to cyclic loading.

REFERENCES

BALADI, G. Y. and ROHANI, B. (1979). An elastic-plastic constitutive model for saturated sand subjected to monotonic and/or cyclic loadings, In: *Numerical Methods in Geomechanics*—Third Intern. Conf., Aachen, Ed. Wittke, W., Publ. A. A. Balkema, Rotterdam, Vol. 1, pp. 383–404.

BAKER, R., FRYDMAN, S. and GALIL, J. (1980). *A plasticity model for the load–unload behaviour of sand*, Paper presented at the 1980 ASCE Convention, Florida, October 27–31, 1980.

BAZANT, Z. P. and BHAT, P. D. (1976). Endochronic theory of inelasticity and failure of concrete, *Journ. Eng. Mech. Div., ASCE*, **102**(EM4), 701–22.

BAZANT, Z. P. and KRIZEK, R. J. (1975). Saturated sand as an inelastic two phase medium, *Journ. Eng. Mech. Div., ASCE*, **101**(EM4), 317–32.

CARTER, J. P., BOOKER, J. R. and WROTH, C. P. (1982). A critical state soil model for cyclic loading, *Soil Mechanics—Transient and Cyclic Loads*, Chapter 9, J. Wiley & Sons, Chichester, pp. 219–52.

182   S. PIETRUSZCZAK AND H. B. POOROOSHASB

CASTRO, G. (1969). Liquefaction of sands, *Harvard University Soil Mechanics Series, No. 81*, Pierce Hall, Cambridge, USA.

DAFALIAS, Y. F. and HERRMANN, L. R. (1982). Bounding surface formulation of soil plasticity, *Soil Mechanics—Transient and Cyclic Loads*, Chapter 10, J. Wiley & Sons, Chichester, pp. 253–83.

DAFALIAS, Y. F. and POPOV, E. P. (1975). A model of non-linearly hardening materials for complex loadings, *Acta Mechanica*, **21**, 173–92.

DAFALIAS, Y. F. and POPOV, E. P. (1977). Cyclic loading for materials with a vanishing elastic region, *Nucl. Eng. Design*, **41**, 293–302.

DUNCAN, J. M. and CHANG, C. Y. (1970). Non-linear analysis of stress and strain in soils, *Journ. Soil Mech. Found. Eng. Div.*, *ASCE*, **96**(SM5), 1629–51.

GHABOUSSI, J. and MOMEN, H. (1979). Plasticity model for cyclic behaviour of sands, In: *Numerical Methods in Geomechanics*—Third Intern. Conf., Aachen, Ed. Wittke, W., Publ. A. A. Balkema, Rotterdam, Vol. 1, pp. 423–34.

GUDEHUS, G., DARVE, F. and VARDOULAKIS, I. (in press) (Eds). *Proceedings of the Intern. Workshop on Constitutive Behaviour of Soils*, Grenoble, Sept. 6–8, 1982, Publ. A. A. Balkema, Rotterdam.

ISHIHARA, K. and OKADA, S. (1978). Yielding of overconsolidated sand and liquefaction model under cyclic stresses, *Soils and Foundations*, **18**(1), 57–72.

ISHIHARA, K., TATSUOKA, F. and YASUDA, S. (1975). Undrained deformation and liquefaction of sand under cyclic stresses, *Soils and Foundations*, **15**(1), 29–44.

KRIEG, R. D. (1975). A practical two-surface plasticity theory, *Journ. Appl. Mech.*, **42**, 641–6.

LADE, P. V. (1977). Elastoplastic stress–strain theory for cohesionless soils with curved yield surfaces, *Int. Journ. Solids and Structures*, **913**, 1019–35.

MITCHELL, R. J. (1970). On the yielding and mechanical strength of Leda clays, *Can. Geotechn. Journ.*, **7**, 297–312.

MROZ, Z. (1967). On the description of anisotropic work hardening, *Journ. Mech. Phys. Solids*, **15**, 163–75.

MROZ, Z. (1980). On hypoelasticity and plasticity approaches to constitutive modelling of inelastic behaviour of soils, *Int. Journ. Num. Anal. Meth. Geomech.*, **4**, 45–55.

MROZ, Z. and NORRIS, V. A. (1982). Elastoplastic and viscoplastic constitutive models for soils with application to cyclic loading, *Soil Mechanics—Transient and Cyclic Loads*, Chapter 8, J. Wiley & Sons, Chichester, pp. 173–217.

MROZ, Z. and PIETRUSZCZAK, S. (1983). A constitutive model for sand with anisotropic hardening rule, *Int. Journ. Num. Anal. Meth. Geomech.*, **7**, 305–20.

MROZ, Z., NORRIS, V. A. and ZIENKIEWICZ, O. C. (1978). An anisotropic hardening model for soils and its application to cyclic loading, *Int. Journ. Num. Anal. Meth. Geomech.*, **2**, 203–21.

MROZ, Z., NORRIS, V. A. and ZIENKIEWICZ, O. C. (1979). Application of an anisotropic hardening model in the analysis of the elastoplastic deformation of soils, *Geotechnique*, **29**, 1–34.

MROZ, Z., NORRIS, V. A. and ZIENKIEWICZ, O. C. (1981). An anisotropic critical state model for soils subject to cyclic loading, *Geotechnique*, **31**, 451–69.

Nova, R. and Hueckel, T. (1982). A constitutive model for soil under monotonic and cyclic loading, *Soil Mechanics—Transient and Cyclic Loads*, Chapter 12, J. Wiley & Sons, Chichester, pp. 343–73.

Nova, R. and Wood, R. (1979). A constitutive model for sand in triaxial compression, *Int. Journ. Num. Anal. Meth. Geomech.*, **3**, 255–78.

Quigley, R. M. and Thomson, C. D. (1966). The fabric of anisotropically consolidated marine clay, *Can. Geotechn. Journ.*, **3**, 61–73.

Pande, G. N. and Pietruszczak, S. (1982). Reflecting surface model for soils, *Proc. Intern. Symp. on Num. Models in Geomech.*, Zurich, Publ. A. A. Balkema, Rotterdam, pp. 50–64.

Pande, G. N. and Pietruszczak, S. (1984). A sideways look at the constitutive concepts for soils, *Proc. Intern. Symp. on Num. Models in Geomech.*, Zurich, Vol. 2, Publ. A. A. Balkema, Rotterdam.

Pietruszczak, S. and Mroz, Z. (1980). Description of anisotropic consolidation of clays, *Proc. Euromech. Coll. on Anisotropy in Mechanics*, CNRS Publ., pp. 598–622.

Pietruszczak, S. and Mroz, Z. (1983). On hardening anisotropy of K_0-consolidated clays, *Int. Journ. Num. Anal. Meth. Geomech.*, **7**, 19–38.

Poorooshasb, H. B. and Pietruszczak, S. (1985). On yielding and flow of sand; A generalized two-surface model, *Computers and Geotechnics*, **1**, 33–58.

Poorooshasb, H. B. and Young, R. N. (1982). On intersecting yield surfaces, *Proc. Intern. Symp. on Num. Models in Geomech.*, Zurich, Publ. A. A. Balkema, Rotterdam, pp. 157–62.

Poorooshasb, H. B., Holubic, I. and Sherbourne, A. N. (1966/67). On yielding and flow of sand in triaxial compression, *Can. Geotechn. Journ.*, *Part 1*, **3**(4), 179–90; *Parts 2 and 3*, **4**(4), 376–97.

Prevost, J. H. (1978). Plasticity theory for soil stress–strain behaviour, *Journ. Eng. Mech. Div.*, ASCE, **104**(EM5), 1177–94.

Sangrey, D. A., Henkel, D. J. and Esrig, M. I. (1969). The effective stress response of a saturated clay soil to repeated loading, *Can. Geotechn. Journ.*, **6**, 241–52.

Tatsuoka, F. and Ishihara, K. (1974). Drained deformation of sand under cyclic stress reversing direction, *Soils and Foundations*, **14**(3), 51–65.

Taylor, P. W. and Bacchus, D. R. (1969). Dynamic cyclic strain tests on clay, *Pro. 7th Intern. Conf. Soil Mech.*, Mexico, **1**, 401–9.

Townsend, F. C. and Mulilis, J. P. (1976). *Liquefaction potential of sands under static and cyclic loading*, Research Report S-76-2, Report 6, US Army Engineer Waterways Experiment Station, CE, Vicksburg, USA.

Valanis, K. C. (1971). A theory of viscoplasticity without yield surface, *Arch. of Mech.*, **23**, 517–55.

Wilde, P. (1977). Two-invariants dependent model of granular media, *Arch. of Mech.*, **29**, 799–809.

Wood, D. M. (1982). Laboratory investigations of the behaviour of soils under cyclic loading: a review, *Soil Mechanics—Transient and Cyclic Loads*, Chapter 20, J. Wiley & Sons, Chichester, pp. 513–82.

Wroth, C. P. and Loudon, P. A. (1967). The correlation of strains within a family of triaxial tests on overconsolidated samples, *Proc. Geotechn. Conf.*, Oslo, pp. 159–63.

YAMADA, Y. and ISHIHARA, K. (1981). Undrained deformation characteristics of loose sand under three-dimensional stress conditions, *Soils and Foundations*, **21**(1), 98–107.

ZYTYNSKI, M., RANDOLPH, M. F., NOVA, R. and WROTH, C. P. (1980). On modelling the unloading–reloading behaviour of soils, *Intern. Journ. Num. Anal. Meth. Geomech.*, **2**, 87–94.

Chapter 6

SOME ASPECTS OF THE BEHAVIOUR OF SOILS IN SIMPLE SHEAR

D. W. Airey,* M. Budhu† and D. M. Wood*

* *Department of Engineering, Cambridge University, UK*
† *Department of Civil Engineering,*
State University of New York at Buffalo, USA

1 INTRODUCTION

The most common piece of equipment for performing laboratory tests to study the stress–strain behaviour of soils is the conventional triaxial apparatus. In this apparatus (Fig. 1) cylindrical samples of soil are subjected to an axisymmetric system of principal stresses

$$\sigma_1 = \sigma_a \qquad \sigma_2 = \sigma_3 = \sigma_r$$

This apparatus is of limited relevance for following the actual stress paths of importance in geotechnical constructions but it is widely available and relatively simple to use.

A particular criticism that may be levelled against the triaxial apparatus is that the applied axial stress and radial pressure are necessarily principal stresses. Their directions are fixed and the principal axes of stress and strain are not able to rotate. A general soil element in the ground can expect to experience varying directions of principal stresses as well as varying magnitudes and it becomes important to study the behaviour of soil samples in the laboratory under stress conditions in which rotation of principal axes can occur.

It turns out to be quite impractical to contemplate applying to samples of soil in the laboratory the general system of stresses and strains shown in Fig. 2, which has six degrees of freedom. While there are research apparatus

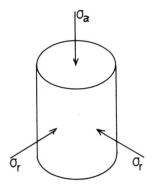

FIG. 1. Stress conditions applied in conventional triaxial apparatus. σ_a = axial stress and σ_r = radial cell pressure.

such as the Directional Shear Cell (Arthur *et al.*, 1977) and the Hollow Cylinder Apparatus (for example, Broms and Casbarian (1965), Hight *et al.* (1983)) which provide four out of the six degrees of freedom, the device which is most widely available is the Simple Shear Apparatus which offers only two degrees of freedom.

Simple shear state of strain is shown in Fig. 3. It is a plane strain mode of shearing so that $\varepsilon_{zz} = \gamma_{yz} = \gamma_{zx} = 0$ and the stress $\sigma_{zz} = \sigma_2$ is a principal stress. It is also an inextensional mode of shearing so that $\varepsilon_{xx} = 0$. The two remaining degrees of freedom are then the shear strain γ_{yx} and the vertical strain ε_{yy}, which is equal to the volumetric strain.

There have been two main approaches to the development of simple shear apparatus. Roscoe (1953) studying the shear box experiments of Hvorslev (1937) realised the importance of studying the behaviour of the soil elements that were actually participating in the narrow zone of failure

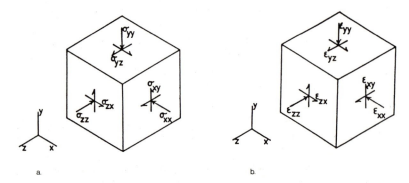

a.   b.

FIG. 2.   (a) General stress state with shear stresses and normal stresses applied to all faces of a cubical element. (b) General strain state.

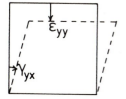

FIG. 3.   Simple shear state of strain $\varepsilon_{zz} = \varepsilon_{xx} = \gamma_{yz} = \gamma_{zx} = 0$.

(Fig. 4(a)). The generations of simple shear apparatus developed at Cambridge thus represent attempts to compel an entire soil sample to become the zone of failure (Fig. 4(b)). The early work on the development of critical state soil mechanics (for example, Roscoe *et al.* (1958)) rests on the results of simple shear experiments.

The Scandinavians have suggested that the strength of clay on thin failure surfaces (Fig. 5) (Aas, 1980) can usefully be studied, at least in part, in the simple shear apparatus (though there is no absolute necessity for such a failure surface to be inextensional (Houlsby and Wroth, 1980)). The simple shear apparatus developed at the Norwegian Geotechnical Institute was developed specifically to test field samples of soil (Bjerrum and Landva, 1966) and Norwegian simple shear apparatus are now much used by the site investigation industry.

The Cambridge simple shear apparatus (Fig. 4(b)) tests a sample which is square in plan and enclosed within rigid platens which are linked together with hinges and sliders in order that the necessary simple shear deformation may develop. The Norwegian simple shear apparatus (Fig. 4(c)) tests a sample which is circular in plan and enclosed within a rubber membrane reinforced with a spiral wire binding in order to encourage the desired inextensional plane strain mode of deformation.

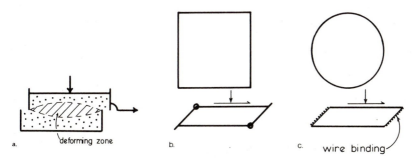

FIG. 4.   (a) Direct shear box. (b) Mechanism of Cambridge simple shear apparatus. (c) Arrangement of Norwegian simple shear apparatus.

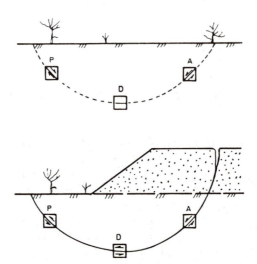

FIG. 5.   Shear stresses on a possible slip surface before and after the placing of a fill
(after Aas (1980)).

This chapter is largely concerned with presenting some of the findings of recent research work at Cambridge using the simple shear apparatus. It is recognised that this gives an incomplete picture of the behaviour of soils in simple shear.

2   UNIFORMITY OF SIMPLE SHEAR SAMPLES

Though simple shear deformation appears simple, practical implementation is faced with a basic problem illustrated in Fig. 6. In order that the sample may be able to change in volume (that is, height) at will it is necessary for the ends of the apparatus to be relatively free from shear stress. As a result the distribution of shear stress over the top and bottom surfaces has to fall towards zero at the ends of the sample (Fig. 6(a)). The resulting unbalancing couple has to be counteracted by an opposite couple generated by a non-uniform distribution of normal stress on the top and bottom surfaces (Fig. 6(b)).

The non-uniformities of boundary stresses are shown schematically in Fig. 6. How severe these will be in practice is a matter for theoretical analysis (for example, Roscoe (1953); Lucks *et al.* (1972); Wright *et al.* (1978)), direct experimental observation (for example, Stroud (1971); Borin

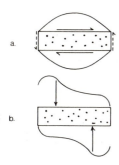

FIG. 6. (a) Non-uniform distribution of shear stresses from absence of complementary shear stress on ends of sample. (b) Non-uniform distribution of normal stress to preserve moment equilibrium of the sample.

(1973); Budhu (1979, 1984); Airey, 1984)), and general discussion (for example, Vucetic and Lacasse (1982)). Direct experimental observation is, however, only possible in apparatus equipped with transducers which can measure the distribution of normal and shear stresses applied to the sample and cannot be done on a routine basis. Recent Cambridge simple shear apparatus have been equipped with an array of contact stress transducers (load cells) for this purpose (Fig. 7). Some of the findings of these load cell measurements will be presented in subsequent sections.

The analyses that have been performed of simple shear deformation, and the experimental observations that have been made, suggest that in the central part of the sample, provided the height to length ratio is sufficiently low (a ratio of about 0·2 is used in the Cambridge simple shear apparatus with a length of about 100 mm), the inhomogeneity of stresses resulting from the non-uniform boundary stresses will be low. An extra advantage of the use of an array of load cells surrounding the sample such as that shown in Fig. 7 is that complete information about the stress tensor in the central part of the sample can be deduced from the load cell measurements. A rational way in which this may be done is described by Wood et al. (1979).

In most commercially available apparatus the only measurements that

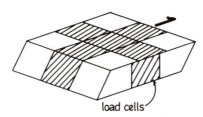

load cells

FIG. 7. Load cells (contact stress transducers) in Cambridge simple shear apparatus.

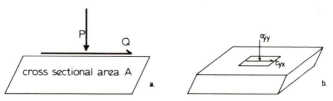

FIG. 8. (a) Stress measurements in simple apparatus. Average normal stress $\sigma_n = P/A$ and shear stress $\tau_h = Q/A$ are the only components determined. (b) Single load cell measuring actual normal stress σ_{yy} and shear stress τ_{yx} applied to soil at the centre of the sample.

are possible are of *total* normal load and *total* shear load (Fig. 8(a)). From these, knowing the cross sectional area A of the sample, the *average* normal stress σ_n and the *average* shear stress τ_h can be calculated and this is not sufficient to describe the stress tensor. It is clear that it would at the very least be desirable in commercial apparatus to measure with a single load cell the actual normal stress σ_{yy} and shear stress τ_{yx} applied to the soil at the centre of the sample (Fig. 8(b)). It is usually found that $\sigma_{yy} > \sigma_n$ and $\tau_{yx} > \tau_h$.

The uncertainty about the stress tensor arises because no information is available about the stress σ_{xx}. Let us suppose that at failure stresses σ_{yy} and τ_{yx} have been deduced (ignoring, for the moment, the probable difference between these and the measured σ_n and τ_h). The horizontal plane on which these stresses act could be a plane of maximum stress obliquity (Fig. 9(a)) so that the angle of friction ϕ_m mobilised in the soil is

$$\tan \phi_m = \tau_{yx}/\sigma_{yy} \tag{1}$$

or it could be a plane of maximum shear stress (Fig. 9(b)) so that

$$\sin \phi_m = \tau_{yx}/\sigma_{yy} \tag{2}$$

A further possibility has been noted by de Josselin de Jong (1971) using a book-stack analogy. Externally observed simple shear deformation of a

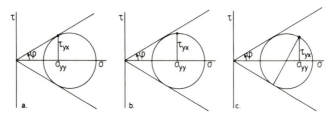

FIG. 9.   Possible Mohr circles for simple shear state of stress.

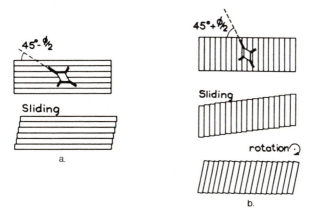

FIG. 10.   Book-stack analogy of simple shear deformation (from de Josselin de Jong (1971)).

pile of books can be produced by the sliding of each book on a horizontal plane (Fig. 10(a)), but the same external effect is found when each book in a row of the same books is allowed to slide on a vertical plane and then the whole row is rotated (Fig. 10(b)). The mode of sliding, shown in Fig. 10(a), corresponds to the state of stress illustrated in Fig. 9(a). The mode of sliding

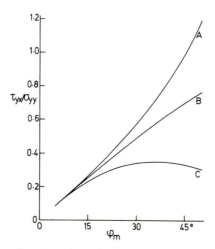

FIG. 11.   Variation of τ_{yx}/σ_{yy} with mobilised angle of friction ϕ_m for different assumed modes of response. A, horizontal plane with maximum stress obliquity; B, horizontal plane with maximum shear stress; C, vertical plane with maximum stress obliquity.

shown in Fig. 10(b) corresponds to the state of stress illustrated in Fig. 9(c) and the mobilised angle of friction is given by

$$\frac{\sin \phi_m \cos \phi_m}{1 + \sin^2 \phi_m} = \tau_{yx}/\sigma_{yy} \tag{3}$$

The three eqns (1), (2) and (3) are plotted in Fig. 11 as variations of expected τ_{yx}/σ_{yy} with mobilised angle of friction ϕ_m. De Josselin de Jong suggests that the third mode—vertical failure planes plus rotation—will usually be the easiest one for the soil to choose. This conclusion is to some extent governed by the initial stress state in the sample at the start of the simple shear deformation.

3 SIMPLE SHEAR TESTS ON SAND

Typical distributions of normal stress observed in a cyclic simple shear test on dry dense 14/25 Leighton Buzzard sand with constant average normal stress σ_n are shown in Fig. 12. The curves represent a smoothed mathematical fit to the load cell data (of normal stresses and 'couple stresses'*); the tensile stresses indicated are clearly fictional. It is evident that the stress distribution matches that anticipated qualitatively in Fig. 6(b). It is also clear that in such a cyclic test the sand at the ends of the sample is being subjected to a dramatically fluctuating stress and this can be expected to influence the internal uniformity of the sample being tested. Over the central section of the apparatus the stresses are more uniform and varying less wildly.

The non-uniformity of boundary stresses is an unavoidable problem associated with simple shear apparatus. Non-uniformity of internal deformations is to some extent governed by the way in which samples are prepared. At the top and bottom boundaries of the sample a rigid flat metal surface is required to transmit shear stresses to a sample of granular soil. A plane surface cannot be forced through a granular soil without disturbing its local void ratio: there is a tendency for a thin loose zone to exist adjacent to the boundary whose importance will depend on the ratio of particle size

---

* It is tempting to see the load cell data, which give information on both the force applied to the load cell and its line of action, as a prime case for the application of the theory of couple stresses (Cosserat and Cosserat, 1909; Mindlin, 1963; Koiter, 1964; Fung, 1965). However, it is difficult for most granular materials to envisage a mechanism by which it is possible for couples, as opposed to forces, to be transmitted across infinitesimal surfaces at a particulate level (Wood, 1980).

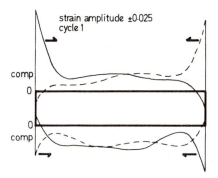

FIG. 12.   Distributions of normal stress on horizontal boundaries at shear maxima
during cyclic test on dense 14/25 Leighton Buzzard sand.

to apparatus height. The technique adopted by Stroud (1971) has been to
coat the top and bottom platens of the simple shear apparatus with a thin
layer of epoxy resin which ensures good transmission of shear stresses by
replacing the smooth metal by a surface that is as rough as the sand itself.

The distribution of stresses *inside* a simple shear sample cannot be
investigated. However, the distribution of deformations within a soil
sample can be studied by radiographic measurement of the position of lead
markers (Roscoe *et al.*, 1963) and for granular soils radiography gives the
possibility of detecting local changes in density because the absorption of
X-rays drops as the soil dilates.

Though the simple shear apparatus applies a uniform strain to the
sample at its boundaries this is no guarantee of internal homogeneity. An
example, taken from Stroud (1971), of a comparison of boundary strains
and the average strain measured radiographically from movements of lead
markers in the central region of a sample is shown in Fig. 13(a). The
agreement is within the accuracy of the measurements.

This same sample was sheared to a high strain and an approximately
horizontal zone of preferential dilation was noted within the sample on the
radiographs (Fig. 15). Analysis of the grid of radiographic markers shown
in Fig. 14(a) enabled the distributions with depth of change in void ratio
and of shear strain shown in Fig. 14(b),(c) to be drawn. For the levels A, B,
C in Fig. 14 radiographic strain paths have been plotted in Fig. 13(b) for
comparison with the boundary strains. The difference is now much greater.
The regions of intense shearing show a much higher rate of dilation and a
constant volume critical state condition is reached at a shear strain between
0·5 and 1.

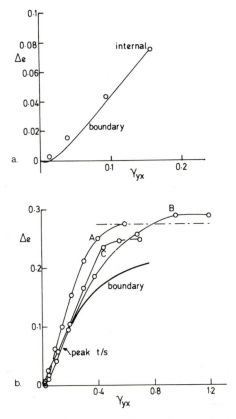

FIG. 13.   (a) Comparison of boundary and internal strains in simple shear test on dense 14/25 Leighton Buzzard sand ($e_0 = 0.53$) with constant $\sigma_n = 172\,\mathrm{kN/m^2}$ ($25\,\mathrm{lbf/in^2}$) (from Stroud (1971)). (b) Strain paths for the most rapidly dilating regions within the sample shown in Fig. 14 (from Stroud (1971)).

Similar observations of the strains required to fully mobilise the critical state condition within a rupture zone have been made by Vardoulakis (1978) in a biaxial plane strain apparatus and by Scarpelli and Wood (1982) in a direct shear box.

Once a rupture has formed the simple shear sample is no longer homogeneous. The analytical work of Vardoulakis (1980) and Vermeer (1982) shows clearly that ruptures can form before the peak stress ratio of the homogeneous material. The formation of ruptures is influenced by the degree of restraint that the apparatus imposes on the soil and this will

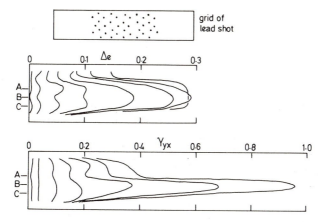

FIG. 14.   Variation of change of void ratio and shear strain with depth from radiographic measurements during simple shear test on dense 14/25 Leighton Buzzard sand ($e_0 = 0\cdot53$) with constant $\sigma_n = 172\,\text{kN/m}^2$ ($25\,\text{lbf/in}^2$) (after Stroud (1971)).

depend on the relative dimensions of the apparatus and of typical particles. Thus Fig. 15(b) shows the much more complex array of ruptures observed in a simple shear test on a fine sand with grain diameter $\sim0\cdot2\,\text{mm}$ (about $\frac{1}{100}$ of the sample height) for comparison with Fig. 15(a). The 14/25 Leighton Buzzard sand has a grain diameter of about 1 mm (about $\frac{1}{20}$ of the sample height).

Comments about non-uniformity of simple shear samples apply primarily at large strains. It seems perfectly appropriate, then, to present data on the simple shear behaviour of sand at lower strains. An extensive series of simple shear tests on dry 14/25 Leighton Buzzard sand has been conducted at Cambridge and some of the findings will be presented here.

It is convenient to study the simple shear behaviour in terms of principal

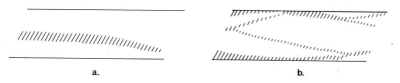

a.   b.

FIG. 15.   (a) Zone of preferential dilation sketched from radiograph of simple shear test shown in Figs 13 and 14. (b) Rupture zones sketched from simple shear test on fine sand (grain size $\sim0\cdot2\,\text{mm}$).

stresses in the plane of shearing $\sigma_1:\sigma_3$ and to use combinations of these parameters

$$s = \tfrac{1}{2}(\sigma_1 + \sigma_3) \tag{4}$$

$$t = \tfrac{1}{2}(\sigma_1 - \sigma_3) \tag{5}$$

to separate the mean stress and the deviatoric or shear stress. Determination of $\sigma_1:\sigma_3$ or $t:s$ is only possible in the fully instrumented Cambridge simple shear apparatus (Fig. 7) but it turns out that in tests on sand a simple relationship exists between the stress ratio mobilised on the horizontal plane

$$R = \tau_{yx}/\sigma_{yy} \tag{6}$$

and the rotation ψ of the major principal stress from the vertical (Fig. 16). Data from many simple shear tests on 14/25 Leighton Buzzard sand (Cole,

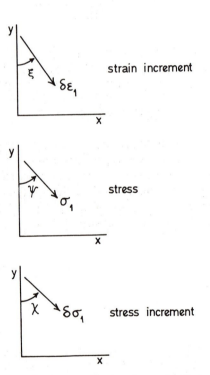

FIG. 16.   Definition sketches for angles ξ, ψ, χ.

1967; Stroud, 1971; Budhu, 1979) are plotted in Fig. 17 and it is seen that a simple relation

$$R = k \tan \psi \qquad (7)$$

(with $k = 0.669$ for this sand) fits the data rather well. This relation has also been proposed by Ochiai (1975) and Oda (1975). Certain relationships can be deduced from eqn (7) and from considerations of the geometry of Mohr's circle of stress

$$\sigma_1/\sigma_{yy} = 1 + R^2/k \qquad (8)$$

$$\sigma_3/\sigma_{yy} = 1 - k \qquad (9)$$

$$t/\sigma_{yy} = (R^2 + k^2)/2k \qquad (10)$$

$$s/\sigma_{yy} = 1 + (R^2 - k^2)/2k \qquad (11)$$

Hence, even for apparatus in which only τ_{yx} and σ_{yy} are measured (Fig. 8) it may be possible to obtain more complete information about the stress tensor for tests on sand. The reliability of predictions made using eqns (7)–(11) is demonstrated by Wood et al. (1979).

The final component of the stress tensor is the intermediate principal stress, $\sigma_{zz} = \sigma_2$. Data collected by Stroud (1971) show (Fig. 18) that the

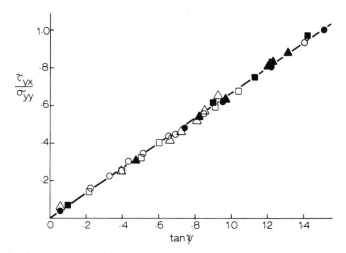

FIG. 17.   Linear relationship between $R = \tau_{yx}/\sigma_{yy}$ and $\tan \psi$ supported by data from a wide range of different simple shear tests on 14/25 Leighton Buzzard sand.

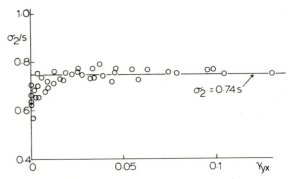

Fig. 18.   Variation of ratio σ_2/s with shear strain (after Stroud (1971)).

ratio σ_2/s rises in simple shear tests on dense and loose sand to an approximately constant value of 0.74. However, a relation of the form

$$\sigma_2 = k_1 s \tag{12}$$

is not as well supported for such a wide range of test paths as eqn (7).

Stroud (1971) performed a number of tests on dense ($e_0 = 0.530$) and loose ($e_0 = 0.780$) samples: some tests with constant average normal stress σ_n and monotonically increasing shear displacement, and some tests with

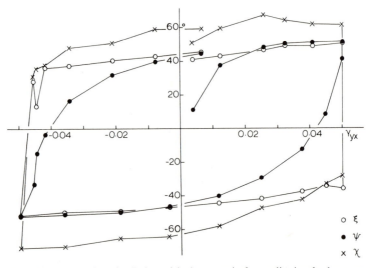

Fig. 19.   Variation of angles ξ, ψ, χ with shear strain for cyclic simple shear test on dense 14/25 Leighton Buzzard sand.

more elaborate paths chosen in order to try and build up a picture of the behaviour of the sand as an elastic:work-hardening plastic material. The description of such a material requires a separation of elastic and plastic strains (El-Sohby, 1964). For many paths the elastic strains of sand are negligible by comparison with the plastic strains.

Preliminary information is required about directions of principal axes of stress, stress increment, and strain increment. For an elastic material coincidence of axes of stress increment and strain increment is expected. For an isotropic plastic material coincidence of axes of strain increment and stress is expected. Variations of the angles ξ, ψ and χ (Fig. 16) during a cyclic test on sand (Budhu, 1979) are shown in Fig. 19. The response can be broadly described as elastic ($\xi = \chi$) at small strains and on stress reversal; and plastic ($\xi = \psi$) at 'large' strains as earlier shown by Roscoe *et al.* (1967). The coincidence of ξ and ψ in fully developed plastic flow at large strains can be used to estimate k in eqn (7): the direction of the principal strain increment ξ can be determined for all simple shear apparatus.

Stroud (1971) shows that the yield loci for Leighton Buzzard sand are virtually identical to the contours of cumulative shear strain expressed as $\sum \mathring{\gamma}$ where $\mathring{\gamma}$ is the diameter of Mohr's circle of strain increment. Typical yield loci, for dense Leighton Buzzard sand are shown in t:s space in Fig. 20. It may be noted that they are concave downward, and hence would cut

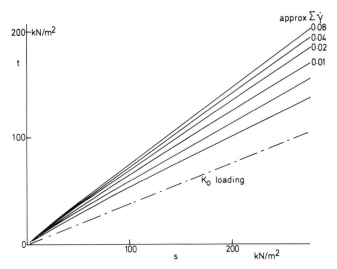

FIG. 20.   Yield loci (and approximate shear strain contours) for dense 14/25 Leighton Buzzard sand (after Stroud (1971)).

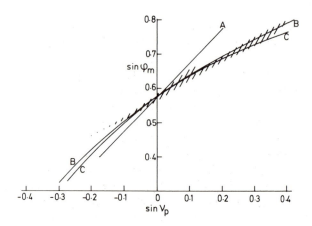

FIG. 21.   Theoretical plastic flow rules and spread of experimental data for 14/25
Leighton Buzzard sand (after Stroud (1971)).

constant t/s lines. Their shape is broadly similar to those found by
Tatsuoka and Ishihara (1974) and by Houlsby (1981) in triaxial tests on
sand.

Stroud's data of plastic strain increment ratios are shown in Fig. 21
together with three theoretical flow rules. In this diagram the plastic rate of
dilatancy,

$$\frac{\mathring{v}_p}{\mathring{\gamma}_p} = -\sin v_p \tag{13}$$

where $\mathring{v}_p$ is a plastic volumetric strain increment, $\mathring{\gamma}_p$ a plastic shear strain
increment, and v_p is the angle of dilation (Fig. 22), is plotted against the
stress ratio

$$t/s = \sin \phi_m \tag{14}$$

where ϕ_m is the mobilised angle of friction in the sand.

Flow rule A is a simple 'Cam clay' type of flow rule (Roscoe and
Schofield, 1963)

$$\sin \phi_m = \sin v_p + \sin \phi_c \tag{15}$$

where ϕ_c is the critical state angle of shearing resistance for shearing at
constant volume and constant stresses ($v_p = 0$).

Flow rule B is a stress:dilatancy flow rule, following Rowe (1962)

$$\sin \phi_m = \frac{\sin v_p + \sin \phi_c}{1 + \sin v_p \sin \phi_c} \tag{16}$$

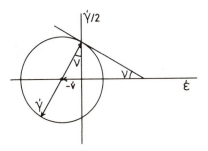

FIG. 22.   Angle of dilation v.

Flow rule C is the 'boundary energy correction' of Taylor (1948) which is simply expressed as

$$R = \sin \phi_c + \tan v \tag{17}$$

where v is the angle of dilation calculated from the *total* strain increments. If the difference between plastic and total strain increments is ignored, and if it is assumed that principal axes of strain increment and stress coincide then

$$R = \frac{\sin \phi_m \cos v_p}{1 - \sin \phi_m \sin v_p} \tag{18}$$

and flow rule C becomes

$$\sin \phi_m = \frac{\sin v_p + \sin \phi_c \cos v_p}{1 + \sin v_p \sin \phi_c \cos v_p} \tag{19}$$

which is the expression plotted in Fig. 21. Evidently either flow rule B or flow rule C is good at matching the experimental data.

The hardening law that Stroud deduces is implicit in the contours of shear strain that are the yield loci in Fig. 20.

The flow rules, eqns (15), (16) and (19), relate dilatancy with mobilised angle of friction. The maximum angle of friction that can be mobilised depends on the void ratio (or relative density) of the sand and the stress level. Critical state conditions, combinations of e and s for constant volume shearing, reached in simple shear tests of Cole (1967) and Stroud (1971) are shown in Fig. 23. The critical state line can be represented by

$$e = G - \lambda \ln s \tag{20}$$

where $\lambda = 0\cdot025$, $G = 0\cdot927$ at $s = 1 \, \text{kN/m}^2$.

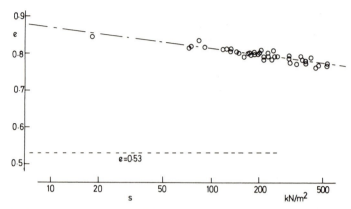

FIG. 23.   Critical state line for 14/25 Leighton Buzzard sand (after Stroud (1971)).

Differences of density and stress level can then be accounted for by plotting, instead of the three quantities $t:s:e$, the two quantities t/s and e_λ where

$$e_\lambda = e + \lambda \ln s \tag{21}$$

Evidently for critical state conditions $e_\lambda = G$ and $t/s = \sin \phi_c$ and a single critical state point can be plotted (Fig. 24). Test paths on loose and dense samples

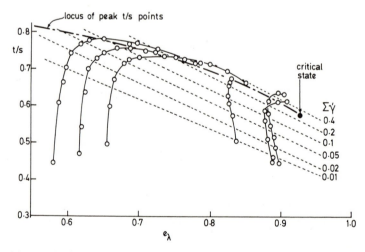

FIG. 24.   Typical paths of constant σ_n tests, locus of peak t/s points, contours of shear strain in $t/s:e_\lambda$ space for 14/25 Leighton Buzzard sand (after Stroud (1971)).

alike can be plotted in $t/s:e_\lambda$ space (Fig. 24) as can a locus of peak t/s points and contours of cumulative shear strain and a unified picture of the behaviour of the sand can be obtained.

4 SIMPLE SHEAR TESTS ON CLAY

Experimental studies of the behaviour of clay in simple shear have been performed at Cambridge by Borin (1973) and Airey (1984). It is in many ways easier to test samples of clay than samples of sand. However, if boundary stresses are to be measured with load cells in contact with the sample (Fig. 7), then wet clay becomes a much less convenient material to test than dry sand, primarily because of the need to prevent moisture from the clay penetrating to the strain gauges on the load cells. There is also a difficulty in preparing and installing samples of the correct size and cuboidal shape in the simple shear apparatus. Whereas Borin, using a simple shear apparatus which was square in plan, consolidated samples in the simple shear apparatus from a slurry within a rubber membrane, Airey used a modification of a circular simple shear apparatus constructed by Budhu (1979), installed preconsolidated disc shaped samples (about 20 mm high and 110 mm diameter) extruded from a separate consolidometer, and surrounded them by a rubber membrane bound with strain gauge wire so that some indication of the lateral stress acting on the samples could be obtained (a technique used also by Youd and Craven (1975) and Moussa (1974), among others). The apparatus used is thus a large version of the Norwegian type of simple shear apparatus (Fig. 4(c))—sufficiently large that load cells can be incorporated in the top and bottom horizontal platens.

Typical normal stresses measured in this apparatus during a simple shear test on kaolin (with plasticity index $I_p = 0.31$) are shown in Fig. 25. It seems that uniformity of boundary stresses improves as the plasticity of the material being tested increases (Airey and Wood, 1984). However, it is still desirable to measure the normal and shear stresses using a load cell in direct contact with the soil at the centre of the sample (Fig. 8(b)) in order to avoid the necessity of correcting the stresses for the membrane restraint and frictional effects in the apparatus.

Uniformity of internal strains can be studied by determining radiographically the positions of lead markers as for sand. It has been found, in tests on kaolin, that adjusting the normal load to prevent any pore water movement into or out of the sample being registered on a

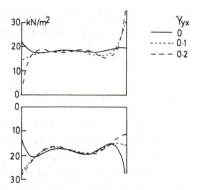

FIG. 25.   Normal stresses on top and bottom boundaries of simple shear apparatus during test on normally consolidated kaolin.

burette produces a truly undrained condition with no detectable internal volumetric strains, at least up to failure. It appears then that the procedure commonly adopted for performing constant volume drained simple shear tests by changing the normal stress to keep the sample height constant (Bjerrum and Landva, 1966) should produce results equivalent to those which would be obtained from actual undrained tests—at least up to failure —though the changes in normal stress will not necessarily be equal to the changes in pore pressure that would have been observed.

Rupture bands in clay are too thin to be detected radiographically as zones of changed density but they can be traced from step discontinuities in threads of lead paste injected into the sample. Typical examples of ruptures sketched from radiographs are shown in Fig. 26 for constant load tests on

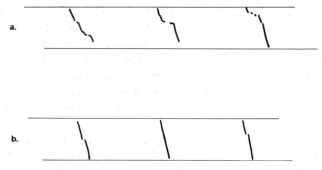

FIG. 26.   Ruptures observed in radiographs of simple shear tests on (a) kaolin; (b) Gault clay. (Sketches of radiographs of threads of lead paste.)

kaolin and Gault clay ($I_p = 0.35$). The ruptures, which in general appear at around peak shear stress, clearly propagate from the regions of normal stress concentration at the top and bottom of the sample. Though the uniformity of stress and strain for clays in simple shear testing may be superior to that of sand, the stress conditions around these ends of the sample are certainly not the average conditions, and statements about the relation of the orientation of the ruptures to the orientation of the principal stresses are not feasible at the ends of the sample. However, in the tests on kaolin the system of ruptures formed almost at the same time throughout the sample and in the central region, away from the stress concentrations, it appears that their orientation lies between the directions of maximum stress obliquity and of zero extension. For the kaolin (Fig. 26(a)) the ruptures extend across the centre of the sample at an angle of 5–15° to the horizontal. For the slightly more plastic Gault clay the ruptures die out— the tip effect is able to diffuse into the surrounding clay.

Once ruptures have been observed then continued shearing provides information relevant to the ruptured and not the intact soil and correct interpretation is unclear. Before peak shear stress, it appears from the data of Borin (1973), who had sufficient load cells around his samples to be able to deduce the complete stress state, that a relation

$$R = k \tan \psi \tag{7}$$

exists (Fig. 27) with $k \simeq 0.4$ for kaolin. This value of k corresponds, through eqn (9), to a value of earth pressure coefficient at rest $K_0 = 0.6$ (slightly lower than the value $K_0 = 0.64$ quoted for kaolin by Nadarajah (1973)). It should be noted that the application of eqn (7) can only be demonstrated for monotonic loading of normally consolidated clay—a much more restrictive set of circumstances than for sand.

Combining eqns (10) and (11) an expression for the mobilised angle of friction ϕ_m can be obtained:

$$\sin \phi_m = (R^2 + k^2)/(R^2 + 2k - k^2) \tag{22}$$

and from considerations of the geometry of Mohr's circle (Fig. 28) the angles to the horizontal of the planes on which this maximum stress ratio is mobilised can be found

$$\left.\begin{array}{c} \theta_1 \\ \theta_2 \end{array}\right\} = \pi/4 + \phi_m/2 \pm \psi \tag{23}$$

The variation of the angles ϕ_m, ψ, θ_1 and θ_2 with the angle of friction mobilised on the horizontal plane, $\tan^{-1} R$, is shown in Fig. 29 for $k = 0.4$ in eqn (7).

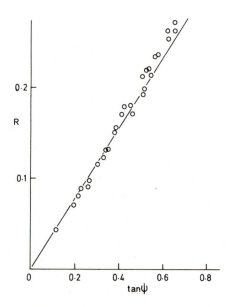

FIG. 27. Relationship between R and $\tan\psi$ for simple shear tests on normally consolidated kaolin (data from Borin (1973)).

Randolph and Wroth (1981) have suggested that de Josselin de Jong's book-stack analogy (Fig. 10) should be invoked for the correct interpretation of undrained simple shear tests on clay so that failure is initiated when the state of stress corresponds to that shown in Fig. 9(c) with the maximum permissible angle of friction being mobilised on vertical rupture planes. They show typical results from a simple shear test on kaolin

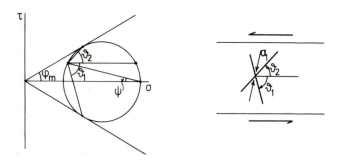

FIG. 28. Orientation of planes of maximum stress obliquity in simple shear sample.

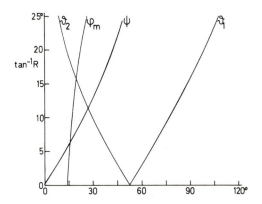

FIG. 29.   Variation of angles ϕ_m, ψ, θ_1, θ_2 with $\tan^{-1} R$ for $k = 0\cdot4$.

of Borin (1973) (Fig. 30) which indicate that the friction mobilised on vertical planes is indeed greater than that mobilised on horizontal planes. Unfortunately Borin did not use radiography to detect the presence of ruptures. The book-stack analogy only really makes sense if it is assumed that ruptures must form along zero extension directions and must be planes along which maximum stress obliquity is mobilised.

An alternative interpretation is now possible for Airey's tests and probably other tests conducted in circular simple shear apparatus with a

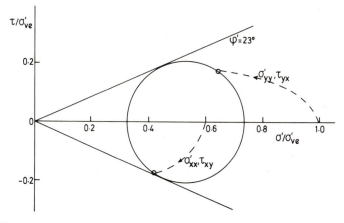

FIG. 30.   Measured stress path and failure state for undrained simple shear test on normally consolidated kaolin (data from Borin (1973); after Randolph and Wroth (1981)).

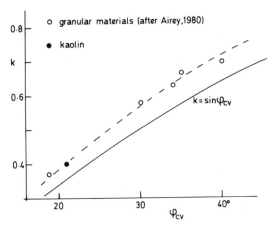

FIG. 31.   Data of constant k in eqn (7) and ϕ_{cv}, the angle of friction for constant volume shearing.

surrounding membrane. The ruptures actually observed in Airey's tests (Fig. 26) are in the sub-horizontal θ_2 direction of Fig. 28. This observation then ties in with the curves of Fig. 29: for $\phi_m = 23°$ (the same value used by Randolph and Wroth in Fig. 30) $\tan^{-1} R = 21°$, $\psi = 43.9°$, and $\theta_2 = 12.6°$.

The use of eqn (7) even for normally consolidated clays requires a value of k. Data collected by Airey (1984) show an approximate relationship between k and ϕ_{cv} the angle of friction for constant volume shearing (Fig. 31). The data lie above the line

$$k = \sin \phi_{cv} \qquad (24)$$

which might be expected if the principal axes of strain increment and stress coincided during constant volume shearing ($\xi = \psi$). However, whereas it was shown above that there were fairly clear rules governing the relative values of ξ, ψ and χ (the direction of the principal stress increment) for sands, Borin's (1973) data show fairly convincingly that such rules do not exist for clays.

For situations where eqn (7) does not apply, an alternative, very approximate estimation of the stress σ_{xx} is possible using measurements of the change in radial stress acting on the membrane (from the change in resistance of the strain gauge wire with which it is bound). Very approximately,

$$\Delta\sigma_r = k_2(\Delta\sigma_{xx} + \Delta\sigma_2) \qquad (25)$$

with k_2 equal to about 0.5, and, also approximately,

$$\sigma_2 = k_3 s \cos^2 \phi_{cv} \qquad (26)$$

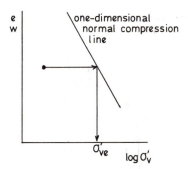

FIG. 32.   Equivalent consolidation pressure σ'_{ve}.

with k_3 lying between 0.9 and 1.0. Equation (26) was discussed by Bishop (1966) with reference to data from plane strain tests on a number of soils. Sketchley (1973) reports $\sigma_2 \simeq 0.83s$ for plane strain, biaxial tests on kaolin.

The comparison of data from different simple shear tests on clays is facilitated if some allowance is made for the differing water contents of different samples and the possibly changing water content during any particular test. The most convenient way, provided some information about the one-dimensional normal compression of the clay is available, is to use the equivalent consolidation pressure σ'_{ve} (Fig. 32) as suggested by Terzaghi (1931) and Hvorslev (1937). This is the pressure which would in one-dimensional normal compression produce the current void ratio or water content of the clay. Evidently, then, $\sigma'_v = \sigma'_{ve}$ during one-dimensional normal compression. Also σ'_{ve} remains constant during an undrained or constant volume test, but in a drained test in which the void ratio steadily drops, the equivalent consolidation pressure steadily rises.

Typical results of a series of drained and undrained simple shear tests on normally consolidated and overconsolidated kaolin are shown in the normalised stress space $\sigma_{yy}/\sigma'_{ve} : \tau_{yx}/\sigma'_{ve}$ in Fig. 33. Though there is still a difference between the paths of constant load (drained) and constant volume (undrained) tests, particularly for the normally consolidated clay, the effect of the normalisation is to bring the two sets of data together. Using this normalisation results of drained tests could be easily used to produce estimates of strength in undrained tests of an acceptable engineering accuracy.

It is a feature of models of soil behaviour such as Cam clay (Roscoe and Schofield, 1963) that similar paths in $s'/\sigma'_{ve} : t/\sigma'_{ve}$ principal stress space are to be expected for drained and undrained tests on, in particular, normally

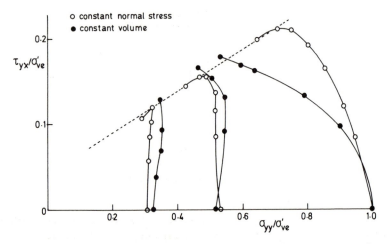

FIG. 33.   Drained (constant normal stress σ_n) and 'undrained' (constant volume) simple shear tests on kaolin.

consolidated samples. These simple shear tests have not provided data of s and t—they can only be inferred. However, there is no a priori reason why even in $s'/\sigma'_{ve} : t/\sigma'_{ve}$ let alone $\sigma_{yy}/\sigma'_{ve} : \tau_{yx}/\sigma'_{ve}$ space identity of paths should be expected. Indeed, there is experimental evidence from conventional triaxial tests to show that the increased kinematic freedom of the drained condition permits soils to exist in normalised principal effective stress states that lie further from the origin than those of undrained tests.

It has become clear from tests on clays in the simple shear apparatus that uniformity of boundary stresses and internal deformations is very much better than for tests on sands. Consequently it is permissible to present with more confidence the results of routine simple shear tests on clays. It may be noted also that in cyclic simple shear tests on clay described by Airey (1984) there is no evidence of the build up of non-uniformity that characterised the tests of Budhu (1979) on sand.

5   CONCLUSIONS

It is not necessary to dismiss the use of simple shear apparatus out of hand. It is the purpose of experimental research with this apparatus to indicate the problems that are associated with it and the ranges of testing capabilities for which these shortcomings may not be significant.

Non-uniformity of boundary stresses, and development of internal inhomogeneities and ruptures have been identified as the principal shortcomings. It is evident that in many tests, particularly on sands, these shortcomings may invalidate the experimental results. It appears from recent work that conditions improve as the plasticity of the soil being tested increases.

Of course, elaborate instrumentation and radiographic examination are only possible under research conditions. In routine use, therefore, the presence of non-uniformities will pass undetected. Care is always needed in the interpretation of the experimental results.

REFERENCES

AAS, G. (1980). Vurdering av korttidsstabilitet i leire på basis av undrenert skjaerfasthet, NGI publication 132, Beretning over NGIs virksomhet fra 1 Jan 1978–31 Dec 1979, pp. 21–30.

AIREY, D. W. (1980). Soils in the circular simple shear apparatus, MPhil thesis, Cambridge University.

AIREY, D. W. (1984). Clays in circular simple shear apparatus, PhD thesis, Cambridge University.

AIREY, D. W. and WOOD, D. M. (1984). Discussion: Specimen size effect in simple shear test, J. Geotechnical Engineering, ASCE, 110(3), 439–42.

ARTHUR, J. R. F., CHUA, K. S. and DUNSTAN, T. (1977). Induced anisotropy in a sand, Géotechnique, 27(1), 13–30.

BISHOP, A. W. (1966). The strength of soils as engineering materials. Sixth Rankine lecture, Géotechnique, 16(2), 91–128.

BJERRUM, L. and LANDVA, A. (1966). Direct simple-shear tests on a Norwegian quick clay, Géotechnique, 16(1), 1–20.

BORIN, D. L. (1973). The behaviour of saturated kaolin in the Simple Shear Apparatus, PhD thesis, Cambridge University.

BROMS, B. B. and CASBARIAN, A. O. (1965). Effects of rotation of the principal stress axes and of the intermediate principal stress on the shear strength, Proc. 6th Int. Conf. on Soil Mechs and Foundation Eng., Montreal, 1, 179–83.

BUDHU, M. (1979). Simple shear deformation of sands, PhD thesis, Cambridge University.

BUDHU, M. (1984). Non-uniformities imposed by simple shear apparatus, Canadian Geotechnical Journal, 21(1), 125–37.

COLE, E. R. L. (1967). The behaviour of soils in the simple shear apparatus, PhD thesis, Cambridge University.

COSSERAT, E. and COSSERAT, F. (1909). Théorie des corps déformables, Librairie Scientifique A. Hermann et Fils, Paris.

DE JOSSELIN DE JONG, G. (1971). Discussion: Session 2. Stress–strain behaviour of soils, Proc. Roscoe Memorial Symp., Ed. Parry, R. H. G., G. T. Foulis & Co., Henley-on-Thames, pp. 258–61.

EL-SOHBY, M. A. (1964). The behaviour of particulate materials under stress, PhD thesis, Manchester University.

FUNG, Y. C. (1965). *Foundations of solid mechanics*, Prentice-Hall, Englewood Cliffs.

HIGHT, D. W., GENS, A. and SYMES, M. J. (1983). The development of a new hollow cylinder apparatus for investigating the effects of principal stress rotation in soils, *Géotechnique*, **33**(4), 355-83.

HOULSBY, G. T. (1981). A study of plasticity theories and their applicability to soils, PhD thesis, University of Cambridge.

HOULSBY, G. T. and WROTH, C. P. (1980). Strain and displacement discontinuities in soil, *Proc. ASCE*, **106**(EM4), 753-71.

HVORSLEV, M. J. (1937). Über die Festigkeitseigenschaften gestörter bindiger Böden, Ingeniørvidenskabelige Skrifter A no 45, København.

KOITER, W. T. (1964). Couple-stresses in the theory of elasticity, *Koninklijke Nederlandse Akademie van Wetenschappen, Proc. Series B (Physical Sciences)*, **67**(1), 17-44.

LUCKS, A. S., CHRISTIAN, J. T., BRANDOW, G. E. and HÖEG, K. (1972). Stress conditions in NGI simple shear test, *Proc. ASCE*, **98**(SM1), 155-60.

MINDLIN, R. D. (1963). Influence of couple-stresses on stress concentrations, *Experimental Mechanics*, January, 1-7.

MOUSSA, A. A. (1974). *Radial stresses in sand in constant volume static and cyclic simple shear tests*, Norwegian Geotechnical Institute, Internal Report 51505-10.

NADARAJAH, V. (1973). Stress-strain properties of lightly overconsolidated clays. PhD thesis, Cambridge University.

OCHIAI, H. (1975). The behaviour of sands in direct shear tests (in Japanese), *Journal of Japanese Society of Soil Mechs and Foundation Eng.*, **15**(4), 93-100.

ODA, M. (1975). On the relation $\tau/\sigma_n = k \tan \psi$ in the simple shear test, *Soils and Foundations*, **15**(4), 35-41.

RANDOLPH, M. F. and WROTH, C. P. (1981). Application of the failure state in undrained simple shear to the shaft capacity of driven piles, *Géotechnique*, **31**(1), 143-57.

ROSCOE, K. H. (1953). An apparatus for the application of simple shear to soil samples, *Proc. 3rd Int. Conf. on Soil Mechs and Foundation Eng.*, Zurich, **1**, 186-91.

ROSCOE, K. H. and SCHOFIELD, A. N. (1963). Mechanical behaviour of an idealised 'wet' clay, *Proc. 2nd European Conf. on Soil Mechs and Foundation Eng.*, Wiesbaden, **1**, 47-54.

ROSCOE, K. H., SCHOFIELD, A. N. and WROTH, C. P. (1958). On the yielding of soils, *Géotechnique*, **8**(1), 22-52.

ROSCOE, K. H., ARTHUR, J. R. F. and JAMES, R. G. (1963). The determination of strains in soils by an X-ray method, *Civil Engineering and Public Works Review*, **58**(684), 873-6 and (685), 1009-12.

ROSCOE, K. H., BASSETT, R. H. and COLE, E. R. L. (1967). Principal axes observed during simple shear of a sand, *Proc. Geotechnical Conf.*, Oslo, **1**, 231-7.

ROWE, P. W. (1962). The stress-dilatancy relation for static equilibrium of an assembly of particles in contact, *Proc. Roy. Soc. A*, **269**, 500-27.

SCARPELLI, G. and WOOD, D. M. (1982). Experimental observations of shear band patterns in direct shear tests, *Proc. IUTAM Symp. on Deformation and failure of granular materials*, Eds Vermeer, P. A. and Luger, H. J., A. A. Balkema, Rotterdam, pp. 473–84.

SKETCHLEY, C. J. (1973). The behaviour of kaolin in plane strain, PhD thesis, Cambridge University.

STROUD, M. A. (1971). The behaviour of sand at low stress levels in the simple shear apparatus, PhD thesis, Cambridge University.

TATSUOKA, F. and ISHIHARA, K. (1974). Yielding of sand in triaxial compression, *Soils and Foundations*, **14**(2), 63–76.

TAYLOR, D. W. (1948). *Fundamentals of soil mechanics*, John Wiley, New York.

TERZAGHI, K. (1931). Festigkeitseigenschaften der Schüttungen, Sedimente und Gele, In *Handbuch der physikalischen und technischen Mechanik*, Eds Auerbuch, F. and Hort, W., Leipzig, Barth, **4**(2), 513–78.

VARDOULAKIS, I. (1978). Equilibrium bifurcation of granular earth bodies, *Advances in analysis of geotechnical instabilities*, University of Waterloo Press, SM Study no 13, Paper 3, 65–119.

VARDOULAKIS, I. (1980). Shear band inclination and shear modulus of sand in biaxial tests, *Int. J. for Numerical and Analytical Methods in Geomechanics*, **4**, 103–19.

VERMEER, P. A. (1982). A simple shear-band analysis using compliances, *Proc. IUTAM Symp. on Deformation and failure of granular materials*, Delft, Eds Vermeer, P. A. and Luger, H. J., A. A. Balkema, Rotterdam, pp. 493–9.

VUCETIC, M. and LACASSE, S. (1982). Specimen size effect in simple shear tests, *Proc. ASCE*, **108**(GT12), 1567–85.

WOOD, D. M. (1980). *Stress states in tests on sand in the Simple Shear Apparatus*, Cambridge University Engineering Dept., Report CUED/D-Soils TR97 (1980).

WOOD, D. M., DRESCHER, A. and BUDHU, M. (1979). On the determination of the stress state in the simple shear apparatus, *Geotechnical Testing Journal*, *ASTM*, **2**(4), 211–22.

WRIGHT, D. K., GILBERT, P. A. and SAADA, A. S. (1978). Shear devices for determining dynamic soil properties, *Proc. ASCE Specialty Conf.*, *Earthquake Engineering and Soil Dynamics*, Pasadena, **2**, 1056–75.

YOUD, T. L. and CRAVEN, T. N. (1975). Lateral stress in sands during cyclic loading, *Proc. ASCE*, **101**(GT2), 217–21.

Chapter 7

BEHAVIOUR OF GRANULAR SOIL SPECIMENS IN THE TRIAXIAL COMPRESSION TEST

I. VARDOULAKIS and A. DRESCHER

*Department of Civil and Mineral Engineering,
University of Minnesota, Minneapolis, USA*

1 INTRODUCTION

The triaxial compression test on cylindrical soil specimens is the most commonly performed test for determining the various mechanical properties of soils. It is used world-wide in design projects as well as in research work to evaluate the strength parameters of soils. Its impact on past and present research is overwhelming, and probably will remain significant in the near future. In fact, the development of modern, non-linear soil mechanics in recent decades heavily depends on experimental findings from the triaxial test. The majority of the sophisticated constitutive models already proposed for soils either originate or exclusively refer to the stress and strain states that are induced in the soil specimen tested in the triaxial apparatus. However, with the increasing interest in a more detailed and accurate description of the mechanical behaviour of soils, some criticism has been raised concerning the relevance of this test in testing soil properties. This criticism points to insufficiently controlled uniformity in the deformation in the soil sample, and consequently to non-uniformity in the induced state of stress.

In this work, we will briefly discuss the objectives of the triaxial compression test on soils, and the assumptions involved. Then, we present an approximate analysis of the influence of the boundary imperfections on the stress state in the cylindrical soil specimen. Making use of bifurcation theory, we discuss the diffuse and localised inhomogeneities that are

215

experimentally observed in the deformation mode. The theoretical analysis and the experimental data are compared, and an idealised description of the material behaviour is discussed. The analysis is restricted to cohesionless soils that are tested when dry or fully drained, i.e. no effect of water pore pressure is incorporated in the analysis. The material presented in this work comprises the results of the authors' recent studies rather than a comprehensive, 'state of the art' literature review. The experimental results were obtained at the Institute of Soil and Rock Mechanics, University of Karlsruhe, within an ongoing research program sponsored by the Deutsche Forschungsgemeinschaft (DFG, Grant No. Gu 103/13,16,20).

2 TRIAXIAL COMPRESSION TEST AS MATERIAL ELEMENT TEST

The fundamental assumption underlying the triaxial test is that the concept of a material continuum may be applied to dispersed media such as soils. Next, it is tacitly assumed that the mechanical behaviour of soils can adequately be described within the framework of local theories, i.e. theories in which physical quantities or notions such as stress, strain, density, etc., are assigned to a point of continuum, and no characteristic dimension or dimensions are introduced. It follows, then, that the mechanical response is exactly the same for an infinitesimal element and for a finite volume of the material, provided all the quantities are uniformly distributed throughout. Thus, the material response can be tested on a uniform soil specimen subject to uniform stress and strain.

In the triaxial compression test, a cylindrical soil specimen is subjected to a uniform axisymmetric confining pressure, and to an axial displacement applied at the ends of the specimen. It is assumed that a uniform, axisymmetric state of stress and strain is induced in the specimen. The validity of this assumption cannot be fully proven, for only the displacements can be measured experimentally, and the resulting strains calculated. However, non-uniformity in the displacement field implies non-uniformity in the stress field; and if this does occur, it renders the significance of the triaxial test questionable.

There are various experimental techniques that permit the displacements at the boundaries and in the interior of the specimen to be determined. Several corrections are made to minimise errors, e.g. membrane penetration and bedding error, in the displacement measurements. Extensive and precise measurements revealed that in general, and especially at large strains, the deformation of the specimen is non-uniform.

Furthermore, various modes of non-uniformity have been identified. Disregarding the non-uniformities induced by inappropriate preparation of the soil specimen, the various modes of deformation depend primarily on the slenderness of the specimen, and on the boundary conditions present at both ends of the specimen. In the standard triaxial compression test, a specimen of the slenderness $H/2R = 2/1$ is used, and the vertical displacements are applied through the upper loading platen, which is pin-connected with the loading piston. The relatively high slenderness and the pin-connection frequently trigger an unsymmetric deformation in the form of buckling. Buckling can be suppressed if shorter specimens and end platens that do not tilt are used. The other modes of non-uniform deformation are strongly influenced by the specimen's inability to displace laterally at the ends. The diameter of the end platens is usually equal to that of the specimen, and the rubber membrane, which encloses the specimen, and the friction at the ends prevent any lateral motion. Enlarged and lubricated end platens reduce the risk of bulging or barrelling. Bulging and shear band formation also depend on the density of the tested material; dense granular materials are more sensitive to these forms of inhomogeneities.

The inhomogeneities in deformation that are observed in the triaxial compression test have stimulated theoretical and experimental work, with the aim of better understanding and eliminating these undesirable phenomena which obscure the true behaviour of the material. For example, there is growing evidence that some of the basic features of the mechanical behaviour of granular soils, namely their softening, may predominantly result from inhomogeneities in deformation. On the other hand, the theory of bifurcation provides a possible explanation of a spontaneous loss of homogeneity in deformation in the tested specimen.

In the following section, we discuss the inhomogeneities in the deformation resulting from the boundary imperfections, and we present an approximate approach for incorporating this influence in the interpretation of the triaxial test. Next, the inhomogeneities spontaneously occurring in the tested specimen are analysed.

3   INHOMOGENEITIES DUE TO BOUNDARY IMPERFECTIONS

3.1 End Platen Friction

Numerous experimental results, obtained from compression tests on soils and other solids, indicate that a specimen's behaviour may be influenced significantly by friction that may develop between the specimen and the loading platens. The friction affects the mode of deformation of the specimen as well as the mechanism of failure. High friction prevents the portions of the specimen in contact with the loading platens from displacing laterally, thus imposing severe boundary constraints on the deformation mode. Uniform, cylindrical deformation is not possible, and a non-uniform mode, in the form of barrelling, occurs, even at relatively small vertical strains. Kirkpatrick and Belshaw (1968) and Deman (1975) used an X-ray technique to investigate the displacement field in cylindrical specimens of dry sand in triaxial compression tests with rough and smooth end platens. These experiments have shown that rough platens support the development of rigid cones at the ends of the specimen (Fig. 1(a)). As soon as the roughness of the end platens (the diameter of which is greater than that of the specimen) is reduced by polishing and by adding a thin layer of lubricant, rigid cones do not develop and a fairly uniform deformation develops for small and moderate strains, Fig. 1(b). At large strains, however, inhomogeneity of deformation in the form of bulging or barrelling may occur. Similar results were obtained by Bishop and Green (1965), who studied how the specimen's slenderness and the end friction influenced the deformation mode of a dry sand in triaxial compression.

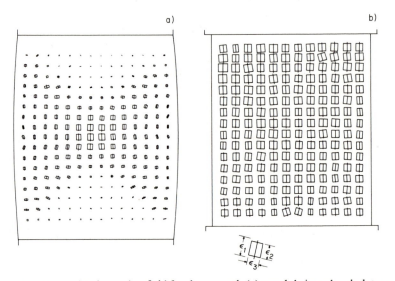

FIG. 1.   Internal deformation field for dense sand; (a) non-lubricated end platens, (b) lubricated end platens (Deman, 1975).

Although it has long been recognised that the friction of the end platens influences the mode of deformation in triaxial compression, little attention has been focused on the quality of the lubricant used in reducing the friction and its working conditions present in the triaxial test on granular material. In fact, the working conditions seem to be complex. The lubricant is placed between the flat, polished metal end platen and a thin rubber disc, which separates the soil particles from the lubricant. This rubber disc is flexible enough for the particles to deform the disc locally, and to produce an uneven gap. The coarser the particles are, the more pronounced are the local irregularities or 'asperities'. No systematic study of the influence of the working conditions in the lubricant layer, and the time effects involved, is available. However, it is interesting to refer to the work by Zangl (1971) and Molenkamp (1983) to illustrate, approximately at least, the significance of the problem. Molenkamp (1983) reports tests with two silicon lubricants of initial thickness $h = 45\,\mu m$, separated by a latex disc with thickness $t = 300\,\mu m$ from a sand of a mean grainsize $D = 160\,\mu m$. Figure 2 presents the variation of the measured coefficient of friction f with the normal stress applied in tests with constant deformation rates. Similar tests, conducted by Zangl (1971) in a direct shear test set-up, yield results depicted in Fig. 3, where f is plotted as a function of the displacement and the normal stress. Interestingly, the coefficient of friction increases with increasing displacement and decreasing normal stress. For very low normal stresses the coefficient of friction is surprisingly high. One may hypothesise that the dependence of f on the displacement and the normal stress can schematically be represented as in Fig. 4.

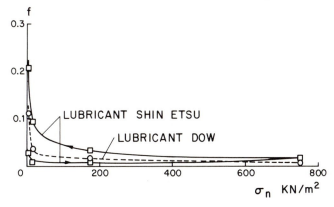

FIG. 2.   Friction coefficient f versus normal stress σ_n (Molenkamp, 1983).

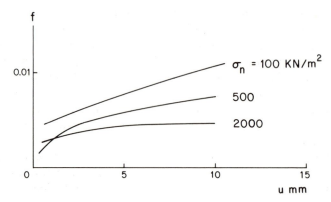

FIG. 3.   Friction coefficient f versus normal stress σ_n and displacement u (Zangl, 1971).

An attempt to incorporate the effect of the platen's friction in the interpretation of the results of the triaxial compression and extension test on granular soils is given by Drescher and Vardoulakis (1982). In the following discussion, their analysis is recapitulated and modified by including the variation of f with the lateral displacement and the normal stress at the platens/specimen interface.

The basis for the analysis presented by Drescher and Vardoulakis (1982) is the so-called method of differential slices. This method originates from the work of Janssen (1895) and has been applied to numerous engineering problems, such as the flow of bulk solids in silos and hoppers, the compression of short cylinders of rock-like materials, and a trap-door problem for a granular soil body.

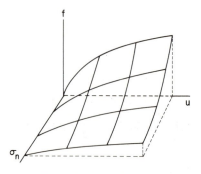

FIG. 4.   Model relationship $f = f(u, \sigma_n)$.

In the slice method, the stresses acting over a finite dimension of the slice cut out from a cylindrical specimen are averaged. This results in ordinary differential equilibrium equations, instead of partial differential equations, for the stresses within the specimen. With an additional assumption relating the average stresses to the stress tensor components at selected points of the slice, the equilibrium equations can be integrated, and the stresses determined, provided that the boundary conditions are specified. The average vertical stress or the total vertical force corresponding to a given confining pressure can then be evaluated. Drescher and Vardoulakis (1982) assumed that locally the granular material can be identified as a rigid, perfectly plastic body that obeys the linear Mohr–Coulomb yield condition and is characterised by the true mobilised angle of internal friction, $\Phi = $ constant, and zero cohesion. In the next sections, we analyse the influence of low and high levels of end platen friction on the measured vertical average stress in triaxial compression.

3.2 Compression at Low Platens Friction

Consider a triaxial compression test on a moderately slender, cylindrical specimen of sand. The specimen is placed between two rigid and flat loading platens, the diameter of which is greater than that of the specimen. The platens are prevented from tilting; thus, uniform vertical displacement can be applied to the ends of the specimen upon loading. If the platens are smooth and a thin layer of lubricant is applied, the specimen deforms fairly uniformly while preserving its cylindrical shape. In spite of reduced end friction, small tangential stresses may still develop between the platens and the soil specimen, depending on the mobilised coefficient of interface friction f. Thus, the stress vector acting at the interface is inclined at an angle v with respect to the normal, given by:

$$v = \arctan f \tag{1}$$

In the presence of tangential stresses at the upper and lower ends of the specimen, the state of stress in the specimen cannot be uniform, although this non-uniformity is not substantial, and probably confined to a small region in the vicinity of the end platens. To account for these tangential stresses, an elemental slice is selected as in Fig. 5(a). At both ends of the slice, normal σ_n and tangential σ_t stresses act, related by:

$$\sigma_t = \sigma_n \tan v \tag{2}$$

Over the height of the slice, however, an average radial $\bar{\sigma}_{rr}$ and circumferential $\bar{\sigma}_{\theta\theta}$ stresses exist. If the Haar–Karman hypothesis,

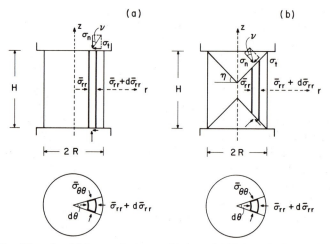

FIG. 5.   Slices for (a) low end platens friction, (b) high end platens friction.

$\bar{\sigma}_{rr} = \bar{\sigma}_{\theta\theta}$, is utilised, the only non-trivial equilibrium equation is:

$$\frac{d\bar{\sigma}_{rr}}{dr} + \frac{2}{H}\sigma_t = 0 \tag{3}$$

Equation (3) can be integrated, provided a relationship between $\bar{\sigma}_{rr}$ and σ_t is known. This relationship can be obtained from the assumption that the soil is at plastic yielding everywhere in the slice, and that the stresses satisfy the Mohr–Coulomb yield condition. At the interface a stress discontinuity is introduced, with the inclination dependent on the current value of v (see Drescher and Vardoulakis, 1982). It turns out that a linear relationship between $\bar{\sigma}_{rr}$ and $\bar{\sigma}_t$ holds:

$$\sigma_t = M\bar{\sigma}_{rr} \tag{4}$$

where

$$M = \frac{\sin\Phi\sin2\gamma_1\sin\gamma_2}{(\sin\Phi - 1)\sin(2\gamma_1 + \gamma_2)}$$

$$\gamma_2 = \arctan\frac{\sin v}{\sin\Phi} - v \tag{5}$$

$$\gamma_1 = \arctan\left\{\frac{\dfrac{1+\cos\gamma_2}{\sin\gamma_2} + \left[\left(\dfrac{1+\cos\gamma_2}{\sin\gamma_2}\right)^2 + \cos^2\Phi\right]^{1/2}}{1+\sin\Phi}\right\}$$

Equation (3) can be written as:

$$\frac{d\bar{\sigma}_{rr}}{dr} + 2\frac{M}{H}\bar{\sigma}_{rr} = 0 \tag{6}$$

where M is in general a function of the lateral displacement u_r and the normal stress σ_n. For $v = $ constant, $M = $ constant, and eqn (6) can easily be integrated with the boundary conditions $r = R$, $\bar{\sigma}_{rr} = \sigma_c$, where σ_c is the confining pressure. Utilising eqn (2), and integrating the normal stresses over the specimen cross-section, the following expression for the average vertical stress $\bar{\sigma}_{zz}$ is obtained:

$$\bar{\sigma}_{zz} = \sigma_c \frac{2\kappa^2}{M\tan v}\left[\exp\left(\frac{M}{\kappa}\right) - \frac{M}{\kappa} - 1\right] \tag{7}$$

where

$$\kappa = \frac{H}{2R} \tag{8}$$

For $v = v(u_r, \sigma_n)$, $M \neq$ constant, and numerical integration of eqn (6) can be performed.

Knowing the average vertical stress $\bar{\sigma}_{zz}$ and the confining pressure σ_c, the apparent angle of internal friction of the tested soil can be evaluated from:

$$\Phi_a = \arcsin\frac{\bar{\sigma}_{zz} - \sigma_c}{\bar{\sigma}_{zz} + \sigma_c} \tag{9}$$

Alternatively, the true angle of friction Φ can be found, if the apparent angle Φ_a is determined from an experiment.

In Fig. 6 the dependence of the apparent angle of friction Φ_a on the ratio $2R/H$, and the true angle of friction Φ for $v = $ constant is presented. Figure 7 shows the dependence of Φ_a on the mobilised angle of interface friction $v \neq $ constant. It was assumed that the function $v = v(u_r, \sigma_n)$, see Fig. 4, can be approximated by a portion of a parabolic-hyperboloid:

$$v = (a^2\sigma_n^2 + b^2u_r^2)^{1/2} - a\sigma_n \tag{10}$$

with a and b selected to match approximately the results of Molenkamp (1983) and Zangl (1971). Figure 8 shows several cross-sections of the selected $f = f(u_r, \sigma_n)$ surface. Linear distribution of u_r over the radius of the specimen was assumed. The initial ratio $2R_0/H_0 = 0.833$, the ratio $d\varepsilon_{rr}/d\varepsilon_{zz} = 1.2$, the true angle of internal friction $\Phi = 30°$, and two values for the confining pressure $\sigma_c = 10\,kN/m^2$ and $\sigma_c = 100\,kN/m^2$, respectively,

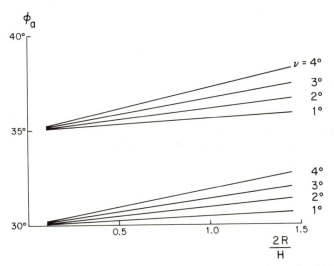

FIG. 6. Apparent angle of internal friction Φ_a versus the ratio $2R/H$ for $v = \text{constant}$; homogeneous deformation.

were selected. As the influence of σ_n on v is significant only for small normal stresses, this effect vanishes for moderate and high confining pressure. Figure 9 illustrates the distribution of the normal stress σ_n and the mobilised angle of interface friction v, over the radius of the interface, for $\sigma_c = 10\,\text{kN/m}^2$ and $\varepsilon_{zz} = 0 \cdot 1$.

3.3 Compression at High Friction

If the friction between the end platens and the specimen is high, then there is no relative lateral displacement at the interface, and most of the deformation takes place outside the rigid cones attached to the platens. A uniform, cylindrical deformation mode cannot be assumed, and the analysis presented in Section 3.2 does not hold. It is possible, however, to modify the analysis by selecting trapezoidal slices in the outer, wedge-shaped region (see Fig. 5(b)). The equilibrium equation in the r-direction is now:

$$\frac{d\bar{\sigma}_{rr}}{dr} + \frac{1}{r + R_1}(\bar{\sigma}_{rr} - \sigma_n + \sigma_t \cot \eta) = 0 \tag{11}$$

where

$$R_1 = \frac{H}{2 \tan \eta} - R \tag{12}$$

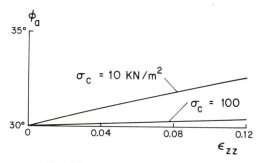

FIG. 7.   Apparent angle of internal friction Φ_a versus vertical strain ε_{zz} for $v = v(u_r, \sigma_n)$, eqn (10); homogeneous deformation.

and η is the angle of inclination of the sloping sides of the ring to the r-direction. In deriving eqn (11), the Haar–Karman hypothesis is utilised. The interface between the cones and the ring can be conceived as a weak discontinuity in the displacement increment field; inside the cone the displacements are vertical, outside the cone both vertical and radial components exist. If the material is treated as rigid and perfectly plastic, it is possible to determine the orientation of the principal stress directions along the discontinuity surface of the displacement increment, provided a flow rule is selected. Drescher and Vardoulakis (1982) considered several flow rules. For the sake of brevity, the associated flow rule is assumed below (see

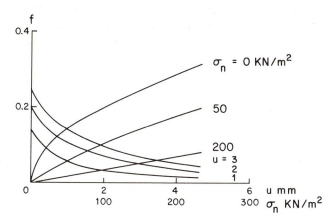

FIG. 8.   Cross-sections of the assumed $f = f(u, \sigma_n)$ surface.

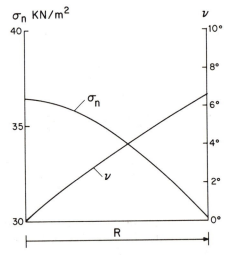

FIG. 9.   Distribution of normal stress σ_n and mobilised angle of interface friction ν over the specimen radius, corresponding to Fig. 7.

Drucker and Prager, 1952); this leads to the inclination χ of the principal stress σ_1 to the cone surface given by:

$$\chi = \frac{\pi}{4} + \frac{\Phi}{2} \tag{13}$$

Assuming, as is the case in the uniform deformation mode, both plastic yielding within the slice and discontinuous stress across the cone surface, the normal σ_n, tangential σ_t and the average radial stress $\bar{\sigma}_{rr}$ are related by:

$$\sigma_t = \sigma_n \tan \Phi$$
$$\sigma_t = M\bar{\sigma}_{rr} \tag{14}$$

where

$$M = \frac{\sin 2\Phi \sin 2\gamma_1}{2(\sin \Phi - 1)\cos(\Phi - 2\gamma_1 - 2\eta)}$$

$$\gamma_1 = \arctan\left\{ \frac{\dfrac{1 - \sin(2\eta - \Phi)}{\cos(2\eta - \Phi)} + \left[\left(\dfrac{1 - \sin(2\eta - \Phi)}{\cos(2\eta - \Phi)}\right)^2 + \cos^2\Phi\right]^{1/2}}{1 + \sin\Phi} \right\} \tag{15}$$

By utilising eqn (14), integrating eqn (11) with the boundary conditions $r = R$, $\bar{\sigma}_{rr} = \sigma_c$, and integrating the vertical components of σ_n and σ_t, the average vertical stress $\bar{\sigma}_{zz}$ acting over the specimens' cross-section can be identified as:

$$\bar{\sigma}_{zz} = 2\sigma_c M(\cot \Phi + \tan \eta) \left[\frac{(1 + \rho_1)^2}{2 - N} + \frac{\rho_1(1 + \rho_1)}{N - 1} - \frac{\rho_1^2(1/\rho_1 + 1)^N}{(N - 1)(2 - N)} \right]$$

(16)

where

$$N = 1 - M(\cot \Phi - \cot \eta)$$ (17)

$$\rho_1 = \frac{R_1}{R}$$

From eqn (16) it is seen that the friction between the specimen and the end platens does not enter the solution. Figure 10 illustrates the dependence of the apparent angle of internal friction Φ_a on the rigid cones' inclination η,

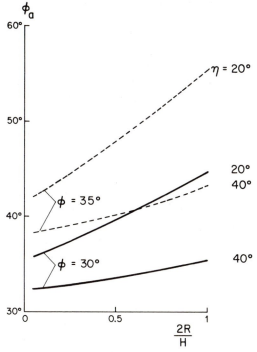

FIG. 10.   Apparent angle of internal friction Φ_a versus the ratio $2R/H$ and cone angle η; inhomogeneous deformation.

and the ratio $2R/H$ of the specimen. The apparent angle of internal friction increases with increasing $2R/H$ and with decreasing η.

The above analysis can be extended to very short specimens, where cones merge and form an inner core surrounded by a wedge-shaped ring. In the inner core, rectangular slices are assumed, whereas in the outer ring the slices are trapezoidal (see Drescher and Vardoulakis, 1982). Both the end friction and the flow rule affect the solution.

4   INHOMOGENEITIES DUE TO EQUILIBRIUM BIFURCATION

4.1 Equilibrium Bifurcation

It has been long anticipated that experiments with perfect boundary conditions (e.g. frictionless end platens) and perfectly homogeneous material should secure a homogeneous deformation within the tested specimen of soil. The inhomogeneities observed in the deformation have been attributed to the boundary imperfections present in the test, and the need to improve the technical realisation of the tests has been emphasised. For example, Roscoe et al. (1963) conclude: '... It has been shown that the distribution of deformation within triaxial specimens during drained compression tests is quite different from that occurring during drained extension tests. It is suggested that the results of these two types of tests cannot be compared for investigating the suitability of any failure criterion for soils. Before this can be achieved, more reliable methods must be developed for submitting soil specimens to uniform strain even as they approach failure...'. Following these suggestions several investigators have since developed a great variety of testing apparatus: for example, the 'independent stress control cell' of Green (1972), the 'biaxial apparatus' of Hambly (1972), or the 'true triaxial apparatus' of Goldscheider and Gudehus (1973). As implied in the above quotation from Roscoe et al. (1963), it was expected that the overall inhomogeneities in the deformation mode would be suppressed by using more refined equipment and specimens carefully prepared and lubricated. It turned out, however, that in general the inhomogeneities in the deformation cannot be avoided, although their appearance can be rendered less dramatic.

A different approach to the non-uniform modes of deformation observed in testing specimens of various materials originates from the fundamental work of Biot (1965) and Hill (1962) (cf. Hill and Hutchinson, 1975). The problem posed by these authors is, in short, whether the observed inhomogeneity may be explained as an inherent property of the material as tested under specified boundary conditions. In fact, any test on a specimen is a boundary value problem, and the boundary conditions, however perfect, may not necessarily guarantee a uniform deformation. Mathematically, the problem reduces to seeking a non-unique solution to the equations describing the equilibrium continuation of the initial mode of deformation for a given constitutive equation of the material. Non-uniqueness, or equilibrium bifurcation, of the deformation process means that at some critical state the deformation process may not follow its 'straight ahead' continuation, but turn to an entirely different mode. Typical examples of such losses of homogeneity are barrelling, bulging, buckling, necking and shear bands, which can be classified as continuous (diffuse) or discontinuous (localised) bifurcation modes.

In order to state properly the bifurcation problem, the constitutive equations describing the material behaviour must first be specified. Furthermore, there is need for a set of differential equations describing continued equilibrium and an exact mathematical description of the corresponding boundary conditions. Using notations and results from Vardoulakis (1983), we will outline in the following discussion the bifurcation analysis of the triaxial compression test.

The mechanical response of a granular material to triaxial compression can be represented by a stress ratio–shear strain curve and a volumetric strain–shear strain curve, Fig. 11(a) and (b). According to these figures, any state S is characterised by the following set of 'state' variables:

—the stress ratio: $\mu = (\sigma_{zz} - \sigma_{rr})/(2\sigma_{rr} + \sigma_{zz})$
—the tangent modulus: $h_t = \mathrm{d}\mu/\mathrm{d}\gamma$
—the secant modulus: $h_s = \mu/\gamma$
—the dilatancy modulus: $\beta = \mathrm{d}\varepsilon/\mathrm{d}\gamma$

where $\varepsilon = -(2\varepsilon_{rr} + \varepsilon_{zz})$ and $\gamma = \varepsilon_{zz} - \varepsilon_{rr}$ are the volumetric strain and shear strain, respectively. For a given granular material it is assumed that the above state variables are known functions of the initial density of the material and of the shear strain, γ. As indicated in Fig. 11, both the shear and volumetric behaviour is assumed to be rigid-plastic.

Let $\dot{\sigma}_{ij}$, $\dot{\varepsilon}_{ij}$ $(\dot{e}_{ij})$ and $\dot{\omega}_{ij}$ denote the Cauchy stress-rate, the strain-rate (deviator), and the spin tensor, respectively. Constitutive equations of the rate-type are correctly expressed in terms of objective stress-rate tensors (cf. Thomas, 1961), for example, the so-called Jaumann stress-rate:

$$\overset{\triangledown}{\sigma}_{ij} = \dot{\sigma}_{ij} - \dot{\omega}_{ik}\sigma_{kj} + \sigma_{ik}\dot{\omega}_{kj} \tag{18}$$

Any axisymmetric continuation of the initial homogeneous and axisymmetric state of stress and strain can be described by the following constitutive equations:

$$\overset{\triangledown}{\sigma}_{rr} = (1 - \mu)\dot{p} + \tfrac{3}{2}ph_s(\dot{\varepsilon}_{rr} - \dot{\varepsilon}_{\theta\theta}) - \tfrac{3}{2}ph_t\dot{e}_{zz}$$
$$\overset{\triangledown}{\sigma}_{zz} = (1 + 2\mu)\dot{p} + 3ph_t\dot{e}_{zz}$$
$$\overset{\triangledown}{\sigma}_{rr} - \overset{\triangledown}{\sigma}_{\theta\theta} = 3ph_s(\dot{\varepsilon}_{rr} - \dot{\varepsilon}_{\theta\theta})$$
$$\overset{\triangledown}{\sigma}_{rz} = 3ph_s\dot{\varepsilon}_{rz} \qquad (19)$$

where $p = (2\sigma_{rr} + \sigma_{zz})/3$ and $\dot{p}$ are the isotropic stress and its rate. Equation (19) also holds for initial homogeneous deformation, with $\dot{\varepsilon}_{rr} - \dot{\varepsilon}_{\theta\theta} = \dot{\varepsilon}_{rz} = 0$.

Following the ideas of Biot (1965), the differential equations for continued equilibrium are expressed in terms of the Jaumann stress-rate and also contain terms that reflect the influence of initial stress. Under axisymmetric conditions of initial stress, continued equilibrium is described by the following equations:

$$\frac{\partial \overset{\triangledown}{\sigma}_{rr}}{\partial r} + \frac{\partial \overset{\triangledown}{\sigma}_{rz}}{\partial z} + \frac{1}{r}(\overset{\triangledown}{\sigma}_{rr} - \overset{\triangledown}{\sigma}_{\theta\theta}) + 2\tau\frac{\partial \dot{\omega}_{zr}}{\partial z} = 0$$
$$\frac{\partial \overset{\triangledown}{\sigma}_{rz}}{\partial r} + \frac{\partial \overset{\triangledown}{\sigma}_{zz}}{\partial z} + \frac{1}{r}\overset{\triangledown}{\sigma}_{rz} + 2\tau\left(\frac{\partial \dot{\omega}_{zr}}{\partial r} + \frac{\partial \dot{\omega}_{zr}}{\partial z}\right) = 0 \qquad (20)$$

where

$$\tau = (\sigma_{zz} - \sigma_{rr})/2$$
$$\dot{\omega}_{zr} = -\frac{1}{2}\left(\frac{\partial V_z}{\partial r} - \frac{\partial V_r}{\partial z}\right) \qquad (21)$$

and V_r and V_z are the velocity (displacement increment) components. The velocity field is assumed to be a linear combination of the form:

$$V_i = \overset{\circ}{V}_i + \Delta V_i \qquad (22)$$

where $\overset{\circ}{V}_i$ corresponds to a continuation of the homogeneous triaxial compression and ΔV_i is an analytical description of the bifurcation mode being considered.

Now there may be introduced a stream function Ψ such that the velocity components are:

$$\Delta V_r = \frac{\partial \Psi}{\partial z} \qquad \Delta V_z = -\frac{1}{\delta^2}\cdot\frac{1}{r}\frac{\partial}{\partial r}(r, \Psi)$$
$$\delta^2 = -2\frac{\dot{\varepsilon}_{rr}}{\dot{\varepsilon}_{zz}} = \frac{1 + \beta}{1 - \beta/2} \qquad (23)$$

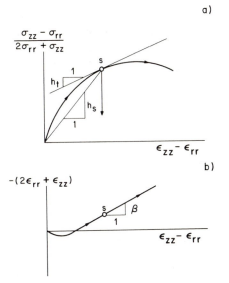

FIG. 11.   Stress ratio–shear strain and volumetric strain–shear strain curves for pressure insensitive granular material.

This means that the strain-rate and spin tensor components can be expressed in terms of the stream function Ψ. Introducing these components into the constitutive equations (19) and the resulting expression into the equilibrium equations (20), two differential equations result which contain a kinematically indeterminate rate of isotropic stress $\dot{p}$. Eliminating $\dot{p}$ from these equations finally results in one 4th order differential equation for the stream function Ψ:

$$L_r^2(\Psi) + A \frac{\partial^2}{\partial z^2} L_r(\Psi) + B \frac{\partial^4 \Psi}{\partial z^4} = 0 \tag{24}$$

where

$$
\begin{aligned}
L_r &= \frac{\partial^2}{\partial r^2} + \frac{1}{r}\frac{\partial}{\partial r} - \frac{1}{r^2} \\
A &= (a_0\gamma + a_1)/(1+\gamma) \\
B &= \lambda^2 \delta^2 (1-\gamma)/(1+\gamma) \\
a_0 &= -\lambda^2 + \delta^2 + a_2 h_t \\
a_2 &= (2+\delta^2)(2+\lambda^2)/3\mu \\
a_1 &= -\lambda^2 - \delta^2 + \lambda^2\delta^2 \\
\lambda^2 &= \frac{\sigma_{zz}}{\sigma_{rr}} = \frac{1+2\mu}{1-\mu}
\end{aligned}
\tag{25}
$$

Equation (24) is of the mixed type; i.e. the type of this equation depends on the value and sign of A and B. These coefficients, are according to eqn (25), functions of the state variables. Thus, the type of the differential equation (24) may change during the deformation process. The type of this equation depends on the type of its principal part (cf. Courant and Hilbert, 1968):

$$\frac{\partial^4 \Psi}{\partial r^4} + A \frac{\partial^4 \Psi}{\partial r^2 \partial z^2} + B \frac{\partial^4 \Psi}{\partial z^4} = 0 \qquad (26)$$

In the following sections, we will outline bifurcation modes that correspond either to an elliptic or to a hyperbolic differential equation (24).

4.2 Diffuse Bifurcation Modes

Diffuse, non-uniform deformation modes in the form of barrelling or bulging have been experimentally studied by Roscoe et al. (1963), Bishop and Green (1965), Kirkpatrick and Belshaw (1968), Deman (1975), Reades and Green (1976), and Hettler and Vardoulakis (1984). As was recognised by Bishop and Green (1973), bulging in the triaxial compression test on sand specimens is mainly controlled by the slenderness of the specimen. Figure 12 demonstrates the non-uniformity of deformation that occurs during the bulging of a cylindrical specimen. This test used lubricated and enlarged end platens and an upper plate that did not tilt. The lateral displacements were precisely monitored (Hettler and Vardoulakis, 1984). Figure 13(a) illustrates how the average vertical stress depends on the actual cross-section of the specimen, here in the case of a densely packed Karlsruhe sand, ($\gamma_t = 16 \cdot 9 \, \text{kN/m}^3$); whereas, Fig. 13(b) pertains to medium dense sand ($\gamma_t = 15 \cdot 6 \, \text{kN/m}^3$). From these results it is quite obvious that the dense sand specimen is more sensitive to bulging than the medium dense specimen. In the latter case, bulging is small and occurs at relatively large vertical strains.

These observations triggered theoretical investigations on diffuse bifurcation phenomena in sand specimens, as presented in a series of papers by Vardoulakis (1979, 1981, 1983). These papers study one of the possible diffuse bifurcation modes, namely, bulging.

The basis for the analysis of the onset of diffuse bifurcation is the differential equation (24). Since a smooth solution for the stream function is assumed for diffuse bifurcation, the stream function is set as:

$$\Psi = u(\rho) \sin \xi$$

$$\rho = \frac{r}{R} \qquad \xi = m\pi \frac{z}{H} \qquad (m = 1, 2, \ldots) \qquad (27)$$

(a)

(b)

FIG. 12.   Triaxial compression test with lubricated end platens; (a) initial state, (b) bulging at $\varepsilon_1 = 0\cdot3$ (Vardoulakis, 1979).

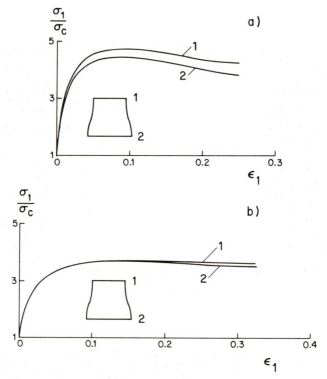

FIG. 13.   Stress ratio versus local strain; (a) dense specimen, (b) loose specimen
(Hettler and Vardoulakis, 1984).

so that the resulting velocity field is a possible description (sinusoidal) of the observed bulging. The resulting velocity field satisfies automatically the boundary conditions at the ends of the specimen; i.e. $\Delta V_z = \Delta \dot{\sigma}_{rz} = 0$. The differential equation (24) is then transformed to a 4th order ordinary differential equation for the unknown function $u(\rho)$. The solution to this equation is given in terms of Bessel functions of the first kind and first order:

$$u = C_1 u^{(1)} + C_2 u^{(2)}$$
$$u^{(i)} = J_1(K\Gamma_i \rho) \tag{28}$$

where C_i are the integration constants. The eigenvalue, K, is related to the slenderness of the specimen, $1/\kappa$ (see eqn (8)), by $K = 2m\pi/\kappa$ and Γ_i satisfies the characteristic equation:

$$\Gamma_i^4 + A\Gamma_i^2 + B = 0 \tag{29}$$

The remaining boundary conditions at the cylindrical surface of the specimen are:

$$\dot{\varepsilon}_{rz}|_{\rho=1} = 0 \qquad \overset{\triangledown}{\sigma}_{rr}|_{\rho=1} = 0 \qquad (30)$$

By introducing the solution of eqn (28) into these boundary conditions and considering non-trivial solutions for C_1 and C_2, an eigenvalue equation for K is derived. It is found that the physically significant solutions are those which correspond to complex characteristic roots of eqn (29), $\pm \Gamma$ and $\pm \bar{\Gamma}$, i.e. to an elliptic differential equation (24). The eigenvalue equation is:

$$\text{Im} \{(\delta^2 - \bar{\Gamma}^2) J_1(K\bar{\Gamma})[(\Gamma^2 + q_1)K\Gamma J_0(K\Gamma) + (q_2 - q_1)J_1(K\Gamma)]\} = 0 \qquad (31)$$

where

$$\begin{aligned}
q_i &= (q_{10}\gamma + q_{i1})/(1 + \gamma) \\
q_{10} &= q_{20} = \delta^2 + a_2 h_t \\
q_{11} &= \delta^2(\lambda^2 - 1) \\
q_{21} &= -\delta^2(\lambda^2 + 1)
\end{aligned} \qquad (32)$$

The bifurcation analysis showed that diffuse bulging takes place in the vicinity of the limiting state ($h_t = 0$), where the stress-ratio and the strain-rate ratio are approximately equal to their maximum (peak) values λ_p and δ_p. Diffuse bulging in triaxial compression was studied for a dense sand with $\lambda_p = 2\cdot145$ and $\delta_p = 1\cdot238$. The results are presented in Fig. 14 in terms of the critical combination of the tangent modulus $h_{t,cr}$ and the shear strain γ_{cr} at which a specimen, with a given slenderness $1/\kappa$, bifurcates. According to Fig. 14, slender specimens bifurcate earlier than more compact ones. The

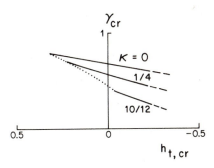

FIG. 14. Critical strain γ_{cr} versus critical tangent modulus $h_{t,cr}$ for bulging bifurcation mode (Vardoulakis, 1983).

critical shear strains, however, are relatively large. This prediction can be improved by assuming anisotropy with respect to the shear moduli in r, z- and r, θ-plane (Vardoulakis, 1983).

In any case, however, diffuse bifurcations of the perfectly lubricated specimen are predicted to occur in the close vicinity of the limiting state, i.e. for small values of the tangent modulus, h_t. In reality, the specimen is never perfectly lubricated, and the upper plate is never perfectly aligned to move parallel to itself. In addition to these imperfections of boundary and geometry, small fluctuations in density are also unavoidable. All these sources of error together result in bulging or barrelling at strain levels prior to the theoretical bifurcation point. According to Fig. 13, this sensitivity to imperfections is more pronounced in dense than in loose specimens. The essence of the diffuse mode bifurcation analysis remains that even under ideal boundary and geometry conditions and for specimens ideally uniform in density, the possibility of spontaneous formation of non-uniformities is mainly governed by the slenderness of the specimen.

4.3 Localised Bifurcation Modes

Localisation of deformation in specimens of granular materials has been studied experimentally by Arthur *et al.* (1977), Vardoulakis *et al.* (1978), Vardoulakis (1980), and more recently by Scarpelli and Wood (1982), Desrues *et al.* (1984) and Vardoulakis and Graf (1985).

Based on a classical treatment of Hadamard (1903), Hill (1962) and Mandel (1963, 1964) proposed that weak stationary discontinuities of the velocity gradient must be understood as localisations of the deformation into shear-bands (see also Hill and Hutchinson, 1975). In searching for discontinuous solutions of the differential equation (24), one considers states for which this equation is hyperbolic, and possesses real characteristics. If eqn (24) is hyperbolic, then the stream function Ψ can be assumed as:

$$\Psi = \Psi(n_1 r + n_3 z) \tag{33}$$

where n_1 and n_3 are real constants. The characteristic direction:

$$\tan \alpha = n_1 / n_3 \tag{34}$$

satisfies the characteristic equation (29):

$$\tan^4 \alpha + A \tan^2 \alpha + B = 0 \tag{35}$$

Following Hill and Hutchinson (1975), shear-band initiation is postulated

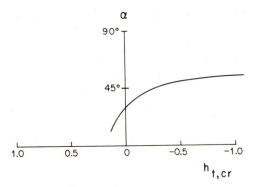

FIG. 15.   Shear band orientation angle α versus critical tangent modulus $h_{t,cr}$ for localised bifurcation mode (Vardoulakis, 1983).

to occur at the first bifurcation with real characteristic directions, i.e. at the state when the discriminant of eqn (35) is:

$$D = 0 \qquad (A < 0) \tag{36}$$

The theoretical result from a shear-band analysis based on the constitutive equation (19) is shown in Fig. 15 (Vardoulakis, 1983); the material properties correspond to the ones of Fig. 14. The present theory (Fig. 15) predicts that realistic values for the angle α correspond to the softening regime of the assumed stress-ratio strain curve ($h_t < 0$). The asymptotic value for α is given approximately by the following formula:

$$\alpha = \alpha_B \approx \pm \arctan (\lambda_p \delta_p)^{1/2} \tag{37}$$

where λ_p and δ_p are the maximum (peak) values of the stress-ratio and strain-rate ratio, respectively. Let α_C denote the so-called Coulomb solution:

$$\alpha_C = \pm (\pi/4 + \Phi_p/2) \tag{38}$$

From Bishop and Green (1965), Fig. 7(a), it follows that a slender and lubricated specimen of medium-dense Ham-River sand has failed along a shear band inclined at an angle $\alpha = 58°$. From Figs 12 and 14 of the same reference, it follows that for the considered sand ($n_0 = 0.414$, $\Phi = 39°$) $\lambda_p = 2.096$ and $\delta_p = 1.186$. Introducing these values into eqns (37) and (38) yields $\alpha_B = 57.6°$ and $\alpha_C = 64.5°$, which means that the bifurcation analysis predicts a value for α fairly close to the one measured experimentally.

5 GEOMETRIC AND MATERIAL SOFTENING

Based on stress–strain data from common triaxial tests, classical soil mechanics teaches that the stress–strain relation for dense and medium-dense sands first hardens to a peak, and then softens. Material strain-softening thus entered computational soil mechanics, and in due course severe questions arose as to whether or not considering strain-softening yields properly posed boundary value problems (cf. Hegemeier and Reed, 1984). And thus, quite naturally, the interpretation of the experimentally observed strain-softening has to be reconsidered.

Drescher and Vardoulakis (1982) used stress–strain data from triaxial compression tests on dry Karlsruhe sand, performed by Deman (1975), to investigate the nature of softening. As shown in Fig. 16, data from a compression test with high end platen friction have been analysed using the theoretical procedure outlined in Section 3.3. The initial dimensions of the specimen were $H_0 = 30$ cm, $2R_0 = 15$ cm, and its density was $\gamma_t = 16\cdot9$ kN/m³. This analysis was feasible because Deman (1975), using X-ray radiography, recorded the evolution of the sloping angle η of the rigid cones (see Fig. 1(a)). The calculated 'true' mobilised friction angle Φ_m shows inappreciable softening as opposed to the strong softening revealed by the apparent mobilised friction angle $\Phi_{a,m}$. This apparent softening, called

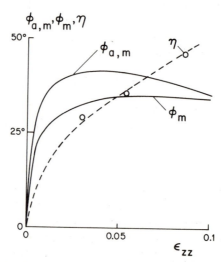

Fig. 16.   Material and geometric softening in test with non-lubricated end platens (based on Deman's experiment, 1975).

geometric softening, is thus a direct consequence of the formation of rigid cones, i.e. the result of inhomogeneous specimen deformation and not a material property. The remaining softening in the corrected $\Phi_m - \varepsilon_{zz}$ curve is perceived as material softening. This assumption is corroborated by analysing data from lubricated tests performed by Deman (1975). Figure 17 presents the comparison between the apparent and the 'true' mobilised angle of friction for a specimen of $H_0 = 17$ cm, $2R_0 = 13$ cm, and $\gamma_t = 17{\cdot}2$ kN/m^3. It was assumed that the angle of interface friction varies with displacement and normal stress, according to eqn (10). From this figure, one can see that both the apparent and the 'true' mobilised angle of friction show the same rate of softening at the same strain level. This is because in this test the deformation is approximately homogeneous, since lubrication prevents rigid cones from being formed. Carefully prepared specimens tested in a triaxial apparatus with parallel guided, enlarged and lubricated end platens show the inappreciable softening (Hettler and Vardoulakis, 1984). By also using compact specimens, diffuse bifurcation in the form of bulging is suppressed, and consequently the observed softening cannot be the result of 'weak', diffuse inhomogeneities. With these precautions in experimentation, the observed post-peak reduction in mobilised friction may be called the global material softening. By this we

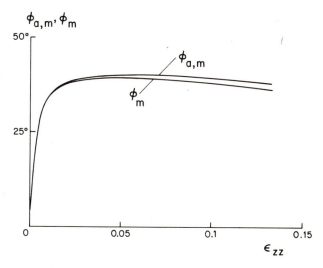

Fig. 17.   Material softening in test with lubricated end platens (based on Deman's experiment, 1975).

mean that the rate in softening is referred to global strains, i.e. strains describing changes in the global dimensions, H and R, of the specimen. This interpretation is no longer true as soon as localised bifurcations (shear bands) destroy completely the uniformity of the specimen.

The assertion that localisation in the triaxial compression test takes place in the softening regime (see Section 4.3) has been corroborated recently by Hettler and Vardoulakis (1984). Triaxial tests were performed with lubricated and enlarged end platens on a large sand specimen ($H_0 = 28$ cm, $2R_0 = 78$ cm). A dense specimen ($\gamma_t = 16\cdot9$ kN/m^3) was strained up to an axial strain of $0\cdot14$. At this strain level, shear bands were observed to intersect the cylindrical surface of the specimen. These localisations are accompanied with pronounced softening as shown in Fig. 18, in a μ versus γ

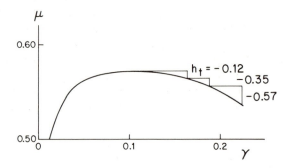

FIG. 18.   Stress ratio versus shear strain in test on dense sand (Hettler and Vardoulakis, 1984).

plot. Beyond the peak, the global softening rate h_t assumes values between $-0\cdot1$ and $-0\cdot6$. According to Vardoulakis (1983), shear-bands for the given density are possible for $h_t < -0\cdot14$, which agrees well with the test. In tests with looser material ($\gamma_t = 16\cdot0$ kN/m^3) and $\gamma_t = 14\cdot3$ kN/m^3), no shear-bands were observed to emerge on the cylindrical surface of the specimen, although the specimens were strained up to an axial strain of $0\cdot16$. This also agrees with the theoretical predictions, because in these tests no significant rate of softening occurred.

By defining the onset of localisation as a failure, we may thus say that post-failure the observed softening refers to a localisation of the deformation into shear bands. Figure 19 shows an X-ray radiography of a fully developed shear band (Vardoulakis and Graf, 1985). This figure demonstrates the well known Roscoe (1967) finding that the shear band

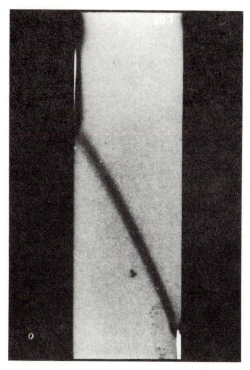

FIG. 19.   Shear band in biaxial test on dense sand (Vardoulakis and Graf, 1985).

thickness d_B is a small multiple of the mean grain size d_{50} of the considered granular material:

$$d_B \approx 10 \div 20 d_{50} \qquad (39)$$

Consequently, post-failure softening can be termed as a localised material softening since it refers to local strains which are calculated by referring displacements measured at the specimen boundaries to the internal length d_B. For the same boundary displacements, global and localised strains refer to each other as, say, H to d_B. For example, for $H = 10\,\text{cm}$ and $d_{50} = 0\cdot33\,\text{mm}$ the apparent rate of softening h_t, referred post-failure to global dimensions, would be about 20 times higher than the true rate of softening, referred to the shear band thickness, d_B. In other words, true material softening evolves with induced strain at an extremely slow pace.

The uncertainty in determining the shear band thickness d_B forces us in post-failure considerations to abandon the continuum model. In fact, it is

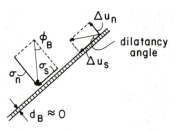

FIG. 20.   Shear band model.

quite possible that the observed shear band thickness is a result of both
dilation due to shear and propagation into surrounding material (Drescher
and Michalowski, 1984; see also Vardoulakis and Goldscheider, 1981).
Assuming that the shear band is described mathematically by a material
line with infinitesimal thickness, its behaviour is described by a relation
between the stress vector, σ_n, σ_s, and the relative displacement vector, Δu_n,
Δu_s, across the shear band (Fig. 20). It is known from biaxial tests
(Vardoulakis and Goldscheider, 1981) that the relative displacement
needed to reach the critical state within the shear band is of the same order
of magnitude as the shear band thickness, thus corresponding to about
100 % of local strain.

6   IDEALISED MATERIAL BEHAVIOUR AND ITS
LIMITATIONS

The theoretical considerations in Sections 3 and 4 are based on the
assumption that mobilised friction and dilatancy in granular material are
independent of the actual stress level. Consequently, a Mohr–Coulomb
hardening rule with associated or non-associated volumetric flow rule is
assumed to be valid, Fig. 21. For a given granular medium it is sometimes
possible to detect an appreciable range of confining pressures,

$$\sigma_c^\ell \le \sigma_c \le \sigma_c^u \tag{40}$$

over which these material assumptions are valid.

   For a medium grained sand, Hettler and Vardoulakis (1984)—see
Section 5—could show that in the range $50 \, \text{kN/m}^2 \le \sigma_c \le 300 \, \text{kN/m}^2$, no
systematic influence of the confining pressure on the friction angle at peak,
$\Phi_{a,p}$, could be detected, Fig. 22. Tests with the same sand performed at
higher confining pressures showed that the friction angle (and dilatancy

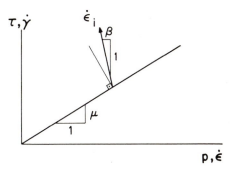

FIG. 21.   Yield condition and flow rule for pressure insensitive frictional material.

modulus) reduced systematically as soon as the confining pressure exceeded a threshold value of $\sigma_c^u \approx 300\,\text{kN/m}^2$. For $\sigma_c > \sigma_c^u$ grain crushing dominates, and the grain size distribution changes during shear. At very low stress levels, on the other hand, the opposite behaviour is observed. Tests with the same sand again revealed the existence of a lower critical confining pressure $\sigma_c^l \approx 50\,\text{kN/m}^2$, below which the friction angle rapidly increased as the confining pressure decreased, Fig. 22. It should be noted that corrections due to end friction (Section 3.2) yielded 'true' friction angles only a few degrees lower than their apparent values. Another reduction in the 'true' angle of friction would result if the confinement of the specimen due to membrane inflation is taken into account. The observed increase of friction angle with decreasing confining pressure can be

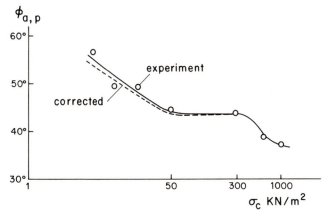

FIG. 22.   Dependence of the peak friction angle on the confining pressure for a dense sand.

interpreted as a result of grain interlocking caused by microscopic asperities of the contact surface of the grains. The resistance against slip caused by these asperities presumably diminishes rapidly as the confining pressure increases.

Based on the results discussed in Section 5, an idealisation concerning the

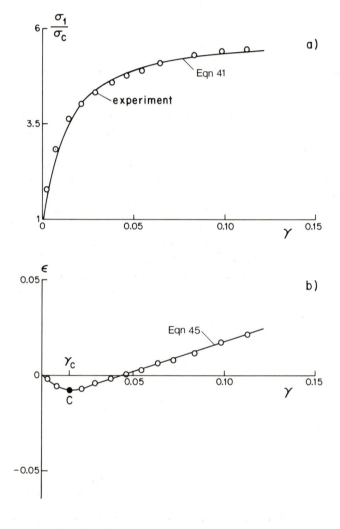

FIG. 23.   Experimental results and curve fits.

stress–strain behaviour of the material can be introduced. For moderately large strains (say for ε_{zz} up to $0\cdot1$) strain-softening may be completely neglected, and the stress–strain curve may very well be replaced by a continuously hardening curve, for example, a hyperbola (Duncan, 1981):

$$\lambda^2 = 1 + \frac{\gamma}{C_1 + C_2\gamma} \tag{41}$$

where

$$\lambda^2 = \frac{\sigma_{zz}}{\sigma_{rr}}$$

$$\gamma = \varepsilon_{zz} - \varepsilon_{rr}$$

$$\varepsilon_{zz} = -\ln\left(\frac{H}{H_0}\right) \tag{42}$$

$$\varepsilon_{rr} = -\ln\left(\frac{R}{R_0}\right)$$

Using, for example, the data from a triaxial compression test performed on lubricated specimens of dry Karlsruhe sand (with $\gamma_t = 17\cdot3\,\text{kN/m}^3$, $H_0 = 5\cdot81\,\text{cm}$, $2R_0 = 6\cdot94\,\text{cm}$, summarised in Table 1) the loading branch of the stress ratio–strain curve is approximated by Duncan's hyperbola, eqn (41) and Fig. 23(a) with

$$C_1 = 2\cdot450E - 3 \qquad C_2 = 2\cdot090E - 1 \tag{43}$$

The volumetric strain–shear strain curve, Fig. 23(b), is also approximated by another 'hyperbolic law':

$$\beta = \frac{C_3\gamma - 1}{C_4 + C_5\gamma} \tag{44}$$

where, again, $\beta = d\varepsilon/d\gamma$. Integration of eqn (44) yields

$$\varepsilon = \frac{C_3}{C_5}\gamma - \left(\frac{1}{C_5} - \frac{C_3C_4}{C_5^2}\right)\ln\left[1 + \frac{C_5}{C_4}\gamma\right] \tag{45}$$

Using the data from Table 1, we obtain:

$$C_3 = 7\cdot650E + 2 \qquad C_4 = 4\cdot590E - 1 \qquad C_5 = 1\cdot817E + 3 \tag{46}$$

From the above curve-fits it follows that, concerning eqn (41) $1/C_1$ is the

TABLE 1

TRIAXIAL COMPRESSION TEST ON DRY SAND

State	ε_{zz} ($E-2$)	$-\varepsilon_{rr}$ ($E-2$)	σ_{zz} (kN/m^2)	σ_{rr} (kN/m^2)	σ_{zz} (corrected) (kN/m^2)
1	0·219	0	174·46	98·1	174·42
2	0·646	0·045	273·64	98·1	273·55
3	1·194	0·229	352·69	98·1	352·45
4	1·633	0·457	392·13	98·1	391·54
5	2·077	0·822	421·75	98·1	420·53
6	2·586	1·186	446·94	98·1	444·84
7	3·068	1·548	466·31	98·1	463·50
8	3·548	1·909	482·22	98·1	478·74
9	4·021	2·313	494·54	98·1	489·13
10	4·536	2·671	505·28	98·1	500·03
11	5·173	3·162	517·15	98·1	510·79
12	5·963	3·870	526·60	98·1	518·38
13	6·774	4·443	532·82	98·1	523·36
14	7·215	4·881	534·17	98·1	523·61

$G_s = 2·66$, $\gamma_t = 17·3\,kN/m^3$, $H_0 = 5·81\,cm$, $2R_0 = 6·94\,cm$.

initial slope of the considered curve, and $(1 + 1/C_2)$ is the asymptotic value of the stress ratio for large γ:

$$h_{t,0} = \frac{1}{C_1} = 408·2$$

$$\lambda_\infty^2 = 1 + \frac{1}{C_2} = 5·786 \qquad (\Phi_\infty = 44·85°) \tag{47}$$

Concerning the curve-fit eqn (45), we identify $1/C_4$ with the slope of the corresponding volumetric curve at large strains:

$$\beta_\infty = \frac{C_3}{C_5} = 4·211 \quad (\arctan \beta_\infty = 22·8) \tag{48}$$

It should be mentioned that correcting for end friction (see Section 3.2) yields slightly lower stress-ratios, which would not be discerned in the displayed graph, Fig. 23. The maximum error of the stress-ratio is 2 % of the apparent value. In terms of the angle of friction,

$$\Phi_a = 43·6° \qquad \Phi = 43·2° \tag{49}$$

The error of $\Delta\Phi \approx 0·5°$ is within the measurement accuracy.

7 CONCLUDING REMARKS

7.1 Summary of Main Results and Recommendations

Following the above analysis of the various inhomogeneities that develop in a cylindrical soil specimen tested in triaxial compression, Hettler and Vardoulakis (1984) suggested an improved version of the triaxial set-up. This version, shown in Fig. 24, incorporates several requirements such as:

(a) flat specimens to avoid bulging; $H/2R = 0.5$ to 1,
(b) lubricated and enlarged end platens to minimise end restraints,
(c) a guided upper plate to minimise load eccentricity,
(d) large overall dimensions to increase strain-measurement accuracy,
(e) high uniformity in the initial porosity and specimen height to support uniform deformation.

Under these conditions, the resulting deformation mode is uniform at least up to the state of maximum principal stress ratio. Correcting the results for low levels of end platens friction (as described in Section 3.2) is meaningful, and will result in more conservative values for the strength of the tested material. For this correction to be feasible, the properties of the lubricant used must be known, i.e. the dependence of the coefficient of friction on loading and displacement.

Despite all possible precautions, however, inhomogeneities due to localised bifurcation cannot be suppressed (see also Desrues *et al.*, 1984). Shear banding in the improved triaxial compression test takes place in the softening regime of the stress–strain curve as soon as the tested material is dense enough to produce sufficient softening rates, at relatively large axial strains, say $\varepsilon_{zz} = 0.1$ (cf. Fig. 13(a)). Presumably, in medium dense and loose sand specimens shear banding does not occur, and the specimen may be deformed homogeneously at even larger strains, say $\varepsilon_{zz} = 0.4$ (cf. Fig. 13(b)).

7.2 Comparison with other Soil Tests

In this closing section, we would like to focus upon some aspects of soil behaviour as revealed in different soil tests, such as the triaxial extension test, and the plane-strain or biaxial compression test. Assuming that all these tests are performed under constant confining pressure, we want now to re-address the question posed by Roscoe *et al.* (1963) with respect to the suitability of any failure criterion for granular soils (see Section 4.1).

In dry or fully drained soil specimens, it is reasonable to identify failure with localised bifurcation. Based on a unique curve hypothesis, Fig. 11,

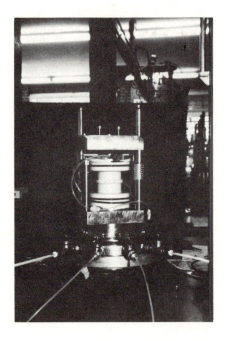

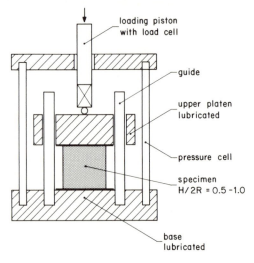

FIG. 24.   Improved triaxial apparatus (Hettler and Vardoulakis, 1984).

Vardoulakis (1980, 1981, 1983) investigated the above question in a series of papers. The results of these theoretical investigations can be summarised as follows:

(a) Triaxial extension test: Failure in the triaxial extension test is manifested by the formation of a localised neck, triggered by diffuse necking. Neck formation will occur in the hardening regime of the assumed stress ratio–strain curve, and in the vicinity of the limiting state of maximum stress ratio. The orientation of the boundaries of the necking region is described again by the bifurcation condition eqn (35). An example of such a computation is shown in Fig. 25 ($\lambda_p^2 = 0.163$, $\delta_p^2 = 0.640$).

(b) Biaxial compression test: Failure in the biaxial compression test is manifested by the formation of shear bands which lie perpendicular to the deformation plane. In the biaxial test, shear banding takes place again in the hardening regime of the stress ratio–strain curve, and in the vicinity of the limiting state. The approximate formula for the shear band orientation angle α in plane strain conditions becomes:

$$\alpha = \alpha_B \approx \pm [\pi/4 + (\Phi_p + \psi_p)/4] \tag{50}$$

where ψ_p is the dilatancy angle of the material at peak.

Following these results, we may finally conclude that failure is not a strict material property. In particular, it may not be possible to defend a failure criterion as a constitutive limiting condition of the form $F(\sigma_{ij}) = 0$, as was proposed, for example, by Tokuoka (1972). In addition, it is not suitable to define a failure criterion in terms of the (effective) stress vector acting across a distinct failure plane, since the orientation of the failure plane does also

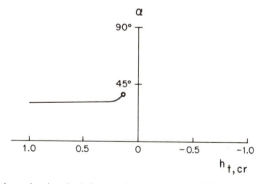

FIG. 25.   Neck angle α in triaxial extension test versus critical tangent modulus $h_{t,cr}$
(Vardoulakis, 1984).

depend on the stress path followed. If failure has to be modelled mathematically, then only a correct bifurcation analysis could yield the desired result. Post failure, the governing differential equations (see eqn (24)) change type. In this case, severe mathematical questions do arise, which are presently not answered at all satisfactorily. Beyond any doubt, research in this area is important and should be pursued with patience and rigor.

ACKNOWLEDGEMENT

This paper is a preliminary study for a research project supported by the National Science Foundation through Grant CEE-8406500, which is gratefully acknowledged. The first author wants also to thank the Deutsche Forschungsgemeinschaft for supporting the experimental part of this research through Grant Gu 103/13,16,20.

REFERENCES

ARTHUR, J. F. R., DUNSTAN, T., AL-ANI, Q. A. J. and ASSADI, A. (1977). Plastic deformation and failure in granular media, *Geotechnique*, **27**, 53–74.

BIOT, M. A. (1965). *Mechanics of Incremental Deformation*, J. Wiley, New York.

BISHOP, A. W. and GREEN, G. E. (1965). The influence of end restraint on the compression strength of a cohesionless soil, *Geotechnique*, **15**, 243–66.

COURANT, A. and HILBERT, D. (1968). *Methoden der Mathematischen Physik II*, Springer Verlag, Berlin.

DEMAN, F. (1975). Achsensymmetrische spannungs- und verformungsfelder in trockenen sand. Veröffentlichungen IBF, No. 62, Dissertation, University of Karlsruhe.

DESRUES, J., LANIER, J. and STUTZ, P. (1984). Localization of the deformation in tests on sand sample, *Int. Symp. Current Trends and Results in Plasticity*, Udine, June 27–30 (in press).

DRESCHER, A. and MICHALOWSKI, R. L. (1984). Density variation in pseudo-steady plastic flow of granular media, *Geotechnique*, **34**, 1–10.

DRESCHER, A. and VARDOULAKIS, I. (1982). Geometric softening in triaxial tests on granular material, *Geotechnique*, **32**, 291–303.

DRUCKER, D. C. and PRAGER, W. (1952). Soil mechanics and plastic analysis or limit design, *Q. Appl. Math.*, **10**, 157–65.

DUNCAN, J. M. (1981). Hyperbolic stress–strain relations, In: *Limit Equilibrium, Plasticity and Generalized Stress–Strain in Geotechnical Engineering. ASCE Spec. Publ.*, 493–60.

GOLDSCHEIDER, M. and GUDEHUS, G. (1973). Rectilinear extension of dry sand: Testing apparatus and experimental results, *Proc. 8th ICSMFE*, Moscow, 1(21), 143–9.

GREEN, M. A. (1972). Strength and deformation of sand measured in an independent stress control cell, *Proc. Roscoe Mem. Symp.*, Cambridge, 285–323.

HADAMARD, J. (1903). *Lecons sur le Propagation des Ondes et les Equations de l'Hydrodynamique*, Chapt. VI, Hermann, Paris.

HAMBLY, E. C. (1972). Plane-strain behaviour of remoulded normally consolidated kaolin, *Geotechnique*, **22**, 301–17.

HEGEMEIER, G. A. and REED, H. E. (1984). Strain softening, *DARPA-NSF Workshop on Theoretical Foundation for Large-scale Computations of Non-linear Material Behaviour*, Northwestern Univ., October 24–26, 1983. Martinus Nijhoff, The Hague, 300–11.

HETTLER, A. and VARDOULAKIS, I. (1984). Behaviour of dry sand tested in a large triaxial apparatus, *Geotechnique*, **34**, 183–98.

HILL, R. (1962). Acceleration waves in solids, *J. Mech. Phys. Solids*, **10**, 1–16.

HILL, R. and HUTCHINSON, J. W. (1975). Bifurcation phenomena in the plane tension test, *J. Mech. Phys. Solids*, **23**, 239–64.

JANSSEN, H. A. (1895). Versuche uber Getreidedruck in Silozellen, *Z. Ver. Dt. Ing.*, **39**, 1045.

KIRKPATRICK, W. and BELSHAW, D. J. (1968). On the interpretation of the triaxial test, *Geotechnique*, **18**, 336–50.

MANDEL, J. (1963). Propagation des surfaces de discontinuite dans un milieu elastoplastique, *IUTAM Symp. Stress Waves in Inelastic Solids*. Brown Univ., 331–41.

MANDEL, J. (1964). Conditiones de stabilite et postulat de Drucker, *IUTAM Symp. Rheology and Soil Mechanics*, Grenoble, 56–68.

MOLENKAMP, F. (1983). Quality of lubrication of endplatens, In: *Constitutive Equations of Soils. Results of a Workshop*, Grenoble (in press).

READES, D. W. and GREEN, G. E. (1976). Independent stress control and triaxial extension tests on sand, *Geotechnique*, **26**, 551–76.

ROSCOE, K. H. (1967). Shear strength of soil other than clay, *Panel Discussion*, *Proc. Geotech. Conf. Oslo, Sess. 3*, p. 198.

ROSCOE, K. H., SCHOFIELD, A. N. and THURAIRAJAH, A. (1963). An evaluation of test data for selecting a yield criterion for soil, *ASTM Spec. Publ.*, **361**, 111–12.

SCARPELLI, G. and WOOD, D. M. (1982). Experimental observations of shear band patterns in direct shear test. *IUTAM Conf. Deformation and Failure of Granular Materials*, Delft, 473–84.

THOMAS, T. Y. (1961). *Plastic Flow and Fracture of Solids*, Academic Press, New York.

TOKUOKA, T. (1972). Yield conditions and flow rules derived from hypoelasticity, *Arch. Rat. Mech. Anal.*, **42**, 239–51.

VARDOULAKIS, I. (1979). Bifurcation analysis of the triaxial test on sand samples, *Acta Mech.*, **32**, 35–54.

VARDOULAKIS, I. (1980). Shear band inclination and shear modulus of sand in biaxial tests, *Int. J. Num. Anal. Meth. Geomech.*, **4**, 103–19.

VARDOULAKIS, I. (1981). Constitutive properties of dry sand observable in the triaxial test, *Acta Mech.*, **38**, 219–39.

VARDOULAKIS, I. (1983). Rigid granular plasticity model and bifurcation in the triaxial test, *Acta Mech.*, **47**, 57–79.

VARDOULAKIS, I. and GOLDSCHEIDER, M. (1981). A biaxial apparatus for testing shear bands in soils, *Proc. 10th ICSMFE*, Stockholm, **4**(61), 819–24.

VARDOULAKIS, I. and GRAF, B. (1985). Calibration of constitutive models for granular materials using data from biaxial tests. *Geotechnique* (in press).

VARDOULAKIS, I., GOLDSCHEIDER, M. and GUDEHUS, G. (1978). Formation of shear bands in sand bodies as a bifurcation problem, *Int. J. Num. Anal. Meth. Geomech.*, **2**, 99–128.

ZANGL, L. (1971). Report to the Minister of 'Wohnungsbau' of GFR (unpublished).

Chapter 8

USE OF THE SELF-BORING PRESSUREMETER IN SOFT CLAYS

G. Wayne Clough

Department of Civil Engineering,
Virginia Polytechnic Institute and State University,
Blacksburg, USA

and

Jean Benoit

Department of Civil Engineering,
University of New Hampshire, Durham, USA

1 INTRODUCTION

Construction and design in soft clays often presents a severe challenge to the geotechnical engineer. In such cases, large deformations are common and margins of safety can be very low. Because of this situation, parameter determination for analysis in soft clays is an important process. Careful research has shown that only through relatively expensive and time-consuming procedures can laboratory testing be expected to yield reasonable values for soft clay parameters. Thus, considerable interest has developed in *in situ* testing methods which might be used for these materials. One of the more promising tools of this type is the self-boring pressuremeter (SBPM). This chapter is devoted to a description of this device along with a summary of results that have been obtained using it.

2 BACKGROUND

The original concept of the pressuremeter is attributed to Kögler, who developed a device consisting of a rubber bladder clamped at both ends and lowered into a predrilled hole. The instrument was gas inflated and a pressure–volume relationship was obtained. Menard (1956), without knowledge of Kögler's work, later developed an improved pressuremeter. The Menard probe consists of a water-inflated rubber membrane positioned between two gas-inflated guard cells which help maintain near plane strain conditions. In application, the Menard approach still suffers from problems inherent in the predrilling process and the empirical interpretation procedures. Recognising this, two research groups in the early 1970s proposed the idea of adding a self-boring capability to the pressuremeter (Baguelin *et al.*, 1972; Hughes, 1973). The resulting devices are usually referred to as the Pressiometre Autoforeur (French version) and the Cambridge Probe (English version). Other SBPM probes have since been developed (Mori, 1981; Johnson, 1982), however their basic characteristics are similar to the original models. Sketches of the French and the English probes are shown in Fig. 1.

Although there are differences between probe types, the basic instrument consists of a long cylinder with a mid-section covered with a flexible rubber

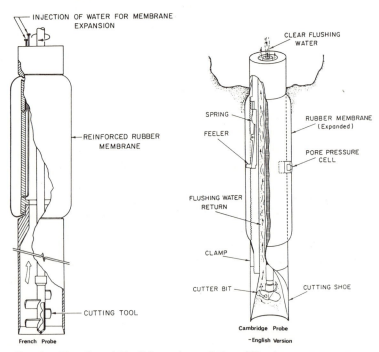

FIG. 1.   French and English versions of the self-boring pressuremeter.

membrane. At the end of the probe a sharp cutting shoe houses a cutter bit able to move relative to the edge of the shoe. The cutter bit is connected to a hollow drilling shaft that runs inside a drilling casing onto which the self-boring pressuremeter is attached. As the instrument is pushed into the ground, drilling fluid is pumped down the drilling shaft, the cutter bit cuts the soil, and the material is flushed to the surface in the annulus between the drilling casing and the drilling shaft.

When a testing location is reached, drilling is stopped and some time is allowed for stabilisation of excess pore pressures. By applying water or gas pressure to the inside of the instrument, the membrane is then expanded against the sides of the borehole. As the cavity is enlarged, movement of the membrane is tracked by either measuring the volume of water in the probe (French) or measuring radial displacement electronically by means of three strain feeler arms set midway along the probe, 120 degrees apart (English). In addition, pore pressures may be measured by transducers which are attached to the membrane to stay in constant contact with the expanding cavity. All of the SBPM are designed to presumably minimise disturbance.

3 RESULTS

The pressuremeter test involves a relatively simple type of loading which consists of a membrane being expanded inside a circular cavity. At a minimum, the results consist of a form of cavity expansion curve. For the SBPM this is commonly presented as a pressure–radial strain relationship. In advanced tests, pore pressures are also measured and cyclic loading is often used to obtain information as to unload–reload behaviour.

Recent advances in data acquisition systems have allowed improvements to be made in the quantity and quality of information obtained in the field. Figure 2 shows pressure–radial strain data recorded using a micro-computer and plotted on a main-frame unit. Although only 120 points are shown in the figure, some 36 times this amount were actually recorded and averaged to arrive at the data plotted.

The results in Figure 2 are typical of a high quality SBPM test in soft clay. Initially, pressure is applied to the membrane, but no radial strain occurs. In this region, the total lateral stress in the ground is still greater than the pressure inside the membrane. Eventually, the membrane begins to lift away from the probe when membrane inertia effects and total lateral pressures are exceeded. After this 'lift-off', the soil around the probe is sheared by the cavity expansion process and a nonlinear curve results.

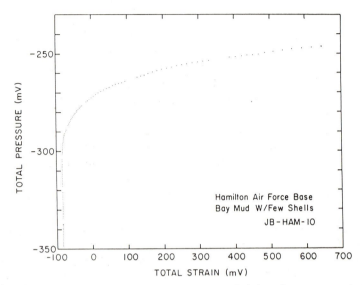

FIG. 2.   Typical pressuremeter results as recorded by the automated data acquisition system (after Benoit, 1983).

Use of an advanced data acquisition unit with the English probe also allows recording of individual readings from each strain arm and each pore pressure cell as well as averaged data. This affords the opportunity of detecting any erratic behaviour of any particular sensor and defining anisotropic effects in the soil as will be shown later in this chapter.

4   INTERPRETATION METHODS

The typical pressuremeter test in clay is supposedly performed rapidly enough to achieve undrained conditions, with the exception of the holding test which is designed to measure pore pressure dissipation. Thus, the basic data most commonly obtained are of the total stress variety. Effective stress information can only be acquired if a pore pressure measuring capability is present.

4.1   *In Situ* Horizontal Stress
All methods are designed to determine horizontal stress from the SBPM lead to a total lateral stress (σ_h). However, it is common for lateral pressure results to be presented in the form of coefficient of lateral earth pressure, k_0, a parameter defined in terms of a ratio of horizontal effective pressure

divided by vertical effective pressure (σ'_h/σ'_v). To obtain k_0 from the pressuremeter test the static groundwater pressure is calculated and removed from the measured σ_h. Next σ'_v is determined by multiplying appropriate unit weight values times the depth. Thus, k_0 is arrived at as a function of parameters which in themselves are not measured in the pressuremeter test. In effect, k_0 is a second order variable, and cannot normally be determined as accurately as σ_h.

There are a number of methods for evaluating σ_h from a SBPM test, and these are compiled in Table 1. The methods may be subdivided along two lines. The first type involves a direct observation of the lift-off pressure from the raw pressuremeter data with correction applied for membrane inertia effects. The second category uses a technique to calculate the horizontal stress from the complete pressuremeter curve. Comparisons between the various methods suggest that most accepted techniques for determining the *in situ* horizontal stress have essentially the same degree of accuracy and that none of them yield any significant improvement over the simple definition of lift-off by inspection (Denby and Hughes, 1982; Lacasse and Lunne, 1982).

Several versions of the SBPM allow measurement of the movement of the membrane at three points located 120 degrees apart. If all three responses are individually measured then the potential exists to determine σ_h in three different locations in the horizontal plane. Should the soil be perfectly isotropic, all three values would be identical. However, a few recent investigations have suggested that this may not be the case, and a degree of anisotropy exists which was heretofore unknown (Dalton and Hawkins, 1982; Ghionna *et al.*, 1982). Dalton and Hawkins (1982) suggest a technique for calculating major and minor principal lateral stresses.

4.2 Coefficient of Consolidation

Where the SBPM has the capability to measure pore pressure response, a special holding test can be performed from which the coefficient of consolidation may be determined (Clarke *et al.*, 1979). The holding test is conducted in the beginning just as a normal test until a radial strain of about ten percent is reached. At this point the expansion is stopped, the membrane held in a fixed position, and the rate of pore pressure dissipation observed. Using the pore pressure data and a closed form solution for consolidation around an expanded cavity, the coefficient of consolidation can be calculated as follows:

$$c_{vh} = \frac{T_{50} r_m^2}{t_{50}} \qquad (1)$$

TABLE 1
TOTAL *in situ* LATERAL STRESS INTERPRETATION METHODS MOST SUITABLE FOR USE WITH THE SELF-BORING PRESSUREMETER

	Horizontal stress determination methods	*References*
From lift-off		
Inspection	First outward movement of the membrane noticeable on the field pressure–strain curve	
Excess pore pressure	First significant change in slope on plot of expansion pressure versus effective pressure	Wroth and Hughes (1974), Wroth (1980)
Modified lift-off	Start of linear portion on plot of strain versus time, to allow for slight overdrilling and deformability of feelers	Lacasse *et al.* (1981)
Logarithm of strain	Break on curve, on plot of field pressure versus logarithm of strain	Law and Eden (1982)
From the pressuremeter curve		
Graphical iteration	Assumes a lift-off pressure value, derives the undrained shear strength, and iterates until value of $s_u + p_0$ is equal to the pressure where yielding occurs	Marsland and Randolph (1977)
Hyperbolic-plastic	Corrects pressuremeter curve for early membrane movement and calculates lift-off from hyperbolic fit	Denby (1978), Denby and Clough (1980)
Double zero shift	Uses hyperbolic model and corrects for pressure and strain zero shift	Arnold (1981)

in which r_m = radius of the expanded membrane; t_{50} = real time required for the measured excess pore to decrease to one half of its value at the end of the membrane expansion phase; T_{50} = time factor for 50 % pore pressure dissipation after cavity expansion (Randolph and Wroth, 1979); c_{vh} = coefficient of consolidation for radial drainage.

4.3 Stress–Strain and Strength Parameters

There are a number of interpretation methods and variations of the method available to determine stress–strain and strength parameters from the pressure–strain (or pressure–volume) relationship obtained from a pressuremeter test in saturated clay. Five basic procedures are compared in Table 2. All assume the clay is homogeneous and isotropic and that the conditions during the test are undrained; i.e., no volume change occurs. The Baguelin et al. (1972), Ladanyi (1972) and Palmer (1972) approach is the only one with no assumption regarding the shape of the stress–strain curve. According to this procedure as the radius of the hole is increased by the pressuremeter expansion, the shear strain induces a difference between the tangential and radial stresses which is a function of the principal strains. From the equation of static equilibrium and the distributions of strain and principal stress difference, the stress–strain relationship simplified for small strains is defined as:

$$\frac{\sigma_r - \sigma_\theta}{2} = \varepsilon_r \frac{\delta \sigma_r}{\delta \varepsilon_r} \qquad (2)$$

where $\delta \sigma_r / \delta \varepsilon_r$ is simply the slope of the pressuremeter curve. A graphical procedure utilising this technique was devised by Hughes (1973), known as the subtangent method. It consists of drawing tangents to the pressuremeter curve (corrected for membrane inertia) and multiplying the slope of the tangents by their corresponding values of radial strain. The procedure is very useful in that a stress–strain curve can quickly be generated from the pressuremeter expansion curve. Benoit (1983) computerised the subtangent method using least squares by cubic splines approximation to fit the pressuremeter curve, and automatically obtaining the slopes of the curve at any strain level. This is important in handling the large quantities of data stored by a microcomputer acquisition system.

Several of the methods in Table 2 have been modified or adapted to improve their accuracy. Ladd et al. (1980) revised the Prevost and Hoeg (1975) procedure for calculating undrained shear strength to account for the possibility of having failure at a strain less than 1 %. Subsequently, Ghionna et al. (1981) altered this approach to incorporate the Marsland

TABLE 2
COMPARISON OF BASIC INTERPRETATION METHODS FOR STRESS–STRAIN AND STRENGTH (ADAPTED FROM DENBY, 1978)

Consideration	Menard (1956)	Gibson & Anderson (1961)	Baguelin et al. (1972), Ladanyi (1972), Palmer (1972)	Prevost & Hoeg (1975)	Denby & Clough (1980)
Stress–strain curve	Assumed to be elastic-plastic	Assumed to be elastic-plastic	Not assumed. Derived by obtaining tangents along pressuremeter curve	Assumed to be a function of fitted curve. Obtained by differentiation of fitted curve	Assumed to be of modified hyperbolic shape. Model defined from parameters obtained on plot of $d\varepsilon_r/d\sigma_r$ vs ε_r
Initial shear modulus	Estimated	Average pressuremeter modulus from elastic stage of test	Measured from pressuremeter curve	Calculated by differentiating stress–strain curve	Measured on plot of $d\varepsilon_r/d\sigma_r$ vs ε_r
In situ horizontal stress	Obtained from pressuremeter curve	Approximate value required	Obtained in self-boring pressuremeter test	Obtained in self-boring pressuremeter test	Calculated from the modified hyperbolic shape
Shear strength	Determined empirically	Computed from elasto-plastic stage of test	Peak value of stress–strain curve	Determined from curve-fitting constants	Measured on plot of $d\varepsilon_r/d\sigma_r$ vs ε_r
Ease of interpretation	Straightforward	Straightforward	Straightforward	Needs computational facilities	Straightforward
Problems	Empirical	Assumption of stress–strain curve. Unrealistic stress–strain curve	Difficulty of obtaining tangents to an experimental curve	Curve-fitting prescribes shape of stress–strain curve	Must obtain slope of pressuremeter curve

and Randolph (1977) method for determining the lateral horizontal pressure, one of the parameters needed to obtain undrained shear strength. Finally, the Gibson and Anderson (1961) procedure for calculating undrained shear strength was modified by Windle and Wroth (1977) to obtain an 'average', rather than a residual value.

All the methods are generally straightforward and equal in ease of interpretation except for the Prevost and Hoeg (1975) technique which requires solving large equations to obtain the entire stress–strain curve. Typically most investigations have shown that the methods of interpretation with the exception of the Menard (1956) empirical approach, lead to generally similar results (Denby, 1978 and Ghionna *et al.*, 1981).

5 PROBE ADVANCE PROCEDURES AND TESTING METHODS

When the SBPM was first introduced very little comment was made in regard to exactly how the probe was being advanced and/or how the test was being performed. Since those early days, a number of investigators have shown that certain aspects of these procedures have a significant effect on the results of the test. The essence of the matter lies in minimising disturbance during probe insertion and achieving the desired undrained conditions during shear. Soil disturbance is influenced by items such as cutter bit position, rate of rotation of the cutter bit, rate of advance of the probe and consistency in component size along the length of the body of the probe. Drainage in the soil mass is influenced by the rate of the membrane expansion. Variations in these parameters can lead to large differences in results derived from the SBPM test as shown by Clough and Denby (1980) and Law and Eden (1980). Disturbance is particularly important because the typical interpretation of the pressuremeter results lead to an overestimate of the undrained shear strength if the soil has been disturbed during insertion (Jamiolkowski and Lancellotta, 1977; Baguelin and Jazequel, 1978; Denby and Clough, 1980).

5.1 Probe Advance Procedures and Configurations

Two potential problems can arise if an improper cutter position is used. If the cutter is set flush with the edge of the cutting shoe, the soil may flow into the shoe around the exposed cutter bit and stresses in the ground can be reduced. This case may be examined from the bearing capacity theory, by which it is possible to assess the conditions where the soil will yield into the face of the shoe. Secondly, if the cutter is set far back into the shoe, clogging can occur because the openings into the exit points are reduced. If this occurs, it would lead to increased stresses ahead of the probe as would a displacement pile. However, this latter phenomenon is erratic in that with the same cutter position, it can occur in some cases and be non-existent in others. An optimal cutter position may be selected based on the evaluation of the yielding and clogging potential or a field trial.

The cutter speed, monitored in revolutions per minute (rpm), usually ranges from 60–120 rpm. This can be important since it affects how the soil is removed and the amount of turbulence in the water exiting from the cutting bit. SBPM tests conducted at 180 rpm suggest that washboring may occur in some soils leading to a relaxation of the soil around the probe shoe (Benoit, 1983). For the ideal case, the cuttings flushed to the surface should appear as small clay chips for moderately sensitive clays and as a slurry for quick clays. Boring in soft clays with an SBPM usually proceeds cautiously with rates of advance generally varying from 1·5–10 cm/min (0·5–4 in/min). A proper combination of rate of advance and cutter revolutions is necessary for smooth drilling. During that process, the chopped material must be flushed to the surface by drilling fluid circulation. Although it is important that the flow be sufficient to prevent the casing from clogging the flow pressure must be small enough to avoid hydraulic fracturing and/or wash-boring of the soil ahead of the pressuremeter probe.

Before inserting the SBPM into the ground, it is important to verify that the section of the probe covered by the rubber membrane has the same diameter as the cutting shoe and the lower membrane clamps. This situation arises since membrane thickness varies depending upon the nature of the membrane. Latex rubber membranes for soft clays are thinner than adiprene membranes used in stiff clays; different diameter cutter shoes and membrane clamps are needed when using latex vs adiprene. Self-boring with an oversized shoe will unload the soil prior to any actual expansion of the membrane, while use of an undersized cutting shoe will produce preloading of the soil. Table 3 provides the results from studies on effects of cutting shoe size. Surprisingly, large effects are caused by small differences in membrane and cutting shoe sizes.

5.2 Testing Procedures

The key parameters relative to a testing procedure are the relaxation period and the expansion rate. A relaxation period is necessary because the drilling operation induces excess pore pressures in the soil which must be allowed to dissipate. The required time period is dependent upon the drilling technique used and the type of soil being tested. Results from various

TABLE 3
EFFECTS OF CUTTING SHOE SIZE

Test site	Ratio of diameters (cutting shoe to membrane)	Effects on		References
		Shear strength	Horizontal stress	
South Gloucester	0·997	Peak and post peak at larger strains	—	Law and Eden (1980)
Coode Island	1·030	—	Reduced by 60–65%	Hughes et al. (1980)
Hamilton Air Force Base	1·011	Increased by 60–100%	Reduced by 20%	Benoit (1983)

testing programs seem to indicate that, generally, most of the excess pore pressures induced from drilling are dissipated in less than 2 h for typical soft clays. Investigations where relaxation periods were less than 30 min led to inconsistent values of horizontal stresses. However, there is apparently a range of opinion as to what the proper relaxation period is and its effect on lateral pressure. More research is needed in this area.

The rate of membrane expansion potentially influences SBPM test results in two ways. First, if the rate is too slow, drainage can occur in the soil. Unfortunately, the operator of the test is normally not aware if drainage is occurring, and the results are subsequently analysed as if no drainage took place. This typically leads to an underestimate of shear strength. In contrast, if the rate is very fast relative to the soil response, rheological effects will occur, leading to an overestimate of the shear strength of the soil relative to long term field loading. The rheological effect to some degree shows up in almost all tests, since we are unable to run tests as slow as most field loadings.

The appropriate rate of membrane expansion will vary with soil type. In a field test program in a soft marine clay located near San Francisco, Benoit (1983) showed that variable rates of expansion had an important impact on predicted undrained shear strengths, but not on *in situ* lateral stresses. At slow rates of loading, drainage was indicated by the presence of unusually low excess pore pressures during the test. Presently, research is underway by the senior author towards developing charts which can be used to estimate a rate of loading which would produce undrained conditions. The proper rate will be chosen based on the charts and the results of a holding test which would be performed early in the test program. The holding test would provide an *in situ* value for the coefficient of consolidation.

TABLE 4
COMPARISON OF PUBLISHED SBPM INVESTIGATIONS IN SOFT CLAY

Test location or soil type	Soil description	Water content (%)	Plastic limit (%)	Liquid limit (%)	Plasticity index (%)	Typical drilling procedures				Relaxation period (min)	Testing procedures Expansion rate		References
						Rate of advance (cm/min)	Drilling flow (l/min)	Cutter position inside cutting shoe (cm)	Cutter speed (rpm)		$kN/m^2/min$	% min	
Porto Tolle clay (Rovigo)	Soft silty clay with silty sand lenses	35-40	—	50-60	25-40					15-120		0·83	Jamiolkowski and Lancellotta (1977) Jamiolkowski et al. (1980)
Guasticce clay (Livorno)	Very soft silty clay	70	—	70-90	50-60					15-120		0·83	Jamiolkowski and Lancellotta (1977)
Onsoy clay (Fredrikstad)	Soft medium plastic homogeneous clay	60-65	—	—	36	2-4	10-12	3	120	90-1300			Lacasse and Lunne (1982) Ghionna et al. (1983)
Drammen clay (Danvikgate)	Plastic and lean clay	50-55	—	—	28	1·5-3	10-12	3	60	90-1300			Lacasse and Lunne (1982) Ghionna et al. (1983)
Panigaglia clay	Silty clay	55-65	—	69-75	44-51								Ghionna et al. (1983)
Leda clay (South Gloucester)	Sensitive soft marine deposit with some silt	40-95	20-25	50-60	—	10	—	0·6-1·3	70	60-1080	9·7		Eden and Law (1980)
Matagami	Highly plastic lacustrine deposit	40-110	20-25	45-70	—	10	—	0·6-1·3	70	60-1080	9·7		Eden and Law (1980)
Coode Island	Silty clay	49-82	35-80	58-103	—					60-960			Hughes et al. (1980)
Boston Blue clay	Medium soft clay	30-50	20-25	40-50	—					10-30		1·0	Ladd et al. (1980)
Northern Coast of Tokyo Bay (Komatsugarva)	CL, MH and CH with 5-20% sand laminations	40-70	20-35	35-55	—					120			Mori (1981)
Young Bay mud (Hamilton Air Force Base)	Some grey clay with some shells and silt lenses, CH-MH	86-90	38-40	85-88	—	2·5-5·0	10-15	2·5	50-60	60-180	1·7-47·6	0·2 0·04-0·99	Denby (1978) Benoit (1983)

6 TESTING PROGRAMS IN SOFT CLAY

A compilation of key factors for published SBPM test programs in soft clays is given in Table 4. The information given illustrates one of the problems associated with comparing findings between different investigations; namely, there are often differences in key parameters from program to program. Further, in many instances the key test and probe parameters are not given. In the future, standardisation will be necessary to obtain repeatable and reliable results.

7 HORIZONTAL STRESSES

Experience in measuring lateral stresses in soft clay using the SBPM has generally been good. In Table 5, results from SBPM test programs are compared to values obtained by alternative procedures. Those cases where relatively unusual results have been reported from SBPM tests can generally be attributed to disturbance effects created during probe insertion. This can be confirmed via test programs where intentional disturbance effects have been induced and poor results are inevitably produced (e.g. see Table 3).

One of the more intriguing findings is that anisotropy may exist in lateral stresses in a single plane. Several investigations have indicated this condition in stiff clay (Dalton and Hawkins, 1982; Ghionna *et al.*, 1982,

TABLE 5
COMPARISON OF LATERAL STRESSES MEASURED BY SBPM AND ALTERNATIVE ESTIMATES

Test site or soil type	Ratio of σ_h from SBPM tests to σ_h from oedometer tests, pressure cells, or empirical methods	References
Porto Tolle clay	0·8–1·1 (French SBPM)	Jamiolkowski and Lancellotta (1977)
Guasticce clay	0·8–1·0 (French SBPM)	Jamiolkowski and Lancellotta (1977)
Onsoy clay	1·0	Lacasse and Lunne (1982)
Drammen clay	0·9	Lacasse and Lunne (1982)
Boston Blue clay	0·7–0·8	Ladd *et al.* (1980)
Hamilton Air Force Base	0·8–1·0	Denby (1978)
	0·8–1·5	Benoit (1983)

1983) and Benoit (1983) found it to exist in soft clay. The major principal stresses were observed to be as much as 20% greater than the minor principal stresses. This phenomenon probably is associated with clay structure or the method by which the clay was deposited. Future investigations using advanced data acquisitions will likely shed more light on the universality of this situation.

8 UNDRAINED SHEAR STRENGTHS

It has been a rather common experience for undrained shear strengths from SBPM testing to exceed those determined by laboratory testing and even vane shear testing. The results summary in Table 6 illustrates this trend. Exact reasons for the high shear strength values obtained in some cases by the SBPM are not clear. However, a number of factors are obvious at this stage. First, it has been a common practice in the past to use SBPM probes with an expanding membrane section for which the length to diameter ratio (L/D) is as low as 2. Theoretical and experimental evidence clearly supports the idea that this leads to an overestimate of the shear strength (Ghionna *et*

TABLE 6

COMPARISON OF STRENGTH OBTAINED FROM SELF-BORING PRESSUREMETER WITH OTHER
in situ AND LABORATORY TESTS

Test site (or soil type) and probe type	Ratios of undrained shear strength—SBPM			References
	Triaxial	Direct simple shear	Field vane	
Porto Tolle clay ($L/D = 4$)	0·9	1·1	1·0	Jamiolkowski and
Guasticce clay ($L/D = 2$)	—	—	1·7–2·0	Lancellotta (1977) Ghionna *et al.* (1983)
Gloucester ($L/D = 6$)	1·1–1·2	—	1·8–1·9	Eden and Law (1980)
Matagami ($L/D = 6$)	—	—	1·3–2·1	
Tokyo Bay ($L/D = 5$) (main cell and guard cells)	0·9–1·0 (one test = 1·1)	—	—	Mori (1981)
Hamilton Air Force Base ($L/D = 6$)	0·93–1·12	—	1·12	Clough and Denby (1980) Benoit (1983)
Boston Blue clay ($L/D = 6$)	2–3	—	—	Ladd *et al.* (1980)
Onsoy clay ($L/D = 6$)	1·4	1·8	—	Ghionna *et al.* (1983)
Drammen clay ($L/D = 6$)	1·6	2·0	—	

al., 1981; Ghionna *et al.*, 1982). For a more reasonable representation of the plane strain environment which is assumed in the data reduction procedures an L/D ratio of 6 is preferable, a value consistent with the dimensions of the English version of the SBPM.

A second important factor is disturbance during probe insertion. Several field and theoretical studies have shown convincingly that disturbance leads to an overestimate of the undrained shear strength (Jamiolkowski and Lancellotta, 1977; Baguelin *et al.*, 1978; Denby and Clough, 1980; Law and Eden, 1980). This effect is at odds with traditional experience with other methods of *in situ* and laboratory testing, and is referred to as the pressuremeter paradox. The effect is generated because the interpretation method assumes the soil to be homogeneous when in fact if there has been disturbance, the soil around the probe has nonhomogeneous properties (see Baguelin *et al.*, 1978 or Denby and Clough, 1980 for a more complete explanation).

If the effects of disturbance and improper probe geometry are removed, it seems that in some cases the shear strength of soft clays is still 'overestimated' (Ghionna *et al.*, 1983). Prevost (1976) has shown that theoretically the SBPM should yield a strength between that found by plane strain compression and plane strain extension. Several investigators have found this to be the case in the field. However, there is not enough independent evidence to confirm the finding. Further work needs to be done using standardised test parameters before a conclusive case can be made. Also additional studies are necessary to produce a definitive means of choosing a membrane expansion rate to ensure undrained conditions in the soil during shear.

9 SOIL MODULUS VALUES

Two types of moduli can be derived from the pressuremeter test: a tangent modulus and a secant modulus. The secant modulus can be directly calculated from the pressuremeter curve, or measured from the stress–strain curve derived from the pressuremeter curve, at different strain levels. The tangent modulus can also be determined from either curve. However, determination of the tangent modulus is difficult because the beginning of the pressuremeter curve is often not well defined. Because of the problems in defining a tangent modulus, a number of investigators advocate using static, cyclic loading results to get a modulus value (Briaud *et al.*, 1983).

In laboratory or *in situ* testing the undrained modulus is very sensitive to disturbance. In SBPM testing, modulus values are also influenced by the L/D ratio of the probe and possible drainage. Typically, published data suggest that SBPM derived modulus values are larger by a factor of two to three times those obtained in laboratory tests. On the whole, SBPM modulus values seem more consistent than those obtained in laboratory tests.

10 COEFFICIENTS OF CONSOLIDATION

Few holding test results have been reported in the literature. This is due in part to the difficulty of making successful pore pressure measurements with the SBPM. The test was first described by Baguelin (1973), but the tests of Clarke *et al.* (1979) are the most extensive to date. Benoit (1983) also successfully carried out several holding tests in a soft marine clay where the pore pressures were monitored closely using a microcomputer data acquisition system. Typical plots generated from one of the Benoit tests are given in Fig. 3. The radial strain increases to 10% and is held constant thereafter. During the holding phase of the test, the pressure applied decreases, as do the pore pressures.

Based on eqn (1) and a value for t_{50} from the test results, the coefficient of consolidation, c_{vh}, is determined. The designation c_{vh} is used to denote that the coefficient refers primarily to a horizontal consolidation process. Table 7 presents the data from published results of holding tests. Where information is available, a ratio is calculated of c_{vh}, to the coefficient of consolidation, c_v, from a conventional oedometer test. This ratio typically falls between 13 and 28, with one result as high as 305. The reason for the c_{vh} value being larger than c_v probably reflects the fact that the horizontal permeability is normally higher than the vertical value for most clays, and the oedometer test reflects the vertical permeability. Also, the pore pressure cells of the pressuremeter is indicative of the response of a very small location in the soil, which in itself could be more sandy than the general soil mass. In any case, the higher permeabilities and coefficients of consolidation measured in the pressuremeter tests are probably more suitable for use in practice, since it is well known that results from oedometer tests give very conservative estimates of the rates of consolidation. In fact, in many practical problems drainage of excess pore pressures takes place mainly in the horizontal direction as is the case of the pressuremeter holding test.

TABLE 7

In situ DETERMINATION OF THE CONSOLIDATION CHARACTERISTICS USING SBPM

Test no.	Soil type	Depth (m)	c_u (kN/m²)	t_{50} (min)	T_{50}	r_m (m)	c_{vh} (m²/year) in situ	c_v (m²/year) oedometer	$\frac{c_{vh}}{c_v}$	References
CA1	Soft grey, organic silty clay	1·85	16	14	1·5	0·0330	61	0·20	305	Clarke et al. (1979)
CA3		3·65	23	128	1·5	0·0340	7	0·25	28	
CA7		7·25	27	24	2·3	0·0344	60	3·0	20	
LB1	Soft, grey silty clay	1·90	60	15	0·33	0·0352	14	No data available		Clarke et al. (1979)
LA2		2·85	26	12	0·52	0·0352	27			
LB3		3·90	38	15	0·55	0·0354	24			
LA4		4·85	38	26	1·11	0·0350	27			
LB5		5·90	34	15	1·5	0·0354	66			
LB7		7·65	44	17	1·5	0·0349	56			
JB-HAM-30		11·9	29·1	53·6	0·51	0·0447	10	0·74–0·93	13	Benoit (1983)
JB-HAM-32		13·4	31·3	45·7	0·53	0·0449	12	0·74–0·93	15	

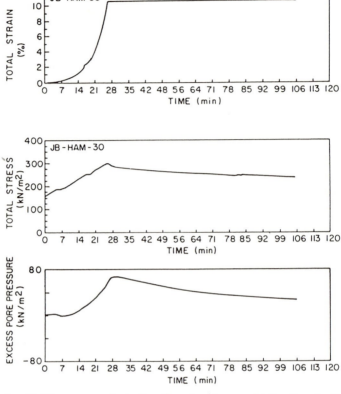

FIG. 3.   Holding test results in San Francisco bay mud (after Benoit, 1983).

11   USE OF THE SBPM IN PRACTICE

At the present stage of its development, the SBPM is just arriving at a point where it can be used reliably in practice. With more effort towards standardisation of the procedures it should find many situations where the results will be of value in analysis and design. To date relatively more use of the SBPM has been made in the United Kingdom and France than the United States. Potential applications include:

(1)   Evaluation of soil stiffness, strength or consolidation properties.
(2)   Determination of *in situ* lateral stress and lateral stress distribution in different directions.

(3) Assessment of changes in soil characteristics or lateral stresses as a result of a construction event (pile driving, excavation, tunnelling, etc.).

(4) Simulation of tunnel closure conditions using a reverse loading test.

(5) Prediction of capacities and deformations of laterally loaded piles.

An example of the use of the SBPM to monitor effects of stress changes produced by construction has been presented by Clough and Denby (1980). SBPM tests were performed at a site with a rubble fill layer overlying a soft clay deposit. A 20 m deep excavation was made at the site which was supported by means of a 0·3 m thick braced, slurry wall. The slurry wall displaced laterally some 0·4 % of the excavated wall height, a value large enough to reduce at-rest earth pressures towards active values. Two SBPM holes were tested at the site, one prior to the excavation and a second after the excavation. The second hole was advanced only 2 m from the slurry wall so as to be within the potential zone of stress relief.

Undrained shear strength and lateral stress values obtained from the two test holes are shown in Figs 4 and 5. Clearly the excavation movements had a manifest effect on the clay since the strengths of the soil and the lateral

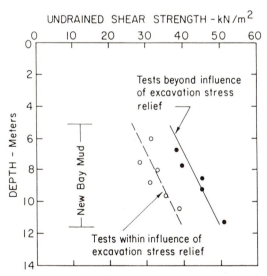

FIG. 4. Comparison of undrained shear strengths of San Francisco bay mud in the active soil zone next to the slurry wall before and after excavation (after Clough and Denby, 1980).

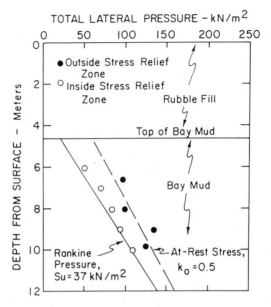

FIG. 5.   Comparison of lateral pressures in San Francisco bay mud in the active soil zone next to the slurry wall before and after excavation (after Clough and Denby, 1983).

pressures in the second hole are lower than those from the first hole. In fact, the lateral stresses from the second hole are consistent with those predicted by the Rankine active earth pressure theory.

These results illustrate the potential of the SBPM as a tool to monitor stress and parameter changes during the course of a construction cycle. Used in this mode the SBPM offers a device which can serve to evaluate predictions of theoretical methods. The example also points out that the SBPM can be more than just a means for determining soil properties.

12   SUMMARY AND CONCLUSIONS

The SBPM is an *in situ* testing tool with considerable potential for use in soft clays. Its capabilities are well matched with new generation analytical tools wherein accurate assessments are needed for *in situ* stresses, strength, stiffness and consolidation characteristics. Further, it can be used as a device to test theoretical predictions by measuring changes in soil parameters and stress states during load application. However, to date, the full potential of the SBPM has not been realised because of the conflicting experiences of various investigators with the probe. Some of the problems which have been reported can be readily explained in terms of a lack of appreciation of the effects of disturbance during probe insertion and unwanted drainage occurring during the actual shear phase. Others are not fully resolved at this time and require further study.

Some key conclusions from the published data on SBPM testing in soft clay are:

(1) Microcomputer data acquisition systems are extremely useful in performing SBPM tests and in providing detailed data sets needed in assessing the results.

(2) Lateral pressures and pressure changes can be reasonably measured using a SBPM.

(3) Lateral stress anisotropy can be detected if the SBPM tests are performed with alternate orientations and multiple sensors are used to monitor deformation of the membrane.

(4) Probe advance procedures and probe geometry and configuration are important in obtaining reliable results.

(5) Undrained shear strength values from a SBPM test can easily be too high if disturbance is induced as a result of improper advance techniques or poorly fitting probe components.

(6) Frequent calibrations should be performed under environmental conditions similar to those in the ground.

(7) The holding test offers a useful extension of the SBPM capability and provides a means of obtaining coefficients of consolidation representative of those needed for most practical problems where predominately lateral drainage occurs.

(8) The holding test results can be useful in evaluating how rapidly the membrane should be expanded to achieve undrained conditions.

ACKNOWLEDGEMENTS

A number of individuals contributed to the material described in this chapter. Thanks go to Drs G. M. Denby, R. C. Bachus and F. Jain. Much of the experimental work performed by the authors was sponsored by the National Science Foundation of the United States, Grant No. CME-8011594.

REFERENCES

ARNOLD, M. (1981). An empirical evaluation of pressuremeter test data, *Canadian Geotechnical Journal*, **18**(3), 455–9.

BENOIT, J. (1983). Analysis of self-boring pressuremeter tests in soft clay, A Thesis presented in partial fulfillment of the Ph.D. Degree, Stanford University, California.

BAGUELIN, F. (1973). Mesure du coefficient de consolidation à l'aide du pressiomèter autoforeur, *Proceedings of the Eighth International Conference on Soil Mechanics and Foundation Engineering*, Moscow, **4.2**, 22–3.

BAGUELIN, F. and JAZEQUEL, J-F. (1978). French self-boring pressuremeters: PAF 68–PAF 72 and PAF 76, *Proceedings of a Symposium on Site Exploration in Soft Ground using in-situ Techniques*, Alexandria, Virginia, Federal Highway Administration, Final report dated January 1980.

BAGUELIN, F., JEZEQUEL, J-F., LEMEE, E. and LE MEHAUTE, A. (1972). Expansion of cylindrical probes in cohesive soils. *Journal of the Soil Mechanics and Foundations Division, ASCE*, **98**(SM11), 1129–42.

BAGUELIN, F., JEZEQUEL, J-F., SHIELDS, D. H. (1978). *The pressuremeter and foundation engineering*, Trans Tech Publications, Clausthal, Germany.

BRIAUD, JEAN-LOUIS, LYTTON, L. ROBERT, HUNG, JUNG-TSANN (1983). Obtaining moduli from cyclic pressuremeter tests. *Journal of the Geotechnical Engineering Division, ASCE*, **109**(5), 657–65.

CLARKE, B. G., CARTER, J. P. and WROTH, C. P. (1979). In-situ determination of the consolidation characteristics of saturated clays, *Proceedings of the Seventh European Conference on Soil Mechanics and Foundation Engineering*, Brighton, **2**, 207–13.

CLOUGH, G. W. and DENBY, G. M. (1980). Self-boring pressuremeter study on San Francisco bay mud, *Journal of the Geotechnical Engineering Division, ASCE*, **106**(GT1), 45–63.

DALTON, J. C. P. and HAWKINS, P. G. (1982). Fields of stress—some measurements of the in-situ stress in a meadow in the Cambridgeshire countryside, *Ground Engineering*, **15**(4).

DENBY, G. M. (1978). Self-boring pressuremeter study of the San Francisco bay mud, A Thesis presented in partial fulfillment of the Ph.D. Degree, Stanford University, California.

DENBY, G. M. and CLOUGH, G. W. (1980). Self-boring pressuremeter tests in clay, *Journal of the Geotechnical Engineering Division, ASCE*, **106**(GT12), 1369–87.

DENBY, G. M. and HUGHES, J. M. O. (1982). Horizontal stress interpretation of pressuremeter tests, *Conference on Updating Subsurface Sampling of Soils and Rocks and Their In-Situ Testing*, Santa Barbara, California.

EDEN, W. J. and LAW, K. T. (1980). Comparison of undrained shear strength results obtained by different test methods in soft clays, *Canadian Geotechnical Journal*, **17**(3) 369–81.

GHIONNA, V., JAMIOLKOWSKI, M., LANCELLOTTA, R. and TORDELLA, M. L. (1981). *Performance of self-boring pressuremeter in cohesive deposits*, Interim Report, USDOT, FHA, Contract No. DOT-FH-11-9264, 182 pp.

GHIONNA, V. N., JAMIOLKOWSKI, M. and LANCELLOTTA, R. (1982). Characteristics of saturated clays as obtained from SBP tests, *Symposium on the Pressuremeter and Its Marine Application*, Editions Technip, Paris.

GHIONNA, V. N., JAMIOLKOWSKI, M., LACASSE, S., LADD, C. C., LANCELLOTTA, R. and LUNNE, T. (1983). Evaluation of self-boring pressuremeter, *Symposium International In-Situ Testing*, Paris, **2**.

GIBSON, R. E. and ANDERSON, W. F. (1961). In-situ measurement of soil properties with the pressuremeter, *Civil Engineering and Public Works Review*, **56**, 615–18.

HUGHES, J. M. O. (1973). An instrument for in-situ measurement of the properties of soft clays, Ph.D. Dissertation, University of Cambridge.

HUGHES, J. M. O., ERVIN, M. C., HOLDEN, J. C. and HARVEY, R. J. (1980). Determination of the engineering properties of the Coode Island silts using a self-boring pressuremeter, *Proceedings of Australian–New Zealand Conference on Geomechanics: 3. Wellington*, **1**, 249–54.

JAMIOLKOWSKI, M. and LANCELLOTTA, R. (1977). Remarks on the use of self-boring pressuremeter in three Italian clays, *Rivista Italiana di Geotechnica*, Anno **XI**(3).

JAMIOLKOWSKI, M., LANCELLOTTA, R. and TORDELLA, M. L. (1980). Geotechnical properties of Porto Tolle NC silty clay, *VI Danube-European Conference of Soil Mechanics and Foundation Engineering*, Scientific-Technical Unions in Bulgaria, Varna.

JOHNSON, G. W. (1982). Use of self-boring pressuremeter in obtaining in-situ shear moduli of clays, Geotechnical Engineering Thesis GT82-1, Geotechnical Engineering Center, Civil Engineering Department, The University of Texas at Austin, Austin, Texas.

LACASSE, S. and LUNNE, T. (1982). *In-situ horizontal stress from pressuremeter tests*, Norges Geotekniske Institutt.

LACASSE, S. M., JAMIOLKOWSKI, M., LANCELLOTTA, R. and LUNNE, T. (1981). In situ stress–strain characteristics of two Norwegian marine clays, *Proceedings of 10th Intl. Conf. on Soil Mechanics and Foundation Engineering*, Vol. II, pp. 507–12.

LADANYI, B. (1972). In-situ determination of undrained stress strain behavior of sensitive clays with the pressuremeter, *Canadian Geotechnical Journal*, **9**, 313–19.

LADD, C. C., GERMAINE, J., BALIGH, M. and LACASSE, S. (1980). *Evaluation of self-boring pressuremeter tests in Boston blue clay*, Federal Highway Administration Interim Report. No. FHWA/RD-80/052.

LAW, K. T. and EDEN, W. J. (1980). Influence of cutting shoe size in self-boring pressuremeter tests in sensitive clays, *Canadian Geotechnical Journal*, **17**, 165–73.

LAW, K. T. and EDEN, W. J. (1982). Effects of soil disturbance in pressuremeter tests, *Proceedings of Symposium on Updating Subsurface Sampling of Soil and Rocks and their In Situ Testing*, Santa Barbara, California (Preprint, Proceedings not yet published).

MARSLAND, A. and RANDOLPH, M. F. (1977). Comparison of the results from pressuremeter tests and large in-situ plate tests in London clay, *Geotechnique*, **27**(2), 217–43.

MENARD, L. (1956). An apparatus for measuring the strength of soils in place, M.Sc. Thesis, University of Illinois.

MORI, H. (1981). Study of the properties of soils in the Northern Coast of Tokyo Bay using a self-boring pressuremeter, *Japanese Society of Soil Mechanics and Foundation Engineering, Soils and Foundations*, **21**(3), 83–96.

PALMER, A. C. (1972). Undrained plane–strain expansion of a cylindrical cavity in clay: A simple interpretation of the pressuremeter test, *Geotechnique*, **22**(3), 451–7.

PREVOST, J-H. (1976). Undrained stress–strain time behavior of clays, *Journal of the Geotechnical Engineering Division, ASCE*, **102**(GT12), 1245–59.

PREVOST, J-H. and HOEG, K. (1975). Analysis of pressuremeter in strain-softening soil, *Journal of the Geotechnical Engineering Division, ASCE*, **101**(GT8), 717–32.

RANDOLPH, M. F. and WROTH, C. P. (1979). An analytical solution for the consolidation around a driven pile, *International Journal for Numerical and Analytical Methods in Geomechanics*, **3**, 217–29.

WINDLE, D. and WROTH, C. P. (1977). In-situ measurement of the properties of stiff clay, *Proceedings of the Ninth International Conference on Soil Mechanics and Foundation Engineering*, **I**, 347–52.

WROTH, C. P. (1980). Cambridge in-situ probe, *Proceedings of Symposium on Site Exploration in Soft Ground Using In-Situ Techniques*, Alexandria, Virginia, Federal Highway Administration, January, pp. 97–135.

WROTH, C. P. and HUGHES, J. M. O. (1974). The development of a special instrument for the in-situ measurement of the strength and stiffness of soils, *Proceedings of Engineering Foundation Conference on Subsurface Exploration for Underground Excavation and Heavy Construction*, M.E. College, Henniker, New Hampshire, pp. 295–311.

INDEX